PSYCHOLOGY
A Complete Introduction

Sandi Mann is a Chartered Psychologist and Associate Fellow of the British Psychological Society. She is Senior Psychology Lecturer at the University of Central Lancashire where she has been teaching a range of psychology topics for over 15 years.

Teach® Yourself

PSYCHOLOGY
A Complete Introduction

Sandi Mann

Also available in ebook

Contents

1

Introduction

Psychology is the study of human mind and behaviour and consists of various subfields and specialities. Psychology is a science because it uses scientific methods of enquiry to develop theories about how humans think and behave. Different types of psychologist work in different settings and using different techniques and client groups in order to develop their knowledge and apply what they know to help people in various ways.

What is psychology?

This is a question that I encounter more than I ever could have imagined when I began my career. Most people have some vague understanding of what psychology is, but I find that very few can really articulate this into anything meaningful (by which I mean something a bit more than 'Something to do with the brain' or even 'It's about people, isn't it?'). In fact, many people seem to see psychologists almost as magicians, capable of reading people's minds, or even controlling them and making them do things they don't want to. Ask any psychologist about the most common response they get at social gatherings when they reveal their profession, and I bet it's this one: 'Oh gosh, I better be careful what I say', accompanied by some awkward body movements, as our conversational partner anxiously imagines we will be analysing their every move or comment to discover their deepest, darkest secrets.

It is true, psychology is about the brain and it is about people (but it's not true that psychologists can uncover your secrets by the way you scratch your nose). In fact, the simplest definition of psychology is that it is the 'science of the mind'.

100 K @ Pg. 3

But what do we mean by the mind? And for that matter, what do we mean by science?

Psychologists study the mind. How? through behaviour

The mind is the source of a whole range of complex and mysterious functions, including attitudes, thoughts, emotions and behaviour. So, psychology is the study of all that. It is a science because psychologists study the mind using the rigorous methods that any other scientist uses. These include observation, experiments, hypothesis testing and more – all of which will be explained in more detail in Chapter 2.

How do they study behaviour? test theories (look @ pg 3)

Obviously, we can't study the mind directly in the same way that physicists can observe neutrons; psychologists can't exactly cut into the brain to see what is going on, and, even if they could, such an investigation would not reveal much. So, instead, we generally have to study human behaviour in order to test theories about how the mind works. Research in psychology, then, seeks to understand and explain how we think, act and feel. Because psychology is a science, it attempts to investigate the causes of human behaviour using systematic, rigorous and objective procedures for observation, measurement and analysis, all supported by theoretical underpinnings, explanations, hypotheses and predictions.

Thus, a better definition of psychology is probably this: 'the scientific study of mind and behaviour'. *new def*

> 'Psychology is the study of the mind and behaviour. The discipline embraces all aspects of the human experience – from the functions of the brain to the actions of nations, from child development to care for the aged. In every conceivable setting from scientific research centres to mental healthcare services, "the understanding of behaviour" is the enterprise of psychologists.'
>
> Definition of psychology as provided by the American Psychological Association (APA)

Interestingly, psychology evolved from the disciplines of philosophy and biology, both of which date back as far as the early Greek thinkers, including Aristotle and Socrates. The word 'psychology' is derived from the Greek word *psyche*, literally meaning 'life' or 'breath', and the Greek word *logia*, meaning the study of something. The groundwork for the study of psychology was laid by the *behaviourists*, who relied on controlled laboratory experiments to identify the causes of human behaviour. Later, *cognitive* psychologists adopted this same rigorous, laboratory-based scientific approach too, with an emphasis on how thought processes play a role in explaining behaviour. Psychologists today explore a wide range of constructs such as perception, thinking, attention, group processes, learning, emotion, motivation, brain functioning, personality, behaviour and interpersonal relationships.

Spotlight: The first psychology laboratory

The German psychologist Wilhelm Wundt (1832–1920) opened the first experimental psychology laboratory in Leipzig in 1879.

The nature–nurture debate

One of the major debates underlying psychology is the so-called 'nature–nurture' one. Put simply, a lot of psychology is concerned with the degree to which our behaviour, attitudes and traits are determined by inherited traits (nature) and the degree to which they are shaped by other influences throughout our lives (nurture). On one side of the debate you have the biological approach, which focuses on physiological processes and structures to explain behaviour. On the other side, there is the behaviourist perspective that states that all behaviour is learned through conditioning. In general, those behaviours or attributes that emerge the earliest are most likely to be hereditary rather than learned. Those that emerge later in life, as a result of maturation, are more likely to be learned.

Those who adopt the most extreme hereditary perspectives are known as *nativists*. Their basic assumption is that the characteristics of the human species as a whole are a product of evolution and that individual differences are due to each person's unique genetic code. At the other end of the spectrum there are the *empiricists* who believe that all behaviour is shaped by experience. For them, maturation applies only to biological processes rather than to the development of such things as personality. For example, Bowlby's (1969) Theory of Attachment (discussed in Chapter 10) takes a nativist perspective, whereby the bond observed between mother and baby is an innate process that is there to ensure the infant's survival. Likewise, Chomsky (1965) proposed that language is gained through the use of an innate (i.e. inborn) language acquisition device (see Chapter 6).

In contrast to Chomsky, the empiricist B. F. Skinner (1957) believed that language is learned from other people via behaviour-shaping techniques (we will come across Skinner more in Chapter 5). Another empiricist approach is Bandura's (1977) Social Learning Theory that states that aggression is learned from the environment through observation and imitation. This is seen in his famous 'Bobo doll' experiment (Bandura 1961), outlined in Chapter 5.

Spotlight: Nature and nuture

Although the phrase 'nature and nurture' had been used by Shakespeare in his play *The Tempest* (1610–11), it was first used in its modern sense by the English Victorian scientist Francis Galton (a cousin of Charles Darwin) in discussions about the influence of heredity and environment on social advancement.

Case study: Identical twins

Thomas J. Bouchard, a professor of psychology, is well known for his valuable work as director of the Minnesota Center for Twin and Adoption Research, which, by examining twins adopted and brought up by different families, has shed important light on the nature vs nurture debate. One particular story of identical twins reared apart is so remarkable that it is known simply as the story of the 'two Jims' (Bouchard et al. 1990).

In 1979 Bouchard came across an account of twins, both named Jim (Jim Springer and Jim Lewis) who had been separated from birth and reunited at age 39. Both Jims grew up not even knowing of the other. The twins were found to have both married women named Linda, then divorced and married a second time to women named Betty. One named his son James Allan, the other named his son James Alan, and both named their pet dogs Toy. They shared interests in mechanical drawing and carpentry; their favourite school subject had been maths, their least favourite spelling. They smoked and drank the same amount and got headaches at the same time of day. Jim Lewis and Jim Springer finally met on 9 February 1979 after 39 years of being separated.

It is important to note that there were also big differences between the pair, too. For example, one Jim had married a third time (to Sandy) and they wore their hair in different styles. However, the case study does suggest the paramount importance of genetics (nature) over environment (nurture).

Subfields of psychology

With its broad scope, psychology covers a wide range of the human experience, such as learning and memory, sensation and perception, motivation and emotion, thinking and language, personality and social behaviour, intelligence, child development, mental illness, and much more. Psychologists can investigate these topics from a variety of different perspectives. Each psychological perspective is underpinned by a shared set of assumptions about what is important to study and how to study it. Some psychologists conduct detailed biological studies of the brain using a range of contemporary tools and techniques; others explore how we process information; still others look at human behaviour from the perspective of evolution, while others study the influence of culture and society on how we behave and think. The different disciplines of psychology described below are thus extremely wide-ranging and examining these can give you a good idea about what psychology is, and what you are likely to learn if you decide to study the subject.

Abnormal psychology: this is the study of people who are different from the 'normal' range in a population and who exhibit abnormal behaviour. Much hinges, of course, on what exactly is meant by 'abnormal'. This speciality is focused on research and treatment of a variety of mental disorders and is linked to psychotherapy and clinical psychology. Clinical psychology is the applied field of abnormal psychology that attempts to assess, understand and treat psychological conditions and mental disorders in clinical practice (such as hospital settings), although clinical psychologists are unlikely to use the term 'abnormal' when they refer to their patients.

Neuropsychology: sometimes called clinical neuropsychology, neuropsychology studies the structure of the brain and its functions, as they relate to specific psychological processes and particular behaviours. This area is closely linked to neuroscience and uses tools such as MRI and PET scans to look at brain injury or brain abnormalities. It thus specializes in looking at how studies of brain injury and disease can shed light on normal as well as abnormal functioning.

Neuropsychologists often work in research settings (universities, laboratories and research institutions), although they may also be found in clinical settings (involved in assessing or treating patients with neuropsychological problems), forensic settings (assessing criminals, for example) or, occasionally, in industry (where their neuropsychological knowledge might be applied to product design or research for drug efficacy).

Clinical psychology: this field is focused on the assessment, diagnosis and treatment of mental health problems. Clinical psychology tends to be underpinned by one of several main theoretical approaches:

▶ The cognitive behavioural perspective: this approach to clinical psychology developed from the behavioural and cognitive schools of thought, so involves examining how a client's feelings, behaviours and thoughts interact.

▶ The psychodynamic approach: this perspective was developed by the psychoanalyst Sigmund Freud, who believed that the unconscious mind played a central role in our behaviour. Techniques such as free association can be used to investigate the client's underlying, unconscious processes that may influence their behaviour.

▶ The humanistic perspective: this approach has its roots in the work of humanist thinkers such as Abraham Maslow and Carl Rogers. This perspective looks at the client holistically and helps people overcome their problems by using approaches such as self-actualization.

These approaches will be examined in more detail in Chapter 16.

Spotlight: A definition of clinical psychology

The American psychologist Lightner Witmer first introduced the term 'clinical psychology' in a 1907 paper. Witmer, a former student of the founder of modern psychology Wilhelm Wundt (1832–1920), defined clinical psychology as 'the study of individuals, by observation or experimentation, with the intention of promoting change'.

Cognitive psychology: the term 'cognitive psychology' was first coined by Ulric Neisser in 1967 with the publication of his book of the same name, and is the study of mental processes such as attention, language use, memory, perception, problem solving, creativity, thinking, attention, learning and decision-making. This branch of psychology is closely related to other disciplines, such as neuroscience, philosophy and linguistics. The discipline grew out of a cognitive shift away from the behaviourist approaches of the 1950s that focused on outward behaviour (that can be seen and thus easily measured) to a more processing approach focusing on internal thoughts to explain that behaviour.

Comparative psychology: this is the branch of psychology concerned with the study of animal behaviour in order to develop a deeper and broader understanding of human psychology. The comparative method involves comparing the similarities and differences among species to gain an understanding of human behaviour. Areas such as heredity, adaptation and evolutionary processes can be studied using the comparative approach. Examples of how the study of animal behaviour can lead to a deeper and broader understanding of human psychology include Ivan Pavlov's research on classical conditioning (see Chapter 5) and Harry Harlow's work with rhesus monkeys that led to the development of Attachment Theory (see Chapter 10).

Developmental psychology: this is an area that looks at human growth and development over the lifespan. It used to focus only on infants and young children, but nowadays also includes teenagers and adults – and the ageing process. Theories often focus on the development of cognitive abilities, morality, social functioning, identity and other life areas. Developmental psychology looks at how people change as they develop and grow, in areas such as cognitive development – which includes problem solving, moral understanding, language acquisition and self-concept and identity formation.

Forensic psychology is an applied field focused on using psychological research and principles in the legal and criminal justice system. It examines the criminal mind and criminality.

Forensic psychology has traditionally been described as the intersection between psychology and justice and many TV and film representations of forensic psychologists have led to an increased interest in this field in recent years. Areas that forensic psychology might cover include eyewitness testimony, jury decision-making, psychological profiling and lie detection.

Industrial-organizational/occupational psychology is a field that uses psychological research, psychological theories and psychological principles to enhance work performance, select employees, improve product design and so on within organizations. Occupational psychologists contribute to an organization's success by improving the satisfaction, safety, health and well-being of its employees. An occupational psychologist might conduct research on employee behaviours and attitudes, and how these can be improved through hiring practices, training programmes, feedback and management systems. The field also helps organizations' and their employees' transition during periods of change and organizational development (e.g. mergers, acquisitions, downsizing, restructuring).

Individual differences research: this looks at the various elements that make up individual personalities. Researchers in this area study the ways in which individual people differ in their behaviour. Although all psychology is ostensibly about individuals, modern psychologists often study groups or the biological underpinnings of cognition rather than examining the differences between individuals per se. Individual differences research typically includes personality, motivation, intelligence, ability, IQ, interests and values. Well-known personality theories include Freud's structural model of personality and the 'Big Five' theory of personality (see Chapter 9).

Social psychology: this is a branch of psychology that is concerned with how social phenomena influence us and how people interact with others. According to the social psychologist Gordon Allport (who might be regarded as the 'father' of social psychology), social psychology is a discipline that uses scientific methods 'to understand and explain how the thoughts, feelings and behaviour of individuals are influenced by the actual, imagined or implied presence of other human beings'

(Allport 1954: 5). Social psychology studies diverse subjects including group behaviour, social perception, leadership, non-verbal behaviour, conformity, aggression and prejudice.

Many people get confused between social psychology and sociology. While there are similarities between them, the differences are important. Sociology deals with the social aspects of humans, while social psychology deals with the behaviour of people in a social setting. Sociology, for example, is more concerned with the study of society as a whole whereas social psychology is the study of the way society affects the way people think and act.

Evolutionary psychology: this looks at how human behaviour has been affected by psychological adjustments during evolution. It seeks to identify which human psychological traits are evolved through adaptations – that is, the products of natural selection or sexual selection. An evolutionary psychologist believes, for example, that language and memory perception are functional products of natural selection. An evolutionary psychologist believes that our human psychological traits are adaptations for survival in the everyday environment of our ancestors. In short, evolutionary psychology is focused on how evolution has shaped the mind and behaviour.

Spotlight: The Theory of Natural Selection

Evolutionary psychology has its historical roots in Charles Darwin's Theory of Natural Selection. In *On the Origin of Species* (1859) Darwin predicted that psychology would develop an evolutionary basis: 'In the distant future I see open fields for far more important researches. Psychology will be based on a new foundation, that of the necessary acquirement of each mental power and capacity by gradation'.

Health psychology: this is the study of psychological and behavioural processes in health maintenance and illness prevention. It tries to understand the relationship between physical health and illness and psychological, behavioural and cultural factors. One approach that health psychology takes is termed the **biopsychosocial** approach. This is where physical health is understood to be the product not only of biological processes (e.g. a virus, a tumour) but also of psychological processes (e.g. thoughts and beliefs), behavioural processes (e.g. habits) and social processes (e.g. socioeconomic status and ethnic background).

It is this understanding of the psychological factors influencing physical health that allows the health psychologist to improve health, either by working with individual patients or indirectly in large-scale public health programmes. Health psychologists might also work directly with other healthcare professionals, by training or advising them on the importance of psychological factors in maintaining health or adherence to health-maintaining schemes or treatment regimes.

What all these different approaches to psychology have in common is a desire to explain the behaviour of individuals based on the workings of the mind. And in every area, psychologists apply scientific methodology. They formulate theories, test hypotheses through observation and experiment, and analyse the findings with statistical techniques that help them make important discoveries.

Other psychology professions

There is a range of professions that psychologists (i.e. people with at least one psychology degree or qualification) can go into, including many that are allied to psychology or that make use of psychology skills. The section here will focus on the main psychology professions as determined by the British Psychological Society's Chartership scheme; these are the professions that the BPS recognizes with its benchmark scheme (see http://www.bps.org.uk/system/files/Public%20files/your_journey_jan_2014_web.pdf). Some are based on the subfields of psychology outlined above such as clinical, health, occupational and forensic psychology. Other professions arising from the various subfields include the following (taken, with permission, from the BPS website):

Counselling psychology: counselling psychologists focus on improving psychological functioning and well-being. Counselling psychologists deal with a wide range of mental health problems concerning life issues including bereavement, domestic violence, sexual abuse, traumas and relationship issues. They work with the individual's unique subjective psychological experience to empower their recovery and alleviate distress.

Counselling psychologists work in hospitals (acute admissions, psychiatric intensive care, rehabilitation), health centres, Improving Access to Psychological Therapy services, community mental health teams and child and adolescent mental health services. They also work within private hospitals, private practice, forensic settings, industry, education, research and corporate institutions.

Educational psychology: educational psychology is concerned with children and young people in educational and early-years settings. Educational psychologists tackle challenges such as learning difficulties, social and emotional problems, and issues around disability as well as more complex developmental disorders. They work in a variety of ways including observations, interviews and assessments and offer consultation, advice and support to teachers, parents and the wider community as well as the young people concerned. They research innovative ways of helping vulnerable young people and often train teachers, learning support assistants and others working with children.

In the UK, local authorities (LAs) employ the majority of educational psychologists working in schools, colleges, nurseries and special units, although increasing numbers are working directly in schools, academies and other educational settings. They regularly liaise with other professionals from education, health and social services. A growing number work as independent or private practitioners.

Sport and exercise psychology: sport psychology's predominant aim is to help athletes prepare psychologically for the demands of competition and training. Examples of the work sport psychologists carry out include counselling referees to deal with the stressful and demanding aspects of their role, advising coaches on how to build cohesion within their squad of athletes, and helping athletes with personal development and the psychological consequences of sustaining an injury. Exercise psychology is primarily concerned with the application of psychology to increase exercise participation and motivational levels in the general public.

Sport and exercise psychologists work in a wide range of settings with a diverse range of clients participating in recreational, amateur and elite levels of competition.

Teaching and research psychology: research in psychology requires the application of skills and knowledge to hypothesize scientifically about an aspect of human behaviour, then to test it, analyse it and communicate the results. Research underpins much of the teaching and practice of psychology as it provides the evidence base for psychological theory and the effectiveness of treatments, interventions, tests and teaching methods. Typically, academics or researchers in higher education undertake both research and teaching and lecturing.

Most researchers are employed in higher education institutions or specialist research units; however, others are employed in a wide variety of contexts – including the food and drink industries, pharmaceutical industries, marketing, government departments and the NHS.

Dig deeper

The BPS website is a good place to get plenty of information on psychology, studying psychology and psychology qualifications: http://www.bps.org.uk/

A more in-depth introductory psychology text is provided by Edward E. Smith, Susan Nolen-Hoeksema, Barbara Fredrickson and Geoffey R. Loftus, *Introduction to Psychology*, 14th revised edition (Wadsworth Publishing, 2003).

To read more about twins separated at birth, see http://www.cbsnews.com/news/twin-brothers-separated-at-birth-reveal-striking-genetic-similarities/

Fact-check

1 What is psychology?
   a   The study of the brain
   b   The study of behaviour
   c   The science of people
   d   The study of mind and behaviour

2 What are nativists?
   a   People who sunbathe naked
   b   People who live in certain parts of the world
   c   People who believe that all behaviour is genetically determined
   d   People who believe that all behaviour is learned

3 What are empiricists?
   a   People who test theories
   b   People who believe that all behaviour is genetically determined
   c   People who believe that all behaviour is learned
   d   People who carry out research

4 What is neuropsychology otherwise known as?
   a   Neuroscience
   b   Clinical psychology
   c   Cognitive psychology
   d   Neurology

5 Which of these theoretical approaches does *not* drive clinical psychology?
   a   The cognitive behavioural perspective
   b   The psychodynamic approach
   c   The humanistic perspective
   d   The social psychology approach

6 Which of the following is studied within the field of individual differences?
   a   Personality
   b   Minority influence
   c   Language acquisition
   d   Social loafing

7 Which of the following is *not* studied in the field of occupational psychology?

   a Employee selection

   b Workplace stress

   c Job satisfaction

   d Attention deficit hyperactivity disorder

8 Where might a health psychologist work?

   a Prisons

   b Schools

   c Sports arenas

   d Hospitals

9 Where might you find a forensic psychologist?

   a Prisons

   b Schools

   c Sports arenas

   d Hospitals

10 Which of the following does *not* reflect scientific methodology?

   a The testing of hypotheses

   b The formulation of theories

   c The analysis of data

   d The use of intuition

2

Psychology research

Having stressed in Chapter 1 that psychology is a science, it is useful to look now at the processes that make psychology a science. These are the processes that have been undertaken to carry out the research in order to produce the knowledge and theories that underpin all of psychological awareness to date – and that will continue to be undertaken to further develop our understanding of the mind and behaviour. The basic process for conducting psychology research involves asking a question, designing a study, collecting data, analysing results, reaching conclusions and sharing the findings. This chapter outlines the key concepts these process involve.

The hypothesis

All scientific research must start with a hypothesis. A hypothesis is just a tentative prediction about what the scientist imagines (through educated guesswork) to be the relationship between two 'variables'. A variable is a factor that can be changed and manipulated in ways that are observable and measurable (more on this later). This prediction, which is based on either previous research or some other logical reasoning, can then be tested.

For example, I might want to study the relationship between ice cream consumption and the weather. My hypothesis might be that 'the higher the temperature, the more people will purchase ice cream'. My variables would be temperature and ice cream consumption. This hypothesis is easily testable by simply measuring both the variables.

People sometimes confuse a theory with a hypothesis. A theory predicts events in general terms, while a hypothesis makes a far more specific prediction about a particular set of circumstances. A theory is developed after extensive testing, while a hypothesis is an educated guess that has not yet been tested. A hypothesis can lead to a new theory, or to proving an existing one.

When talking about hypotheses, there are a couple of other terms that readers might come across. The 'null hypothesis' is the suggestion that there is no relationship at all between two or more variables. This is the default option that a piece of research will usually aim to reject (unless the research is aimed at proving there is no relationship). In the ice cream example, the null hypothesis would be that there is no relationship between ice cream consumption and outside temperature (which would probably be rejected by the findings).

Other terms in psychological research that you should be aware of are 'one-tailed' or 'two-tailed' hypotheses. Put simply, a one-tailed hypothesis specifies the direction that the predicted effect will have, whereas a two-tailed hypothesis does not specify the direction at all.

Thus:

- **One-tailed:** Increased outside temperatures will lead to increased consumption of ice cream.

- **Two-tailed:** Outside temperature will be related to ice cream consumption.

One-tailed hypotheses are used when we are pretty sure of the direction we are expecting, while two-tailed hypotheses are useful when we expect an effect but are not entirely sure what that effect might be.

The experiment

Once a psychology researcher has their hypothesis, they will need to test that with some kind of experiment. An experiment is what we do to test hypothesized relationships between variables. These experiments can be very complex with many different variables, or fairly simple cause-and-effect studies. Even a simple experiment will be made up of various components:

- **The experimental hypothesis:** this is the statement that predicts what effect is expected (see above) and is not simply a guess, but is developed by examining previous research or literature in the area.

- **The variables:** These are the factors that are to be measured or manipulated in the experiment. There are two types of variable – independent and dependent. The *independent variable* (IV) is the thing that you change or manipulate and it is this change that you expect to lead to the hypothesis effect. The *dependent variable* (DV) is the factor that changes as a result of the IV. For example, if I were to conduct an experiment to test my ice cream hypothesis (above), I could manipulate the temperature (IV) in a shopping mall and measure how much ice cream was purchased (DV) at different temperatures. The amount of ice cream bought is *dependent* on the temperature in the mall.

- **The control group:** to carry out a rigorous experiment, it is necessary to have two groups of participants in the study: those who are subject to the manipulation of the IV and those who are not. Thus, I would need to measure ice cream consumption on a group of shoppers where the mall is kept at a constant temperature. This is the control group, and controls for the possibility that *extraneous* variables might have accounted for the findings. Extraneous variables are those unexpected factors that might influence the outcomes. For instance, there may be factors that influence ice cream consumption other than temperature, such as shop displays and time of day. The control group allows these extraneous factors to be controlled for.

▶ **The experimental group:** this is the group receiving the treatment or intervention and can be compared to the control group.

Once the data from the simple experiment has been collected, the researchers will perform a number of statistical tests to determine whether any differences found between the control and the experimental group are statistically significant (or whether they could have occurred by chance).

We could make the experiment more complex by adding another IV to the mix – or another DV. Another IV might be placing adverts for ice cream around the mall to see whether this affects ice cream consumption. Another DV might be a measure of which flavours or types of iced treat are preferred.

An experiment could also involve either **independent** or **repeated** measures. In the ice cream example, we are comparing different groups of people in each condition, experimental and controls – the two groups are independent of each other and thus this is an independent measure. We could do, however, a repeated measures experiment where we use only one group of participants; for example, we could, in theory, measure ice cream consumption before increasing temperature, during, then again once the temperature went back to normal.

Of course, this would make no sense as most people don't eat that much ice cream! But imagine a different experiment, such as one to measure the effect of violent computer games on aggression in children; here, an independent measures experiment would have one group of children play the games and one group play non-violent games – and then compare the amount of aggression between the two groups. A repeated measures experiment would take a baseline measure of aggressive behaviour of one group of children, have them play violent computer games, then measure aggression again. Here the measure after the intervention would be compared with that before it.

Correlational research

Not all psychology research is conducted by carrying out experiments. An alternative is to use correlational methods to look for relationships between variables. Such relationships, or correlations, can be found to be either **positive, negative** or **non-existent**. Positive correlation means that as the amount of one variable increases, the other one does, too. For example, age of children is correlated with height (in that, on average, older children will be taller than younger ones, though there will always be exceptions). Negative correlation means that as one variable increases the other decreases; for example, as age of adults increases, elasticity of their skin decreases (sadly). If no correlation is found, this means that the two variables have no relationship with each other; for example, head circumference does not correlate and thus has no relationship with intelligence.

Spotlight: Correlation and causality

A word of warning: correlation does not imply causality! This means that just because two variables may correlate, we cannot say for sure that one causes the other. Increasing A may cause B to rise, or increasing B may cause A to rise. Or an entirely different variable, C, might be responsible for both A and B rising together.

Correlation can be quantified by using a mathematical measure called the **correlation coefficient**. Once calculated, a correlation coefficient will have a value ranging from -1 to $+1$. A value close to one indicates a strong positive correlation. A value close to -1 indicates a strong negative relationship.

Statistical tests of significance can work out how likely any correlation found is to have occurred by chance, and how likely it is a real reflection of a relationship between the two variables.

Spotlight: Experiments and correlational studies

Be alert to the difference between experiments and correlational studies.

An experiment isolates and manipulates the independent variable to observe its effect on the dependent variable (while attempting to control for any extraneous variables that could be responsible for the effect). Experiments can thus establish cause and effect.

A correlational study, on the other hand, identifies variables and looks for a relationship between them. It cannot predict cause and effect.

Observational methods

All psychological research involves observation to some extent, but observational studies are investigations where the researcher observes a situation and records what happens but does not manipulate an independent variable. There is no intervention and the researcher does not influence the proceedings in any way. These methods can be useful when it is not ethical to manipulate a variable or when there is a need to minimize **demand characteristics** (whereby participants feel the need to provide the researcher with what they think they are looking for in an experiment – we will look at this further below). There can be, however, the problem of **observer bias,** whereby the researcher inadvertently skews their recording according to the results they expect to find. Observational studies can also be quite invasive in terms of privacy and there is the whole issue of whether people react differently when they know they are being observed (again, we will look more at this later in this chapter). Sometimes this can be overcome by not informing the participants that they are being observed, perhaps by having the researcher join in with the activities they are observing.

There are generally two ways that observations can be carried out: using time sampling methods or situation sampling.

Time sampling involves observing participants at different time intervals. These time intervals can be chosen *randomly* or *systematically*. Using systematic time sampling allows the information obtained to only really apply to the one time period in which the observation took place (e.g. mornings). In contrast, the random time sampling would allow greater generalizability across all time periods.

Time sampling is not useful if the event pertaining to your research question occurs infrequently or unpredictably (e.g. buying a car or going on holiday), because you will often miss the event in the short time period of observation. In this scenario, *event sampling* is more useful. In this style of sampling, the researcher lets the event determine when the observations will take place.

Situation sampling involves the study of behaviour in many different locations, and under different circumstances and conditions. By sampling different situations, researchers reduce the chance that the results they obtain will be particular to a certain set of circumstances or conditions, and this significantly increases the generalizability of findings. Researchers may determine which subjects to observe by selecting them either systematically (every tenth student in a cafeteria, for example) or randomly, with the goal of obtaining a representative sample of all subjects (see the later section on the Hawthorn Effect).

Reliability and validity

Any psychology research must be both reliable and valid for it to be considered scientific. Reliability is sometimes used to mean 'consistency'; a reliable research technique will yield the same results consistently if we were to repeat the measure time after time. Thus, if I were to measure intelligence, the technique I use should roughly yield the same results for the same people each time (of course, there are factors that could affect reliability, such as practice effects, but more on that later).

Validity refers to the extent to which a research technique actually measures the behaviour it claims to measure. Thus, I could use a tape measure to measure head circumference as a measure of intelligence; this would be reliable (in that the tape measure is likely to yield a very similar circumference of a head each time I was to repeat the measurement) but not valid as a measure of intelligence (but perfectly valid as a measure of head circumferences).

There are ways to test for reliability and validity in order to produce a 'score' that can indicate whether the technique has good or weak reliability and validity, but discussion of this in great detail is beyond the scope of this book. Suffice it to say, reliability tests look for consistency or correlation between measures, so one way would be to correlate scores of a test at time point 1 with scores on the same person at time point 2; a high correlation indicates high reliability. There are various ways to obtain these two sets of data with which to correlate.

For validity, researchers are also looking for correlations, but this time with something that will tell us that what we are measuring is what we intend to measure. Imagine we want to measure intelligence – one way to check that our measure is valid would be to see whether scores correlate with other existing measures of intelligence or other indicators of intelligence (such as exam grades). Again, scores nearer to 1 indicate the highest correlation and thus validity.

Internal and external validity

There are several different types of validity, and psychologists talk about factors that may *threaten* the validity of their research. These threats can affect *internal* validity or *external* validity. Internal validity refers to how much we can be sure that the findings are due to the variables under consideration rather than to extraneous variables, while external validity considers how much the results from psychological study can be generalized more widely.

Threats to internal validity: Psychology researchers Campbell and Stanley (1966) identify and discuss various types of extraneous variables that can, if not controlled, jeopardize an experiment's internal validity:

▶ *History* These are the unique experiences subjects have between the various measurements done in an experiment that could influence outcomes. Thus, tests of aggression in children might be subject to history effects if some children access violent video games at home and others don't.

▶ *Maturation* These are natural (rather than experimenter-imposed) changes that occur as a result of the normal passage of time. For example, the more time that passes in a study the more likely subjects are to become tired and bored, more or less motivated as a function of hunger or thirst, older and so on. Reading tests on children, for example, will always be subject to maturation effects.

▶ *Testing* The actual testing itself might change people; for example, taking an IQ test might improve people's ability to do well at IQ tests so it might be the actual measure that leads to an apparent increase in IQ before and after an intervention, not the intervening experimental intervention.

▶ *Selection* If the comparison groups are different from one another at the beginning of the study, the results of the study are biased. For example, testing a depression intervention on two groups of volunteer patients might be influenced by the difference in the types of people who volunteer.

▶ *Experimental mortality* Subjects drop out of studies. If one comparison group experiences a higher level of subject withdrawal/mortality than other groups, then observed differences between groups become questionable.

Threats to external validity: There are a few major issues around external validity:

▶ *Population* Can we generalize from a relatively small sample (e.g. of psychology students or middle-aged shoppers, or people walking on a particular street at a particular time) to the population as a whole?

- *Location* Can the results obtained in a laboratory setting really tell us how people will behave in real life?

- *History* Are findings from older studies still valid today?

Demand characteristics and the Hawthorne Effect

There are a number of other important threats to the validity of research that every serious research psychologist must try to counter.

Demand characteristics occur when participants figure out the purpose of the experiment and unconsciously (or even consciously) change their behaviour to fit the aim. They might do this in order to 'help' the researcher or in order to make themselves look good (sometimes called the **social desirability** effect). Alternatively, the participants might try to skew their responses so they don't fit what is being looked for, to try to ruin the study (some people are like that!). One way to avoid demand characteristics, then, is to deceive participants about the nature of the study, or to omit to tell them what you are hoping to find. However, there might be ethical considerations about their giving informed consent if they don't know enough about the study (see the section on 'The ethics of research' later in this chapter).

Spotlight: A definition of demand characteristics

The concept of 'demand characteristics' originated in the work of Martin Orne in 1962. Orne more recently defined demand characteristics as 'the totality of cues and mutual expectations which inhere in a social context ... which serve to influence the behaviour and/or self-reported experience of the research receiver' (Orne and Whitehouse 2000).

Double-blind studies are another way to counter demand characteristics; this is where neither the experimenter nor the participants know which experimental group they are in/ dealing with so cannot consciously or unconsciously tailor their behaviour or responses (sometimes the experimenter themselves can be the source of demand characteristics as they imagine or look for results that will prove their theories).

In the late 1920s early 1930s a series of experiments took place at Western Electric's factory at Hawthorne, a suburb of Chicago. The original purpose of the experiments was to study the effects of physical conditions on productivity. Two groups of workers in the Hawthorne factory were used as guinea pigs. One day the lighting in the work area for one group was improved dramatically while the other group's lighting remained unchanged. The researchers were surprised to find that the productivity of the more highly illuminated workers increased much more than that of the control group. The employees' working conditions were changed in other ways, too (their working hours, rest breaks and so on), and in all cases their productivity improved when a change was made. Indeed, their productivity even improved when the lights were dimmed again. In fact, even when the conditions were returned to how they were at the start, productivity increased.

It was concluded that it wasn't actually the changes in physical conditions that were producing the increase in productivity. Rather, it was the attention that they were being given by the researchers that produced the improvements. They felt happy to be singled out and to feel that someone cared about their working conditions.

'Careful studies of this ... group showed marked increases in production which were related only to the special social position and social treatment they received. Thus, it was the 'artificial' social aspects of the experimental conditions set up for measurement which produced the increases in group productivity.'

J. R. P. French, on the Hawthorne Experiments, 'Experiments in field settings', Chapter 3 in L. Festinger and D. Katz, *Research Methods in the Behavioral Sciences* (New York: Holt, Rinehart & Winston)

What became known as the Hawthorne Effect stated, then, that individuals may change their behaviour as a result of the attention they are receiving from researchers rather than because of any manipulation of independent variables. In other words, we behave differently when we know we are being observed.

The ethics of research

'Psychological investigators are potentially interested in all aspects of human behaviour and experience. However, for ethics reasons, some areas of human experience and behaviour may be beyond the reach of experiment, observation or other form of psychological intervention. Ethics guidelines are necessary to clarify the conditions under which psychological research can take place.'

British Psychological Society Code of Human Research Ethics, p. 4

Psychologists who conduct research must carry it out ethically. Today there are strict ethical codes in place from bodies such as the British Psychological Society and the American Psychological Association governing research. In addition, researchers wanting to conduct studies usually have to seek ethical approval from their own institution. These ethical guidelines are designed to protect participants in research and include adherence to the following principles:

▶ **Principle of Positive Self-regard:** this states that research participants should have as high an opinion of themselves at the end of the process as they did at the start and should not be harmed either physically or emotionally by the process. Part of this involves ensuring that they are fully debriefed at the end; participants must be given a general idea of what the researcher was investigating and why, and their part in the research should be explained. They must be told whether they have been deceived and given reasons why. They must be asked whether they have any questions and those questions should be answered honestly and as fully as possible.

- **Principle of Informed Consent:** participants have the right to know what they are letting themselves in for. Participants must be given information relating to the purpose of the research, the procedures involved in the research, any foreseeable risks and discomforts involved, length of time the subject is expected to participate and whom to contact for answers to questions about the study. Deception for the purposes of the study should be balanced carefully against the need for informed consent.

- **Principle of Competence:** researchers should conduct high-quality research which meets high technical and professional standards.

- **Principle of Confidentiality:** information should be guarded so it cannot be used in a way that would be detrimental to the participant.

- **Principle of Voluntary Participation:** participants should be free to withdraw from the study if they choose to. This causes ethical issues sometimes when students are expected to take part in research in order to gain credits, but care should be taken to adhere to this principle as far as possible.

Many classic psychological experiments would never gain ethical clearance today, for example 'Little Albert' (see Chapter 14), Harlow's monkey experiments (see Chapter 10), the Stanford Prison Experiment (Chapter 12) and the Milgram Experiment (Chapter 12). See the 'Dig deeper' section at the end of this chapter for more on this.

Spotlight: Participants or subjects?

When I was a student (admittedly, many years ago), we referred to those who took part in research as 'subjects'. In recent years, there has been a move away from talking about them as 'subjects' and instead to referring to them as 'participants'. The word 'subject' was thought to be demeaning and failed to give the appropriate respect to individuals who had kindly agreed to *participate* in a research study. In fact, researchers owe a debt of gratitude towards them, and referring to them as mere 'subjects' seems to objectify and dehumanize them.

Dig deeper

Classic psychological experiments that could never be carried out today for ethical reasons:
http://mentalfloss.com/article/52787/10-famous-psychological-experiments-could-never-happen-today

BBC Radio programme about the Hawthorne Effect:
http://www.bbc.co.uk/programmes/b00lv0wx

BPS Code of Human Research Ethics:
http://www.bps.org.uk/sites/default/files/documents/code_of_human_research_ethics.pdf

Fact-check

1 What is a hypothesis?
 a A random expectation about what will happen in an experiment
 b An educated guess about a relationship between variables in an experiment
 c A statement of fact about two variables
 d A demand characteristic

2 What is an experiment?
 a What we do to test hypothesized relationships between variables
 b Where we see what will happen if we do something to someone
 c A set of hypotheses
 d A prediction about what will happen

3 What is a control group?
 a The group whose behaviour is controlled by the researcher
 b The group who don't meet the criteria for taking part in the study
 c The group who don't get the intervention that the experimental group gets
 d A group who don't know the aim of the study

4 If A and B correlate, this means that:
 a A causes B
 b B causes A
 c A and B cause something else
 d A and B are related to each other

5 Observational methods are useful when:
 a We don't know what is going to happen
 b We don't have a hypothesis
 c It is not ethical to manipulate a variable
 d We are worried about the Hawthorne Effect

6 Reliable studies are those that:
- **a** Can be replicated
- **b** Measure what they are meant to measure
- **c** Reject the null hypothesis
- **d** Are one-tailed

7 Which of the following is not a threat to internal validity?
- **a** History
- **b** Maturation
- **c** Testing
- **d** Location

8 Double-blind studies are those where:
- **a** No one knows what the hypothesis is
- **b** The experimenter knows what the hypothesis is but the participants don't
- **c** The experimenter knows what treatment group the participants are in but they don't
- **d** Neither the experimenter nor the participants know what treatment group they are actually in

9 The Hawthorne Effect states that:
- **a** People act differently when they are being watched
- **b** People act differently when they are taking part in psychological studies
- **c** People act differently when they are at work than when they are at leisure
- **d** People act differently with psychologists than other types of researchers

10 Psychological research studies may not be ethical if they:
- **a** Don't have well-thought-out hypotheses
- **b** Have too many variables
- **c** Are two-tailed
- **d** Do not fully inform the participant about what the study involves

3

Perception and attention

Perception refers to how we make sense of our world;
sensation alone is not enough – we have to interpret the
sensory input in order to understand it. This is the process
of perception and various theorists differ in how they believe
these processes work. Understanding the process of perception
helps us understand phenomena such as visual illusions,
how we perceive depth and distance and even phantom pain.
Of course, in order to perceive, we have to attend to the
stimulation first, so this chapter also discusses various theories
of attention.

Perception refers to the organization, identification and interpretation of sensory information in order to make sense of and understand the environment. Perception involves attending to signals from the nervous system, which in turn result from physical or chemical stimulation of the sense organs. For example, vision involves light striking the retina of the eye, smell is mediated by odour molecules, and hearing involves pressure waves. However, perception is not merely seeing or hearing, but making sense of what these sensations tell us.

Perception, then, is not the passive receipt of these signals but is shaped by learning, memory, expectation, and attention. Perception involves these 'top-down' effects as well as the 'bottom-up' process of processing sensory input. The 'bottom-up' processing transforms low-level sensory information to higher-level psychological information (e.g. extracts shapes for object recognition). The 'top-down' processing refers to a person's concept and expectations (knowledge), and selective mechanisms (attention) that influence that perception.

A good example of this difference is illustrated by a recent experience of mine; I asked my husband for a lemonade and when I received the beverage I recoiled at its taste – 'Urgh!' I exclaimed, 'It's flat and tastes awful!' My husband pointed out that it was meant to be flat as he had given me a still drink (traditional lemonade), not a carbonated one. I sipped it again and then decided it was actually quite nice. My 'top-down' processing had conflicted with my 'bottom-up'.

Visual perception theory

This idea of perception as being a way to make sense of and to interpret our sensations goes some way to explain many visual phenomena such as illusions. Psychologists are divided on the extent to which we engage in top-down vs bottom-up processing, with Richard Gregory (1970) arguing that perception is a constructive process that relies on top-down processing and James J. Gibson (1966, 1972) taking a bottom-up view of perception. For Gregory, our memories and other processes play a crucial role in how we see things.

This top-down approach explains visual illusions such as the Necker cube or other images whereby the object can be seen in different ways (even though there is no change in sensory input) as our brain flips between different interpretations of the data. It also explains why we have a tendency to 'see' faces in mundane objects (see the case study below).

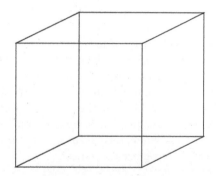

The Necker cube: which is the front of the box? There are two ways to visualize this and our brains can allow us to flip between each.

Gibson in 1966 argued strongly against the idea that perception involves top-down processing and criticized Gregory's discussion of visual illusions on the grounds that they are artificial examples and not images found in our normal visual environments. He argued that we don't need to 'make sense' of the visual world but can perceive it directly as there is enough information in the environment to do this. For Gibson, sensation is perception: what you see is what you get.

Case study: Face pareidolia

In 2004 a decade-old toasted cheese sandwich said to bear an image of the Virgin Mary was sold on the eBay auction website for $28,000, according to a report on the BBC. The original owner of the sandwich, a Mrs Duyser, says she noticed the image burned into her sandwich as she was about to tuck into it in autumn 1994. 'I went to take a bite out of it, and then I saw this lady looking back at me,' she said, in the *Chicago Tribune* newspaper. The item has apparently inspired others to place dozens of spin-off items on the online auction site, including attempts at replica burnt toast, T-shirts, ornamental plates and domain names.

Other places where Jesus has apparently popped up include a Walmart receipt, a frying pan in Salford, UK, and a pizza in Brisbane, Australia.

According to a study published in the journal *Cortex* (Jiangang Liua et al. 2014), it is 'perfectly normal' to 'see' such images because of a phenomenon called 'face pareidolia, the illusory perception of non-existent faces' caused by the interaction between the frontal cortex, the part of the brain that helps produce 'expectations' of what an object should look like, and the posterior visual cortex, the part that processes the image. That is, we are wired to interpret data that we see as something recognizable – primarily faces – and familiar faces will be 'recognized' the most.

Three important components of Gibson's 'Theory of Direct Perception', as his views came to be referred to, are Optic Flow Patterns (changes in the flow of the visual array provide important information about the perception of movement), Invariant Features (such as texture that always occurs in the same way and thus gives us valuable data), and Affordances (environmental cues such as the knowledge that objects look smaller the further away they are). According to Gibson, these components, and others, are what help us make sense of our visual world.

The Gestalt Theory of Perception

If the key to Gregory's top-down approach to understanding perception is inference, and the key to Gibson's bottom-up approach is direct perception of unchanging elements, then the key to the Gestalt approach to perception is organization. Gestalt psychology was founded by Germans Max Wertheimer, Wolfgang Kohler and Kurt Koffka and focused on how people interpret the world. According to Gestalt psychology, the whole is different from the sum of its parts. Based upon this belief, Gestalt psychologists developed a set of principles to explain perceptual organization, or how smaller objects are grouped to form larger ones. These principles are often referred to as the 'laws of perceptual organization'. For example, when we see a person, we do not see them as a collection of body parts – arms, legs, nose, ears and so forth. We organize them into a person and recognize them as such. In fact, we might barely notice the individual parts, even though we can see them (which is why changed features, such as new eyewear or a moustache, often fail to be noticed).

The Gestalt Theory of Perception is based on six main principles that govern how we organize sensations so that they make sense:

▶ The **principle of proximity** (or contiguity) states that things that are closer together will be seen as belonging together, as here:

XXXXXXX X X

Thus the Xs grouped together look like part of a cluster rather than separate; this prevents us having to analyse each stimulus separately.

▶ The **principle of similarity** states that things which share visual characteristics – such as shape, size, colour, texture, value or orientation – will be seen as belonging together.

▶ The **principle of figure and ground** states that we see objects as either figure (distinct elements of focus) or ground (background on which the figure rests). For example, the writing on this page is the 'figure' and the white background is the 'ground'.

- The **principle of good continuation** states that we prefer continuous figures rather than separate ones (so we will see an X as a letter rather than four separate lines)

- The **principle of closure** is a tendency to close simple figures. This results in a effect of filling in missing information to make a whole, as shown, for example, in the World Wildlife Fund panda logo and the IBM logo.

- The **principle of symmetry** describes the instance where the whole of a figure is perceived rather than the individual parts that make up the figure. The mind perceives objects as being symmetrical and forming around a central point. It is perceptually pleasing to divide objects into an even number of symmetrical parts. Therefore, when two symmetrical elements are unconnected, the mind perceptually connects them to form a coherent shape. For example, consider:

$$[ ]\{ \} [ ]$$

We tend to see the above as three pairs of symmetrical brackets rather than as six individual brackets.

PERCEPTUAL CONSTANCY

How do we know that a building in the distance is tall and not as tiny as it appears in our field of vision? Perceptual constancy refers to our ability to understand that objects stay constant even if we perceive them differently. There are typically three constancies:

- **Size constancy** refers to our ability to see objects as maintaining the same size even when our distance from them makes things appear larger or smaller. This holds true for all of our senses. As we walk away from our radio, the song appears to get softer. We understand, and perceive it as just as loud as before, the difference being our distance from what we are sensing.

- **Shape constancy** allows us to perceive a plate as still being a circle even though the angle from which we might view it appears to distort the shape; we recognize a coin even if we see it from side on, and so on.

- **Brightness constancy** refers to our ability to recognize that colour remains the same regardless of how it looks under different levels of light. We know that the bright-green T-shirt we are wearing has not changed colour even though it looks darker indoors than outside.

PERCEPTION OF DEPTH AND DISTANCE

We perceive distance using both monocular and binocular cues.

Monocular cues are those cues that can be seen using only one eye and include:

- **Size:** larger images are perceived as closer to us.

- **Texture:** objects with more detailed textures are perceived as being closer because the texture of objects tends to become smoother as the object gets farther away.

- **Overlap:** those objects covering part of another object are perceived as closer.

- **Shading:** closer objects cast longer shadows that will overlap objects which are farther away.

- **Clarity:** objects tend to get blurry as they get farther away; therefore clearer or more crisp images tend to be perceived as closer.

Binocular cues refer to those cues in which both eyes are needed to perceive. There are two important binocular cues:

- **Convergence:** the closer an object, the more inward our eyes need to turn in order to focus. Thus, we know that the more our eyes converge, the closer the object must be.

- **Retinal disparity:** each eye sees a slightly different image and these are then sent to our brains for interpretation; the distance between these two images, or their retinal disparity, thus provides another cue regarding the distance of the object. Retinal disparity thus marks the difference between two images and increases as the eyes get closer to an object.

Visual attention

> 'Everyone knows what attention is. It is the taking possession
> by the mind in clear and vivid form, of one out of what seem
> several simultaneously possible objects or trains of thought...
> It implies withdrawal from some things in order to
> deal effectively with others.'
>
> William James, *Principles of Psychology*
> [New York: Henry Holt & Co., 1890]

Visual perception is more than seeing. It is more than making sense of what we see. It is also about what we see – and why we see or pay attention to some aspects of our visual field and not to others. We can't attend to everything – there is far too much material bombarding our senses (not just our vision) and we would suffer from sensory overload. Our brains cope by selectively attending to what we consider important.

Advertisers and those in marketing know this. They know that we don't see everything in a visual field equally and work hard at making certain areas salient to us, or by working with those features that are most likely to grab our attention. Our attention is determined by both 'bottom-up' and 'top-down' factors:

▶ **Bottom-up factors** are those elements of the visual field that attract attention due to their properties (e.g. colour, contrast and orientation).

▶ **Top-down factors** are elements outside those within the visual field that influence how we perceive things and include goals, memories and interests.

Selective attention and hearing

Related to the idea of visual attention is the wider concept of selective attention. This refers to the processes by which we attend or notice one part of a stimulus but not another. This is usually studied in relation to auditory perception rather than visual, and psychologists are interested in why we attend to what we do and why we might be less attentive to other things going on around us.

Many theories of selective attention take a bottleneck approach, whereby it is assumed that there is some kind of filter or bottleneck that prevents all information getting through. Perhaps the best-known of these theories is Broadbent's Filter Model. Broadbent (1958) argued that information from all the stimuli presented at any given time enters what is termed a **sensory buffer**. Inputs are then selected on the basis of major physical characteristics for further processing by being allowed to pass through a filter. Because we have only a limited capacity to process information, this filter is designed to prevent the information-processing system from becoming overloaded. The inputs not initially selected by the filter remain briefly in the sensory buffer and, if they are not processed, they decay rapidly.

Broadbent used dichotic listening techniques to reach his conclusions. This is an experimental method aimed at investigating selective auditory attention. Messages are sent to each ear simultaneously and the participant is asked to repeat back what they have heard. Using this method, Broadbent discovered that we prefer to repeat ear by ear – that is, we can only process one 'channel' of information at a time, leading to what he called the 'single-channel model'.

According to Broadbent, the meaning of the messages is not taken into account at all by the filter. All semantic processing (i.e. processing of the meaning of the information) is carried out after the filter. So whatever message is sent to the unattended ear is not understood – even though parts of it might be remembered. For example, we might recall that a female voice spoke in the unattended ear but not what she said.

Broadbent's theory and the research it was based on have attracted criticisms:

▶ Listening to two channels at the same time is quite hard for people not accustomed to doing this, so this difficulty could account for Broadbent's findings rather than the attentional system.

- It is possible that the unattended message is analysed thoroughly but that participants simply forgot it; this could be a memory issue rather than an attentional one.

- Analysis of the unattended message might occur below the level of conscious awareness (see the 'Spotlight' below).

- The Cocktail Party Phenomenon disproves Broadbent's theory; this is when we can pick out our own name in a background buzz of noise even when we are not attending to the general noise.

 Spotlight: Unconscious information processing

Von Wright et al. (1975) found that we might process information even when we are not aware of doing so. In this research, a word was presented to participants alongside a mild electric shock. When the same word was later presented to the unattended channel, participants registered an increase in galvanic skin response (indicative of emotional arousal and analysis of the word in the unattended channel).

A slightly different perspective is taken by Treisman (1964). She maintains in her Attenuation Model that the filter that Broadbent referred to doesn't eliminate stimulation, but attenuates it (or turns down its volume) so that it is still available for further processing. Thus, if there are several sources of noise in a room (e.g. the TV, your kids talking, the baby crying), we can turn down the volume of all except the one we are attending to (e.g. the kids). This would explain why, if we heard our name, we would pick up on that.

Treisman, then, puts the filter at a slightly different place in the bottleneck. She suggested that messages are processed in a systematic way, beginning with analysis of physical characteristics, syllabic pattern and individual words. Only after this are grammatical structure and meaning processed. It will often happen that there is insufficient processing capacity to permit a full analysis of unattended stimuli, in which case later analyses will be omitted. This theory neatly predicts that it will usually be the physical characteristics of unattended inputs that are remembered rather than their meaning.

To get through the filter, items have to reach a certain threshold. All the attended/selected material will reach this threshold. Some items will retain a permanently reduced threshold, for example your own name or words/phrases like 'help' and 'fire' – this is why we will hear these against a background of noise.

Selective attention can be hampered by poor sleep, brain injury or disorders such as autism, learning disabilities or attention deficits. Selective attention can also be used to purposely draw attention to an object or person and ad agencies are always trying to think of clever ways to draw a person's selective attention to their products.

Perception of pain

Compared to our understanding of vision and hearing, the perception of pain and exactly what factors influence it are not well understood. There are cases of people experiencing pain without any physiological reason. Different people also have different pain thresholds that make pain perception hard to understand and research. Three of the best-known pain theories are discussed here, although none of them explain all of the phenomena associated with pain perception.

'The perception of pain involves far more than mere sensation. The affective and evaluative components of pain are often as important as the production and transmission of the pain signal.'

George R. Hansen and Jon Streltzer, 'The psychology of pain', Emergency Medical Clinics of North America 23 (2005): 339

Specificity Theory: this was one of the first modern theories to explain how we perceive pain. It holds that specific pain receptors transmit signals to a 'pain centre' in the brain and that it is this centre that produces the perception of pain. However, the theory does not account for the wide range of psychological factors that affect our perception of pain.

Pattern Theory: this holds that pain signals are sent to the brain only when stimuli group together to produce a specific combination or pattern. The theory does not suggest specialized receptors for pain. Rather, the brain is merely viewed as a message recipient. Despite its limitations, the Pattern Theory did set the stage for the Gate Control Theory that has proved the most influential and widely accepted pain theory so far.

Gate Control Theory: Ronald Melzack and Patrick Wall proposed the Gate Control Theory in 1965. The theory can account for both 'top-down' brain influences on pain perception (see 'Factors that affect the perception of pain' below) as well as the effects of other bottom-up stimuli in appearing to reduce pain. It proposed that there is a 'gate' or control system in the spinal cord through which all information regarding pain must pass before reaching the brain. According to British researchers from University College London, this explains why rubbing a scraped knee or banged elbow really does make the pain go away. It seems that the nerve signals from this tactile stimulation can interact, at the spinal cord level, with those signals transmitting painful sensations. When there is pain from a peripheral site of the body, such as the hand or foot, this painful signal travels along a peripheral nerve until it arrives at the spinal cord for transmission to the brain. However, at the spinal cord level there may be many different types of sensations coming in from around the body (such as touch, vibration and heat) that will 'compete' for transmission to the brain. It is thus believed that the brain's perception of pain could be reduced by multiple sensory signals arriving at the spinal cord at the same time.

Spotlight: Pain as a 'signal'

It has been shown in cancer patients that the affective component of pain can be completely blocked by frontal lobectomy (which involves cutting nerves to the frontal cortex). Lobectomized patients still register severe pain, but it doesn't 'bother' them. Pain can thus be viewed as merely a 'signal' that something is wrong somewhere in the body, until it reaches the emotional brain, where this signal becomes what we feel as pain.

FACTORS THAT AFFECT THE PERCEPTION OF PAIN

▶ **Context:** the perception of even acute pain is highly dependent on the context in which it occurs. There are, for example, reports of soldiers in battle who suffer a compound fracture and report only twinges of pain.

▶ **Attention:** focusing one's attention on pain makes the pain worse. Patients who are hypochondriacs are thought to be over-vigilant about bodily sensations. It has been found that by attending to these sensations, they amplify them to the point of that they feel painful. Conversely, distracting patients is highly effective in reducing their pain.

▶ **Anxiety:** anxiety, fear and a sense of loss of control contribute to pain. Treating anxiety and providing psychological support have been shown to improve pain and reduce analgesic use. Improving patients' sense of control and allowing them to participate in their care is also helpful. For painful medical procedures, it is advised to prepare needles and other equipment out of sight from the patient. It is also helpful to distract patients with conversation about subjects that interest them, such as their hobbies or family.

▶ **Learned pain:** pain can be a learned response, rather than a purely physical problem. In some cases, pain can be entirely 'in the mind'; I recall an experience as a small child when I fell and cut my knee. My older brother asked me whether it hurt, to which I responded that I was fine. Only when I saw blood gushing out of the knee did I start to feel the pain (as I had, presumably, learned to associate blood with pain).

Case study: Phantom pain

Phantom pain sensations are described as perceptions that an individual experiences relating to a limb or an organ that is not physically part of the body (e.g. through amputation). It has been known that at least 80 per cent of amputees experience phantom sensations at some time in their lives. They may experience some level of this phantom pain and feeling in the missing limb for the rest of their lives. Little is known about the true mechanism causing phantom pains, and it used to be thought that the pains were 'psychological'; experts now recognize that these are real sensations originating in the spinal cord and brain.

Early accounts for phantom pain claimed that the pain was the result of neuromas formed from injured nerve endings at the stump site that were able to fire abnormal action potentials. It is now thought that phantom pain can be at least partially explained as a response to mixed signals from the brain. After an amputation, areas of the spinal cord and brain obviously lose input from the missing limb but the brain adjusts to this loss in unpredictable ways. The result can trigger the body's most basic message that something is not right – which we feel as pain.

Studies also show that, after an amputation, the brain may remap the part of the body's sensory circuitry that relates to the missing limb to another part of the body (often the face, surprisingly). In other words, because the amputated area is no longer able to receive sensory information, the information is referred elsewhere – from a missing leg to a still-present lip, for example. So when the lip is touched, it's as though the missing leg is also being touched. Because this is yet another version of tangled sensory wires, the result can be pain. This is referred to as cortical remapping and there is some evidence from functional MRI scans to support this.

Phantom pain can be treated with drugs, or, more recently, a technique called Mirror Box therapy. The patient places the good limb into one side of the box and the stump into the other. The patient then looks into the mirror on the side with the good limb and makes 'mirror symmetric' movements, as we do when we clap our hands. Because the subject is seeing the reflected image of the good limb moving, it appears as if the phantom limb is also moving. Through the use of this artificial visual feedback it becomes possible for the patient to 'move' the phantom limb, and to unclench it from potentially painful positions.

▶ **Expectations:** studies have shown that minor whiplash injuries can affect people differently, depending on the expectations of their culture and location. Similarly, if people believe that they should find something painful, they are more likely to do so.

Dig deeper

Listen to Donald Broadbent talk about the Cocktail Party Phenomenon:
http://www.bbc.co.uk/programmes/b01gvkw7

Learn more about selective attention by watching the Invisible Gorilla clip or reading the book it inspired:
http://www.theinvisiblegorilla.com/videos.html

For more on optical illusions:
http://www.bbc.co.uk/news/magazine-11553099

Fact-check

1 What is perception?
   a   Seeing things that are not there
   b   Hearing things that we cannot understand
   c   Making sense of our sensations
   d   When we hear our name in a crowded room against
       background noise

2 We see faces in patterns because:
   a   Faces jump out at us
   b   We are hallucinating
   c   We imagine the faces
   d   We have a natural tendency to perceive familiar objects in
       patterns

3 Which of the following is not a component of Gibson's Theory
   of Direct Perception?
   a   Optic Flow Patterns
   b   Clarity
   c   Invariant Features
   d   Affordances

4 Which of the following is not a Gestalt Theory of Perception
   principle?
   a   Principle of longitude
   b   Principle of proximity
   c   Principle of similarity
   d   Principle of closure

5 Which of the following does not help us perceive depth and/or
   distance?
   a   Texture
   b   Size
   c   Shading
   d   Symmetry

6 The sensory buffer is:
  a Where visual illusions happen
  b The basis for understanding constancy
  c Where our sensations are filtered
  d The name for top-down processing

7 Selective attention is unlikely to be hampered by:
  a Poor sleep
  b Brain injury
  c Learning disabilities
  d Exercise

8 Which of the following is not a theory of pain?
  a Pattern Theory
  b Gate Control Theory
  c Specificity Theory
  d Context Theory

9 Which of the following is not a factor that can affect the perception of pain?
  a Context
  b Expectations
  c Closing the eyes
  d Anxiety

10 Phantom pain is:
  a When amputees imagine that they can feel pain
  b When amputees are distressed about their missing limb
  c When amputees can feel pain from the missing limb
  d Psychological

4

Memory

Memory is at the heart of cognitive psychology and underlies everything: how we talk, walk, learn and feel. What we call memory is actually a three-stage process involving 1) encoding of information (laying down the memories), 2) storage of that information and then 3) retrieval of those memories.

'Memory is the means by which we draw on our past experiences in order to use this information in the present.'

R. J. Sternberg, 'The theory of successful intelligence', *Review of General Psychology* 3 (1999): 292–316

Encoding

In Chapter 3 we talked about how sensory information reaches our brains via the process of perception. Encoding is the way that this information is processed, ready for storing. There are three main ways in which information can be encoded:

1 **Visual** (picture): for example, we store the memory by visualizing it as an image.

2 **Acoustic** (sound): here we store the information as a sound (this explains why we sometimes get words that sound the same mixed up when we try to remember them).

3 **Semantic** (meaning): here the object is stored in terms of what it means rather than as an image or sound.

It is thought that we use acoustic coding more in the short term but semantic memory for longer-term memory storage.

It should be noted that we are not always aware of encoding – this is not something that always takes place at a conscious level; encoding happens automatically. For example, if I were to ask what you ate for your evening meal last night, you will probably remember, even though you made no effort at the time to encode the information. However, such unconscious encoding is likely to result only in short-term memory; if we are to recall material in the longer term, we need to work at encoding it (as any student will know).

Storage

Memory storage affects how long memories last (duration) and how much is stored (capacity). The way information is stored affects the way it is later retrieved. There are a number of different theoretical approaches to how these storage systems work.

ATKINSON AND SHIFFRIN'S (1968) MULTISTORE MODEL

According to this approach, there are three primary types of memory storage system:

▶ **Sensory memory:** this is the storage system that occurs as the initial stage in the memory process. However, this sensory information is 'stored' only for a very short time (less than half a second for visual stimuli and three to four seconds for auditory) because it is 'raw' (i.e. unprocessed). This is to prevent us being overloaded – we are bombarded with so many sensory stimuli that we couldn't possibly store them all. Only those bits of information that we attend to and process will pass from sensory memory to deeper storage systems. The ability to look at an item, and remember what it looked like with just a split second of observation, is an example of sensory memory. It is out of our control and is an automatic response. There are thought to be two types of sensory memory: **visual sensory memory** (also known as iconic memory) and **auditory sensory memory** (echoic memory).

▶ **Short-term memory (STM):** our short-term memory, or working memory, is where our active processing happens and information can be held here for around 20–30 seconds. Our STM capacity is very limited (see the 'Spotlight' below). We can keep the information in STM longer if we rehearse it, but otherwise the data will then be lost – unless we pay further attention to it, in which case it will pass to the next stage of long-term memory.

Spotlight: Seven, plus or minus two

Short-term memory has a limited capacity: it can store about seven pieces of information, plus or minus two pieces. George A. Miller (1956), when working at Bell Laboratories, conducted experiments showing that the store of short-term memory was 7±2 items (the title of his famous paper was 'The Magical Number 7±2'). A method called 'chunking' can help to increase the capacity of short-term memory by combining small bits of information into bigger chunks – but we can still recall only around seven such chunks.

▶ **Long-term memory (LTM):** The information in our LTM is largely outside of our awareness, but it can be pulled into our working memory when needed. Some of this information is fairly easy to recall, while other memories are much more difficult to access. Our ability to access and retrieve the information from our LTM is what allows us to recall facts, to solve problems, to interact with others and make decisions. Long-term memory has an almost infinite capacity, and information in long-term memory usually stays there for the duration of a person's life. However, this doesn't mean that people will always be able to remember what's in their long-term memory – they may not be able to retrieve information that's there (see the section on 'Retrieval' below).

There is a wealth of evidence for the existence of Atkinson and Shiffrin's multi-modal storage system. For example, the Primacy-Recency Effect (Rundus and Atkinson 1970) states that, when presented with lists to remember, we recall first and last items best because the first items have time to be rehearsed into LTM and the last items can be recalled from STM. Studies of amnesiacs whose condition has been caused by Korsakoff's syndrome (brought on by chronic alcoholism) also provide evidence that suggests the existence of separate and distinct storage systems because they display good STM functioning but impaired LTM.

BADDELEY AND HITCH'S (1974) WORKING MEMORY MODEL

An alternative storage model is suggested by Baddeley and Hitch (1974) and this puts far more emphasis on STM or working memory. In this model, rather than the STM being a single inflexible store, Baddeley and Hitch suggest that the STM is made up of several subsystems, each having a specialized function and each being involved in complex cognitions/thought processes, including analysis and judgements about information input. Evidence for this approach is that people are able to carry out more than one task at once where both tasks involve STM functions.

Although Baddeley and Hitch suggested the existence of several subsystems in STM, they emphasized two in particular, which are governed by a central controlling mechanism that they termed the **Central Executive**. The Central Executive essentially acts as an attention sensory store. It channels information to two (later three) component processes: the **phonological/articulatory loop** and the **visuo-spatial sketchpad**; in 2000 the model was expanded with the introduction of the **multimodal episodic buffer.**

The **visuo-spatial sketchpad** deals with visual and spatial information – what information looks like and how it is laid out. It is engaged when performing spatial tasks (such as judging distances) or visual ones (such as counting the windows on a house or imagining images).

The **phonological/articulatory loop** is the part of working memory that deals with both auditory and written information. It is made up of the phonological store that organizes spoken material by silently rehearsing sounds or words in a continuous loop in what is known as the articulatory process (for example the repetition of a telephone number over and over again). The phonological loop holds spoken information for about 1.5 to 2 seconds. Written words must be converted to spoken words to enter the phonological loop.

The **multimodal episodic buffer** is dedicated to linking information across domains to form integrated units of visual, spatial and verbal information and chronological ordering (e.g. the memory of a story or a movie scene). The episodic buffer is also assumed to have links to long-term memory.

CRAIK AND LOCKHART'S (1972) LEVELS OF PROCESSING MODEL

This model of memory storage gives LTM a greater role, in particular with regard to the semantic processing that takes place there. Rather than just suggesting that information is transferred to the LTM from the STM through the process of repetition (as in Atkinson and Shiffrin's multi-modal model), this model suggests that the depth or level at which we process information determines its place in the LTM and also how well we recall that information. In other words, the more we think about it, the more we will remember it (even if we don't rehearse it). Craik and Lockhart didn't object to there being different subsystems in

LTM, just that the level of processing (shallow, deep or deepest) is key to memory storage.

As an example, consider these three questions:

1 Does the word CAT appear in capital letters or lower case?

2 Does the word CAT rhyme with HAT?

3 Is a CAT a bovine creature or feline?

According to Craik and Lockhart, the first question involves shallow processing as it considers only the appearance of the word. The second question involves deeper processing, looking at how the word sounds. The third question is at the deepest level as this involves semantic (meaning) processing.

Craik and Lockhart suggested that semantic processing can operate at different depths of analysis, some being more complex than others, which they referred to as **Elaborate Semantic Processing.** They also proposed that the method of learning is important in later recall as well. For example, organizing items into categories helps later recall, making items distinctive in some way helps, and items that have more information associated with them can also be recalled better.

Retrieval

In order for us to remember things, we need to be able to retrieve stored information from our memory. If we can't remember something, it could be because we are struggling to retrieve it (although it may also be due to the fact that we haven't encoded it properly or it is not stored effectively).

We retrieve material in different ways dependent on whether the information is stored in short- or long-term storage. It is thought that STM is stored and retrieved sequentially; we need to go through the sequence of memorized information before we get to the bit we need. LTM, however, is stored and retrieved by association. The way we organize information can thus help us with retrieval. For example, we might use the technique of clustering to organize related information into groups.

Types of memory

Two main types of memory are sometimes distinguished:

DECLARATIVE MEMORY

Declarative memory, which requires conscious recall, is when we 'declare' information that we have recalled (e.g. in an exam). It is sometimes called explicit memory, since it consists of information that is explicitly stored and retrieved.

Declarative memory can be further subdivided into semantic memory, which concerns facts taken independent of context; and episodic memory, which concerns information specific to a particular context, such as a time and place. **Semantic memory** allows the encoding of abstract knowledge about the world, such as 'London is the capital of the UK'. **Episodic memory**, on the other hand, is used for more personal memories, such as the sensations, emotions and personal associations of a particular place or time. **Autobiographical memory** – memory for particular events within one's own life – is generally viewed as either equivalent to, or a subset of, episodic memory.

PROCEDURAL MEMORY

In contrast, procedural memory (or implicit memory) is not based on the conscious recall of information, but on implicit learning. Procedural memory is primarily employed in learning motor skills. It is revealed when one does better in a given task due only to repetition – no new explicit memories have been formed, but one is unconsciously accessing aspects of those previous experiences.

A characteristic of procedural memory is that the things that are remembered are automatically translated into actions, and thus sometimes difficult to describe. Some examples of procedural memory are the ability to ride a bike or drive a car.

Memory failures

Psychologists are interested in why we forget. There are usually three reasons for memory failures. We either did not encode the information effectively, or we struggle to retrieve it, perhaps because the information we are trying to recall is rarely accessed (causing the memory trace to decay). Interference can also affect memory – this is where competing memories interfere with existing ones. There are two types of interference:

▶ **Proactive interference** occurs when what we already know interferes with what we are currently learning – where old memories disrupt new memories.

▶ **Retroactive interference** occurs when later learning interferes with earlier learning – where new memories disrupt old memories.

The psychologist Hermann Ebbinghaus was one of the first to scientifically study memory failures (otherwise known as forgetting). In 1885 he conducted experiments using three-letter nonsense syllables such as FHG, KYT and so forth. He used these nonsense words because using known words would have made use of existing knowledge and associations in memory and would have allowed a less pure examination of the memory process.

Ebbinghaus tested his own memory for periods of time ranging from 20 minutes to 31 days and plotted his findings in what is now known as the **Ebbinghaus Forgetting Curve.** The results showed a relationship between forgetting and time, but this relationship was not as straightforward as might have been expected; initially, information is lost very quickly, with factors such as how the information was learned and how frequently it was rehearsed influencing the speed at which these memories are lost. However, at a certain point, the amount of forgetting levels off, presumably because the data that was last to be lost was laid down in the long-term memory, which is surprisingly stable.

The tip-of-the-tongue phenomenon

The tip-of-the-tongue (TOT) phenomenon is the failure to retrieve a word from memory, combined with the feeling that retrieval is imminent. People can often recall one or more features of the forgotten word, such as the first letter or a word similar sounding or in meaning. People often feel anguish when trying to find the word that is on the 'tip of their tongue' and great relief when they locate it.

There are two major competing explanations for the occurrence of TOT phenomenon: the **direct-access view** and the **inferential view.** Direct-access view posits that, although the forgotten word does not have enough memory trace to be recalled, it has enough to signal its presence. The inferential view claims that TOTs aren't completely based on inaccessible, yet activated targets; rather, they arise when the rememberer tries to piece together different clues about the word.

An occasional tip-of-the-tongue state is normal for people of all ages. TOT becomes more frequent as people age.

Spotlight: Deaf people and TOT

Deaf people using sign language experience TOT (or, more accurately, tip-of-the-fingers) phenomenon just as much as speakers. Furthermore, just as speakers can often recall the first letter of the word, signers can sometimes think of part of the sign.

Effects on memory: smell, emotions and stress

MEMORY AND SMELL

It is well known that smells and odours can have a powerful effect on memory. It is thought that the olfactory bulb is located very close to the amygdala, the area of the brain that is connected to the experience of emotion as well as emotional memory. In addition, the olfactory nerve is very close to the hippocampus, which is also associated with memory. So closely are the two related that when people suffer from memory loss (due to ageing or damage) they often suffer from loss of sense of smell, too. But smells would not trigger memories if it weren't also for conditioned responses. When you first smell a new scent, you link it to an event, a person, a thing or even a moment. Your brain forges a link between the smell and a memory. When you encounter the smell again, the link is already there, ready to elicit a memory or a mood. Because we encounter most new odours in our youth, smells often call up childhood memories.

Spotlight: The power of smells

A well-known idea called the 'Proustian phenomenon' proposes that distinctive smells have more power than any other sense to help us recall distant memories. The theory is named after the French writer Marcel Proust, who in his novel *A la recherche du temps perdu* (*In Search of Lost Time*) describes a character vividly recalling long-forgotten memories from his childhood after smelling a tea-soaked madeleine.

MEMORY AND EMOTION

Emotion can have a powerful impact on memory. Numerous studies have shown that the most vivid autobiographical memories tend to be of emotional events, which are likely to be recalled more often and with more clarity and detail than neutral events. Memories seem to be treated differently depending on whether they are associated with pleasant positive emotions or unpleasant negative ones. Specifically, pleasant emotions appear to fade more slowly from our memory than unpleasant emotions, partly because they tend to be associated with more contextual cues. Interestingly, among those with mild depression, there is little difference in how long negative and positive memories take to fade.

Mood also affects memory, specifically at the time of encoding or retrieving. Mood congruence theory suggests that we remember events that match our current mood, which is why when we feel happy we remember other happy times, but when we are feeling sad we can recall only other sad events in our lives (and thus get more depressed). Related to this is mood dependence theory, which suggests that remembering is easier when your mood at retrieval matches your mood at encoding.

MEMORY AND STRESS

Stress has a significant effect on memory formation and learning. In response to stressful situations, the brain releases hormones and neurotransmitters that affect memory encoding processes in the hippocampus. In 2009 the German cognitive psychologists Lars Schwabe and Oliver T. Wolf showed that learning under stress decreases memory recall; the researchers suggest that stress experienced during learning distracts people by diverting their attention during the memory encoding process.

However, the impact of stress on memory can be reduced; when the material to be recalled is linked to the learning context, memory is enhanced, even when this learning occurs under stress. This was shown by a separate study by Schwabe and Wolf who found that when memory testing is performed in a context similar to the original learning task (i.e. in the same room), memory impairment and the detrimental effects of stress on learning can be reduced. The researchers gave stressed and non-stressed participants items to learn in a room with the smell of vanilla; their later recall was enhanced in a similar room (i.e. with the vanilla scent) but diminished in a non-similar room (i.e. no vanilla scent). This was true for both stressed and non-stressed participants.

This research may have practical implications; students may perform better when tested in their usual classroom rather than an exam room and eyewitnesses may recall details better at the scene of an event than in a courtroom.

False memory

'It's easy enough to explain why we remember things: multiple regions of the brain – particularly the hippocampus – are devoted to the job. It's easy to understand why we forget stuff too: there's only so much any busy brain can handle. What's trickier is what happens in between: when we clearly remember things that simply never happened.'

T. Thean, 'Remember that: no you don't', *Time*, 19 November 2013 (http://science.time.com/2013/11/19/remember-that-no-you-dont-study-shows-false-memories-afflict-us-all/)

False memory is the psychological phenomenon in which a person recalls a memory of an event that did not actually occur. Memory is not like a video-recorder; it is very prone to fallacy. False memory is often considered in legal cases regarding childhood sexual abuse. **False memory syndrome** recognizes false memory as a prevalent part of one's life in which it affects the person's mentality and day-to-day life. False memory syndrome differs from false memory in that the syndrome has a strong influence on the person's life, identity, beliefs and values (and on their relationships with other people), while false memory can occur without this significant effect. The syndrome occurs because the person believes the influential memory to be true.

Case study: Language and false memory

In 1974 Elizabeth Loftus conducted a study to investigate the effects of language on the development of false memory. The experiment involved two separate studies. In the first test, 45 participants were randomly assigned to watch different videos of a car accident, in which separate videos showed collisions at 20 miles per hour, 30 miles per hour and 40 miles per hour. Afterwards, participants filled out a survey. The survey asked the question, 'About how fast were the cars going when they smashed into each other?' The question always asked the same thing, except that the verb used to describe the collision varied. Rather than 'smashed', other verbs used included bumped, collided, hit and contacted. Participants estimated collisions of all speeds to average between 35 miles per hour to just below 40 miles per hour. If actual speed were the main factor in estimate, it could be assumed that participants would have lower estimates when they saw the lower-speed collisions. Instead, the word being used to describe the collision seemed to better predict the estimate in speed rather than the speed itself.

The second experiment also showed participants videos of car accidents, but the critical manipulation was the wording of the follow-up questionnaire. One hundred and fifty participants were randomly assigned to three groups. Those in the first groups were asked the same question as in the first study using the verbal form 'smashed'. The second group was asked the same question as in the first study, replacing 'smashed' with 'hit'. The final group was not asked about the speed of the crashed cars. The researchers then asked the participants if they had seen any broken glass, knowing that there was no broken glass in the video. The responses to this question had shown that the difference between whether broken glass was recalled or not heavily depended on the verb used. A larger number of participants in the 'smashed' group declared that there was broken glass.

These studies show that the words used to phrase a question can heavily influence the response given. The second study indicates that the phrasing of a question can create memories of events that did not happen (false memories).

Loftus's studies paved the way for research into other ways in which 'false memories' can be induced. Even the smallest adjustment in wording a question, for example, such as using 'the' can alter the responses. So, asking someone if they had seen 'the' stop sign, rather than 'a' stop sign, provides the respondent with a presupposition that there was a stop sign in the scene they are trying to recall. This presupposition increases the number of people responding that they had indeed seen the stop sign. Similarly, using presupposition can create memories of things that were not there: 'What shade of blue was his jacket?' assumes that the jacket was blue, for example, and thus encourages the individual to 'remember' the jacket being blue. Asking someone 'How tall was the gunman?' will lead to greater estimates of height than asking how short he was. This shows how easily memories can be manipulated.

Suggestion then, can lead to the creation of false memories, but so can misinformation, existing memories and misattribution.

Dig deeper

Read more on false memory syndrome at the British False Memory Society:
http://bfms.org.uk/

Read more about memory and smell in a newspaper article:
http://www.telegraph.co.uk/science/science-news/9042019/
Smells-can-trigger-emotional-memories-study-finds.html

An excellent website on human memory:
http://www.human-memory.net/disorders_age.html

Fact-check

1 The three stages of memory are:
- **a** Encoding, storage and retrieval
- **b** Long-term memory, short-term memory and sensory memory
- **c** Visual, acoustic and semantic memory
- **d** Working, multistore and levels of processing

2 The three main ways in which information can be encoded are:
- **a** Encoding, storage and retrieval
- **b** Visual, acoustic and semantic
- **c** Working, multistore and levels of processing
- **d** Long-term memory, short-term memory and sensory memory

3 The three stages of Atkinson and Shiffrin's (1968) Multistore Model are:
- **a** Encoding, storage and retrieval
- **b** Long-term memory, short-term memory and sensory memory
- **c** Visual, acoustic and semantic memory
- **d** Working, multistore and levels of processing

4 The three subsystems in Baddeley and Hitch's (1974) Working Memory Model are:
- **a** The phonological/articulatory loop, the visuo-spatial sketchpad and the multimodal episodic buffer
- **b** The central executive, the phonological/articulatory loop and the visuo-spatial sketchpad
- **c** Declarative, procedural and episodic systems
- **d** Iconic, echoic and sensory systems

5 Which of the following is not an example of procedural memory?
- **a** Riding a bike
- **b** Driving a car
- **c** Reciting a learned poem
- **d** Using a new computer program

6 Which of the following is not a reason for memory failures?
- **a** Failure to encode
- **b** Failure to retrieve
- **c** Interference effects
- **d** Selective attention

7 Smells evoke emotions because:
- **a** Smells are a powerful sense
- **b** Smells reach primitive parts of the brain
- **c** Every scent has an emotion associated with it
- **d** The smell receptors are closely linked to areas of memory within the brain

8 Mood congruence theory suggests that:
- **a** We remember events that match our current mood
- **b** Remembering is easier when your mood at retrieval does not match your mood at encoding
- **c** Moods are often congruent with emotions
- **d** Moods are often evoked by smells

9 What is false memory?
- **a** When we fail to remember things that happened
- **b** When other people remember things that happened to us but we don't
- **c** When we remember things that did not actually happen
- **d** When people imagine historic sexual abuse

10 Which of the following is not a factor in leading to false memories?
- **a** Suggestion
- **b** Misattribution
- **c** Misinformation
- **d** Sexual abuse

5

Learning

Learning refers to the changes that occur as the result of experience or exposure to stimuli, and much of what we know about how we learn originates in the theories of classical and operant conditioning. But there are other forms of learning, too, and social learning suggests that we don't always have to learn by doing things ourselves but just by watching others.

Learning is defined as a relatively lasting change in behaviour as a result of experience. We can't see learning, but can infer it only from observable behaviour. Changes sometimes take place in behaviour that are not the result of learning, but these are usually short-lasting (e.g. drugs or temperature might change behaviour in the short-term but this is not the result of learning).

Of course, not all permanent change is due to learning, either. For example, brain damage, maturation and so on can change behaviour. For change in behaviour to be classed as 'learning', then, it has to have come about through some kind of experience that the person has undergone.

Learning as a psychological discipline has its roots in behaviourism. Behaviourism is a psychological approach developed by the American psychologist John B. Watson (1878–1958) that was concerned with measurable behaviours (as oppose to internal mental processes that could not be measured). Behaviourism can perhaps be best summed up by the following quote from Watson:

> 'Give me a dozen healthy infants, well-formed, and my own specified world to bring them up in and I'll guarantee to take any one at random and train him to become any type of specialist I might select – doctor, lawyer, artist, merchant-chief and, yes, even beggar-man and thief, regardless of his talents, penchants, tendencies, abilities, vocations, and race of his ancestors.'
>
> John Watson, *Behaviorism* (Chicago: University of Chicago Press, 1930)

By this he meant that most behaviours that can be measured can be trained, changed or 'conditioned' – and that virtually any behaviours can be produced with the right training. Watson's theory was based on the idea that all behaviours are acquired through the conditioning that occurs when we interact with our environment. Two types of conditioning are identified and these form the basis of all learning according to the behaviourist perspective: classical conditioning and operant. Each of these will be considered in turn.

Classical conditioning

Classical conditioning is a learning process in which an association is made between a previously neutral stimulus (i.e. one that didn't provoke a response) and a stimulus that naturally evokes a response.

Spotlight: Ivan Pavlov and his dogs

Although classical conditioning is one of the building blocks of psychology, the man who first noted the phenomenon was not a psychologist at all. Ivan Pavlov was a Russian physiologist who, in 1904, won a Nobel Prize for his advancement of knowledge in the field of digestion. It was his work in this area on dogs that led to the now-famous Pavlovian response.

Ivan Pavlov was born in Russia in 1849 and was the eldest of 11 children. Turning down the chance to be a priest like his father, he instead became a scientist and by the early 1900s he was busy studying the production of saliva in dogs as part of his ongoing work in the field of digestion. He gave his dogs a range of edible and non-edible items and then measured the amount of saliva they produced. Salivation, he knew, was an automatic reflex that was outside the conscious control of the animals. Saliva is produced when animals taste or smell food and is designed to aid digestion.

However, he noted that, after a few experiments, the dogs began to produce saliva as soon as his assistants opened the door and entered the room – that is, before any food had been produced to see, smell or taste. Pavlov realized that the dogs must have learned to produce saliva as soon as the assistants appeared because they had come to associate the appearance of the assistants with the production of food. Unlike the salivary response to the presentation of food, which is an unconditioned reflex (in that it doesn't need to be learned), salivating to the expectation of food was, he claimed, a conditioned or learned reflex.

When Pavlov made this discovery, he devoted the rest of his life to studying more about this type of learning, called classical conditioning because it is the first systematic study of basic laws of learning. His most famous experiments involved pairing a neutral stimulus (a bell) with the food that produced the unconditioned response (salivation) to the food; after a few pairings, the bell alone was enough to produce salivation even without pairing it with the food (conditioned response).

In classical conditioning, it is important to distinguish between the main components:

▶ **The unconditioned stimulus (US):** this is the stimulus that naturally produces a response to something that does not need any learning to achieve (e.g. feeling hungry at the sight of food – the US is the food).

▶ **The conditioned stimulus (CS):** this is the previously neutral stimulus that, after becoming associated with the unconditioned stimulus, eventually comes to trigger a conditioned response (e.g. feeling hungry when the clock strikes 1 p.m. irrespective of whether your stomach is empty or not – the CS is the clock).

▶ **The unconditioned response (UR):** this is the automatic response elicited by the unconditioned stimulus (e.g. hunger or salivation at the sight of food).

▶ **The conditioned response (CR):** this is the learned response to the previously neutral stimulus (e.g. hunger when the clock strikes one).

THE BASIC PRINCIPLES OF CLASSICAL CONDITIONING

There are a number of different phenomena associated with all examples of classical conditioning. These include:

▶ **Extinction:** in classical conditioning, extinction happens when a conditioned stimulus is no longer paired with an unconditioned stimulus. Just as pairing the two leads to a conditioned response, when the pairing stops, eventually the response will stop, too – it will become extinct. Thus, if Pavlov's dogs stopped hearing a bell before each presentation of food, eventually a bell on its own would no longer be enough to produce salivation.

- **Spontaneous recovery:** even after extinction, the conditioned response can sometimes come back at random times, even years later.

- **Stimulus generalization:** this is the tendency for events similar to the conditioned stimulus to evoke the conditioned response. For example, if a child has been bitten by a Yorkshire Terrier he may develop a conditioned fear to all Yorkies that may generalize to all dogs – and possibly even to all animals.

- **Discrimination:** this is the opposite of generalizability as it is the ability to differentiate between a conditioned stimulus and other stimuli that have not been paired with an unconditioned stimulus. For example, if schoolchildren pair the sound of the lunch bell with feeling hungry, they won't feel hungry at the sound of a different bell.

- **Contiguity:** the more closely in time two events occurred, the more likely they are to become associated; as time passes, association becomes less likely. This is why a dog owner who returns home from work to find his dog has soiled the carpet will not succeed in punishing the dog then – too long has passed since the event for the dog to make the connection between his soiling and the punishment.

SCHEDULING THE CS AND THE US

There are different ways in which the conditioned and the unconditioned stimulus can be paired. Using Pavlov's dogs as an example, we can see various possible schedules:

- **Delayed/forward conditioning:** this is where the CS (bell) is presented first and while the bell is still ringing the dog is given the US (food). This is the fastest way to get acquisition (the term used for conditioning a stimulus).

- **Trace conditioning:** this is where the CS (bell) is presented but it is followed by a short break before the US (food) appears.

- **Simultaneous conditioning:** here the CS (bell) and the US (food) are presented at the same time and continue for the same amount of time.

▶ **Backward conditioning:** In this case the US (food) is presented first and is followed by the CS (bell).

HIGHER-ORDER OR SECOND-ORDER CONDITIONING

Classical conditioning might seem simple but it actually gets a little more complicated. Imagine pairing a bell with the appearance of food for one of Pavlov's dogs. Classical conditioning occurs whereby eventually the bell alone will produce salivation without the need for food to be present at all. So far so clear. Now, imagine that every time we ring the bell, we also present the dog with a flash of light. Eventually, the flash of light becomes weakly conditioned to produce the salivation even without the bell. This is second-order conditioning.

And it can go further: another stimulus can be paired with the flash of light and salivation can be conditioned to occur with that, too (third-order conditioning). And so it goes on.

A good real-life example is this. A child has a kind aunt who has no children of her own so indulges her nieces and nephews instead. The aunt starts as a neutral figure but the treats and presents that she gives to the child soon turn her into a conditioned stimulus: the child feels happy whenever he sees his aunt. It just so happens that this aunt wears a particular perfume and one day the child smells that perfume in a store – and feels really happy. The perfume has become a second-order conditioned stimulus.

Operant conditioning

'*The only way to tell whether a given event is reinforcing to a given organism under given conditions is to make a direct test. We observe the frequency of a selected response, then make an event contingent upon it and observe any change in frequency. If there is a change, we classify the event as reinforcing to the organism under the existing conditions.*'

B. F. Skinner, *Science and Human Behavior*
(New York: Simon & Schuster 1953)

Operant conditioning (or instrumental conditioning) is a type of learning in which an individual's behaviour is changed by its antecedents (things that preceded it) and consequences (things that follow it). Operant conditioning is distinguished from classical conditioning in the following ways:

▶ **Classical conditioning** involves placing a neutral stimulus before a reflex (i.e. a response that does not need to be learned) and focuses on involuntary, automatic behaviours. It involves making an association between an involuntary response and a stimulus. The learner does not actively learn – but is passive in the whole process.

▶ **Operant conditioning**, on the other hand, involves applying reinforcement (reward) or punishment after a behaviour and focuses on strengthening or weakening voluntary behaviours. Operant conditioning is about making an association between a voluntary behaviour and a consequence. Operant conditioning requires the learner to actively participate and perform some type of action in order to be rewarded or punished.

Operant conditioning then focuses on using either reinforcement or punishment to increase or decrease a behaviour. Through this process an association is formed between the behaviour and the consequences for that behaviour. The 'father' of operant conditioning was B. F. Skinner (1904–90), although his theories were based on the work of Edward Thorndike (1874–1949), whose studies of learning in animals using a puzzle box led to his 'Law of Effect'. The puzzle box consisted of an arrangement into which a cat was placed and from which it had to work out a way to escape in order to obtain its reward (scraps of fish). The boxes would contain a lever which, when pressed, opened the exit door. The cats would stumble around until they happened to press the lever accidentally. This would happen for a few trials until the cat realized that there was a connection between their pressing the lever and the door opening. Then they would immediately press the lever to escape. Thorndike's 'Law of Effect' stated that any behaviour that is followed by pleasant consequences is likely to be repeated, and any behaviour followed by unpleasant consequences is likely to be stopped.

Almost half a century later, this Law of Effect provided a framework for Skinner to develop his principles of operant conditioning. He used an updated version of Thorndike's puzzle box, called the operant chamber, or Skinner box (1948), which has contributed immensely to our understanding of the Law of Effect in modern society and how it relates to operant conditioning. Skinner introduced a new addition to the Law of Effect – **reinforcement.** This concept stated that behaviour that is reinforced tends to be repeated (i.e. strengthened) while behaviour that is not reinforced tends to die out or be extinguished (i.e. weakened).

While Thorndike used cats, Skinner used rats (which allowed for smaller puzzle boxes to be designed). The principle of the puzzle was the same: the rat had to press a lever in order to obtain a pellet of food. At first this would happen accidentally when the rat brushed against the lever, but the rat soon learned what action to take in order to obtain its reward. This was termed **positive reinforcement,** which strengthens a behaviour (in this case pressing the lever) by providing a consequence (food) that an individual finds rewarding.

The removal of an unpleasant reinforcer can also strengthen behaviour. Skinner introduced electric shocks to the rats in his boxes – these shocks could be removed by pressing the lever in the same way that the food was released in the positive reinforcement trials. The rats learned to press the lever to escape the unpleasant stimulus, just as they learned to press it to gain a pleasant reward. This is known as **negative reinforcement** because it is the removal of an adverse stimulus that is 'rewarding' to the animal. Negative reinforcement strengthens behaviour because it stops or removes an unpleasant experience.

Punishment is another operant term and this is different from negative reinforcement. In fact, punishment is the opposite of reinforcement since it is used to stop a behaviour or weaken the likelihood of it occurring. Punishment can either be negative or positive: positive punishment is when an unfavourable outcome results from performing some action, whereas negative punishment is when a favourable outcome is stopped after the action is performed.

Some reinforcement can be simultaneously positive and negative, such as a drug addict taking drugs for the added euphoria (a positive feeling) and eliminating withdrawal symptoms (which would be a negative feeling). Or, in a warm room, a blast of air conditioning serves as positive reinforcement because it is pleasantly cool and as negative reinforcement because it removes uncomfortable hot air. Both positive and negative reinforcement *increase* behaviour. Most people, especially children, will learn to follow instruction by a mix of positive and negative reinforcement.

PRIMARY AND SECONDARY REINFORCERS

A primary reinforcer, sometimes called an unconditioned reinforcer, is a stimulus that does not require pairing to function as a reinforcer and most likely has obtained this function through evolution and its role in survival. Examples of primary reinforcers include sleep, food and water. The reinforcing value of primary reinforcers can vary. Thus, one person may prefer one type of food while another hates it. Or one person may eat lots of food while another eats very little. So even though food is a primary reinforcer for both individuals, the value of food as a reinforcer differs between them.

A secondary reinforcer, sometimes called a conditioned reinforcer, is a stimulus or situation that has acquired its function as a reinforcer after pairing with a stimulus that functions as a reinforcer. Money is a secondary reinforcer that has only learned value.

Spotlight: The Premack Principle

The Premack Principle is a special case of reinforcement coined by David Premack (1959). This states that a highly preferred activity can be used effectively as a reinforcer for a less preferred activity. The principle is often considered in parenting situations, such as 'If you clear the table, you can go and play outside' or 'Eat your vegetables and you can have ice cream.' As a result, it is sometimes called Grandma's Law.

BEHAVIOUR MODIFICATION

Behaviour modification is a set of therapies/techniques based on operant conditioning (Skinner 1938, 1953). The main principle comprises changing environmental events that are related to a person's behaviour – for example the reinforcement of desired behaviours and ignoring or punishing undesired ones. This is used in workplaces, in schools and other environments to *shape* behaviour.

Shaping is when reinforcement is used to build up desired complex behaviours: the behaviours are broken into smaller parts and each part is reinforced before moving on to the next segment in the sequence. For example, a child who is afraid of dogs might be rewarded for being in the same room as a dog. Once that behaviour becomes accepted, he might then be rewarded for sitting near the dog. Eventually, he will be reinforced for stroking the dog and so on.

A **token economy** is a system of behaviour modification based on the systematic reinforcement of target behaviour. The reinforcers are symbols or 'tokens' that can be exchanged for other reinforcers. Token economies are often used in schools and mental health settings to shape appropriate behaviour.

REINFORCEMENT SCHEDULES

Schedules of reinforcement are the rules that are used to decide when reinforcers (or even punishers) are presented in relation to a specified operant behaviour. These rules are defined in terms of the time and/or the number of responses required in order for the reinforcement or reward to appear. A reinforcement schedule is a tool in operant conditioning that allows the experimenter or trainer to control the timing and frequency of reinforcement in order to elicit a target behaviour series from a participant. There are three main types of schedule: continuous, ratio and interval.

<u>Continuous reinforcement</u> is a schedule of reinforcement in which every occurrence of the instrumental or operant response is followed by the reinforcer. For example, if Skinner's rats received a food pellet each time they pressed the lever, that would be continuous reinforcement. Parents toilet training their toddlers usually start with continuous reinforcement. This type of schedule is the least resistant to extinction since as soon as the reinforcement stops, the behaviour will stop too (unless it becomes its own reward, as tends to happen with toilet training – children usually find accidents distressing and thus maintain toileting behaviour even when the external rewards have stopped).

With **ratio schedules,** the presentation of the reward depends on the number of operant responses that the individual has performed. There are two types of ratio schedule:

▶ **Fixed ratio schedules:** these deliver reinforcement after a set number of responses. Thus Skinner's rat might receive a food pellet after every fifth press. In real life, this might work by rewarding an estate agent with a bonus for every five houses sold. Extinction will occur when the reward is stopped.

▶ **Variable ratio schedules:** here the reinforcement occurs after a variable number of responses. A real-world example is slot machines (because, though the probability of hitting the jackpot is constant, the number of lever presses needed to hit the jackpot is variable). The variable ratio schedule is the most resistant to extinction.

Interval schedules require a minimum amount of time that must pass between successive reinforced responses (e.g. five minutes). Responses that are made before this time has elapsed are not reinforced. There are also two types of interval schedule:

▶ **Fixed interval:** this is where there is a fixed amount of time between each reinforcer; a real life example of this is when someone is paid hourly. Extinction will occur quickly if the reinforcer is stopped.

> **Variable interval:** reinforced on an average amount of time that varies from trial to trial. Fishing is a good example of a variable interval schedule: the fisherman/woman knows that they might have to wait a long time before they catch their fish. This schedule is resistant to extinction in that the behaviour will continue for quite a while after reinforcement stops.

Social Learning Theory

'Learning would be exceedingly laborious, not to mention hazardous, if people had to rely solely on the effects of their own actions to inform them what to do. Fortunately, most human behavior is learned observationally through modeling: from observing others one forms an idea of how new behaviors are performed, and on later occasions this coded information serves as a guide for action.'

Albert Bandura, *Social Learning Theory* (Englewood Cliffs, NJ: Prentice-Hall, 1977)

Taking a different perspective to the behaviourist view of learning as outlined so far in this chapter is Albert Bandura's Social Learning Theory (SLT; 1977). Albert Bandura (born 1925) is an eminent psychologist at Stanford University. SLT states that people can learn from one other, via observation, imitation and modelling, not just through conditioning. Unlike Skinner, Bandura believed that humans are active information processors and think about the relationship between their behaviour and its consequences. Observational learning could not occur unless cognitive processes were at work; because the social learning approach takes into account the cognitive factors that mediate between stimuli and responses, it addresses one of the most important criticisms of behaviourism – that is, its neglect of thinking or cognitive processes.

These are the key tenets of Social Learning Theory:

▶ Learning is not just behavioural, based on conditioning; rather, it is a cognitive process that takes place in a social context.

▶ Learning can occur vicariously, through the observation of a behaviour and the consequences of that behaviour.

▶ Learning can occur without an observable change in a person's behaviour.

While the role of reinforcement in learning is acknowledged, SLT states that there are other factors that contribute, too.

Reciprocal determinism states that, just as an individual's behaviour is influenced by the environment, the environment is also influenced by the individual's behaviour. Thus, for example, a child may have learned by their home life to be aggressive, but by being aggressive they also change the way others act towards them.

Case study: Bobo doll experiments

Both of the shooters of the Columbine School massacre in 1999 watched violent movies and played violent video games, and many blamed these types of media for what happened. But what exactly is the impact of violent media on the behaviour of children and youth? Can children really learn to be violent by watching others? In 1961 Bandura and colleagues conducted the now-famous Bobo doll experiments. The Bobo doll was a child-sized inflatable doll with a weighted bottom that causes it to pop back up after being knocked down. Preschool-aged children were divided into three groups: one group that observed an adult behaving aggressively towards the Bobo doll (punching, kicking, striking with a mallet, yelling), another group that observed the adult playing peacefully, and a control group.

Later, the children were allowed to play independently in the playroom, which contained a variety of aggressive and non-aggressive toys, including the Bobo doll. Participants' acts of verbal and physical aggression towards the Bobo doll were then recorded. Results revealed significant group differences, one of which was that the children exposed to the aggressive model were more likely to imitate what they had seen and behave aggressively towards the doll. Bandura and colleagues argued that the results supported the idea that children can rapidly learn new behaviours through the process of observation and imitation, and that this occurs even in the absence of any kind of reinforcement.

Some critics of these studies, however, argue that the behaviour of the children in Bandura's studies was significantly influenced by demand characteristics and that they were, in effect, deliberately producing the behaviour they thought the experimenters wanted to see.

Observation is the central tenet of SLT but observational learning can be influenced by a variety of factors. For example, the degree of modelling (or copying the behaviour of a model) can depend on who that model is; we are more likely to learn from and copy the behaviour of someone we like and who is similar to us (something that advertisers and marketers will use to their advantage where possible). Learning is also influenced by the learner themselves; the learner has to be paying attention to the model, be able to retain the information they observe, be capable of reproducing it and be motivated to do so. All these factors can influence the likelihood of social learning taking place.

Spotlight: The fate of Bandura's Bobo doll

The original Bobo doll can be seen in the Center for the History of Psychology at the University of Akron, after being donated by Bandura in 2010. It is one of their most popular exhibits.

Dig deeper

See Thorndike's puzzle box in action at
http://www.simplypsychology.org/edward-thorndike.html

Can birds read? Watch a bird demonstrate operant conditioning in a Skinner box:
http://www.simplypsychology.org/operant-conditioning.html

To see Bandura's Bobo doll study, see:
https://www.youtube.com/watch?v=dmBqwWlJg8U

Fact-check

✗ 1 What is learning?

    a A permanent change in behaviour as a result of experience

    b A permanent change in attitude as a result of experience

    c A temporary change in behaviour as a result of experience

    ⓓ A relatively lasting change in behaviour as a result of experience

✗ 2 What is classical conditioning?

    a The process by which dogs salivate

    ⓑ A learning process in which an association is made between a previously neutral stimulus and a stimulus that naturally evokes a response

    c A type of learning in which an individual's behaviour is modified by its antecedents (things that preceded it) and consequences (things that follow it)

    d A procedure that focuses on using either reinforcement or punishment to increase or decrease a behaviour

3 What is operant conditioning?

    a The process by which dogs salivate

    b A learning process in which an association is made between a previously neutral stimulus and a stimulus that naturally evokes a response

    ⓒ A type of learning in which an individual's behaviour is modified by its antecedents (things that preceded it) and consequences (things that follow it)

    d A procedure that focuses on using either reinforcement or punishment to increase or decrease a behaviour

4 Thorndike's 'Law of Effect' states that:

a Any behaviour that is followed by pleasant consequences is likely to be repeated, and any behaviour followed by unpleasant consequences is likely to be stopped

b Any behaviour that is followed by unpleasant consequences is likely to be repeated, and any behaviour followed by pleasant consequences is likely to be stopped

c A highly preferred activity can be used effectively as a reinforcer for a less preferred activity

d Reinforcement can be used to build up desired complex behaviours

5 The removal of an unpleasant reinforcer to strengthen behaviour is referred to as:

a Positive reinforcement

b Negative reinforcement

c Punishment

d Extinction

6 Shaping is:

a When reinforcement is used to build up desired complex behaviours

b A token economy

c Used with ratio schedules

d Used with interval schedules

7 Fixed schedules of reinforcement are:

a The most efficient

b Used in schools

c Where there is a fixed amount of time or number of responses before a reward appears

d Where there is a variable amount of time or number of responses before a reward appears

8 With which of the following processes does social learning *not* occur?

a Observation

b Imitation

c Modelling

d Change in behaviour

9 Reciprocal determinism is the process by which:

   a   There is a variable amount of time or number of responses before a reward appears

   b   Just as an individual's behaviour is influenced by the environment, the environment is also influenced by the individual's behaviour

   c   A highly preferred activity can be used effectively as a reinforcer for a less preferred activity

   d   Shaping occurs

10 Which of the following factors does *not* influence the likelihood of social learning taking place?

   a   Who the model is

   b   How similar we are to them

   c   How motivated we are

   d   How old we are

6

Language and thought

Language and thinking processes are thought by many to go hand in hand; while it is theoretically possible to have thought without language (and language without thought), the two processes certainly interact quite early in development. Most psychologists are of the view that the two processes are very much interlinked, which is why they are presented together in this chapter. Other aspects of cognition that depend on these processes, such as reasoning, problem-solving and creativity, are also explored in this chapter.

Language acquisition

Language acquisition is the process by which we learn to perceive and understand language, as well as to use words and construct sentences to communicate (this is distinguished from second-language acquisition, which deals with the acquisition, in both children and adults, of additional languages). It is the complex linguistical skill that humans have that sets them apart from other animals; while other species do communicate using a limited number of meaningful vocalizations, there is no other species known to date that can express infinite ideas (sentences) with a limited set of symbols (speech sounds and words) as humans can.

The capacity to successfully use language requires one to acquire a range of complex tools including phonology, morphology, syntax, semantics and an extensive vocabulary. Language need not be verbally expressed – sign language would come in the same category in terms of the processes of acquisition.

There are thought to be two main guiding principles in first-language acquisition:

▶ Speech perception always precedes speech production (children understand language before they can speak it; this understanding is sometimes called receptive language, as oppose to expressive language, which is spoken)

▶ Language is a gradually evolving system by which a child learns a language one step at a time, beginning with the distinction between individual phonemes (the smallest unit of sound in a language).

A major debate in understanding language acquisition is how these capacities are picked up by young children. Behaviourists such as Skinner (1957) argue that children learn language based on behaviourist reinforcement principles (including imitation and reinforcement), by associating words with meanings. Correct utterances are positively reinforced when the child realizes the communicative value of words and phrases; for example, a child who can say the word 'drink' is more likely to be rewarded with what they want than a child who cannot articulate the word (or an approximation of the word). According to this view, children learn words by associating sounds with objects, actions and events. They also learn words and syntax by imitating others. Adults enable children to learn words and syntax by reinforcing correct speech.

Nativists, such as Noam Chomsky (born 1928), however, disagree with this approach, arguing that children would never acquire the tools needed for processing the infinite number of sentences that we can process, if the language acquisition mechanism was dependent on language input alone; as there are infinite ways of putting sentences together, these cannot possibly all be learned by imitation. In addition, learning alone cannot account for the rapid rate at which children acquire language. When you consider the hugely complex nature of human language with its complicated grammatical structures, and compare this with the relatively limited cognitive ability of a small child, you can appreciate why Chomsky felt that there must be something other than learning that drives language acquisition. Chomsky decided that the process of language acquisition in infants must be biologically driven. Otherwise, he argued, it is hard to explain how children, within the first five years of life, are able to grasp the complex, grammatical rules of their native language – complexities that most adults are unable to master anywhere near as well. Indeed, the 'critical period' for language acquisition seems to be in the first five years; after the age of seven, our ability to learn a language declines dramatically.

Chomsky argues that human brains have a language acquisition device (LAD), an innate mechanism or process that allows children to develop language skills. According to this view, all children are born with a universal grammar, which makes them receptive to the common features of all languages. Because of this hard-wired background in grammar, children easily pick up a language when they are exposed to its particular grammar.

'When we study human language, we are approaching what some might call the "human essence", the distinctive qualities of mind that are, so far as we know, unique to man.'
Noam Chomsky, *Language and Mind* (New York: Harcourt Brace Jovanovich, 1972)

Evidence for an innate human capacity to acquire language skills comes from a number of observations:

▶ The various stages of language development occur at roughly the same ages in most children, even across different cultures.

▶ Children generally acquire language skills quickly and effortlessly (unlike adults).

Some researchers believe that both nature and nurture are important in language acquisition. These theorists believe that while humans do have an innate capacity for acquiring the rules of language, children develop language skill through interaction with others.

The relationship between language and thought

In the 1950s Edward Sapir and his student Benjamin Lee Whorf proposed the **Linguistic Relativity hypothesis** (sometimes referred to as the Sapir–Whorf hypothesis, despite the fact that the two never actually co-authored anything). This claimed that language determines the way people think. Differences in the way languages encode cultural and cognitive categories affect the way people think, so that speakers of different languages will tend to think and behave differently depending on the language they use. Thus, the theory controversially claims that there are certain thoughts of an individual in one language that cannot be understood by those who live in another language.

'No two languages are ever sufficiently similar to be considered as representing the same social reality. The worlds in which different societies live are distinct worlds, not merely the same world with different labels attached.'

Edward Sapir, 'The status of linguistics as a science',
Language 5/4 (1929): 207

The hypothesis is generally understood to have two different versions:

▶ the strong version (sometimes called linguistic determinism), in which language totally determines thought and in which linguistic categories limit and determine cognitive categories

▶ the weak (and less controversial) version (linguistic relativism), in which linguistic categories and usage merely influence thought and certain kinds of non-linguistic behaviour.

Non-verbal communication

Not all language is communicated verbally. Non-verbal communication (NYC) is the process of communication through sending and receiving wordless (mostly visual) cues between people and includes the use of voice (paralanguage), touch (haptics), distance (proxemics) and physical environments/ appearance. Even speech contains non-verbal elements known as paralanguage, including voice quality, rate, pitch, volume and speaking style, as well as prosodic features such as rhythm, intonation and stress. It is thought that up to two-thirds of a message is communicated non-verbally.

The development of these non-verbal linguistic skills involves being able to both encode and decode non-speech cues. Encoding is the act of generating the information through facial expressions, gestures and postures. Decoding is the interpretation of information from received sensations from previous experiences. Babies learn non-verbal communication from social–emotional communication, with the face rather than words being the major route of communication (because they don't understand the words). As children become verbal communicators, they begin to look at facial expressions, vocal tones and other non-verbal elements less consciously; it could be said that they go from being non-verbal to verbal communicators.

Spotlight: Darwin and non-verbal communication

Scientific research on non-verbal communication and behaviour was started in 1872 with the publication of Charles Darwin's book *The Expression of the Emotions in Man and Animals*. In this book Darwin argued that all mammals, both humans and animals, showed emotion through facial expressions. Darwin attributed these facial expressions to behaviours that earlier in our evolutionary history had specific and direct functions. For example, animals that bare their teeth when angry do so because it communicates an intent to bite. Wrinkling the nose is a sign of disgust for humans but in our evolutionary past it would have helped reduce the inhalation of foul odour. According to Darwin, humans continue to make facial expressions even though they no longer serve the original purpose that they were 'designed' for, because they have acquired communicative value throughout evolutionary history.

NVC expert Michael Argyle (1925–2002) discussed the function of NVC in 1970 and suggested that, whereas spoken language is normally used for communicating information about events external to the speakers, non-verbal codes are used to establish and maintain interpersonal relationships. In 1988 Argyle concluded that there are five primary functions of non-verbal bodily behaviour in human communication:

1 To express emotions

2 To express interpersonal attitudes

3 To accompany speech in managing the cues of interaction between speakers and listeners

4 Presentation of one's personality

5 Rituals (greetings).

Some NVC is clearly learned behaviour while some is not. Learned non-verbal cues require a community or culture in order for infants to learn them. For example, table manners are learned examples of non-verbal communication. Dress code is a non-verbal set of symbols that must be established by society – and will vary from culture to culture. Hand symbols, too, vary between cultures and are not innate non-verbal cues. <u>Learned cues must be gradually reinforced by punishment</u> (such as being admonished for putting elbows on the table) or <u>positive feedback</u>.

Case study: Children's comprehension of NVC

Speakers can influence how recipients will interpret their utterances by using non-verbal 'markers'. If they wish some other, less obvious interpretation other than the spoken one, they may 'mark' their utterance (e.g. with special intonations or facial expression). A groundbreaking study reported in the *Journal of Child Language* identified this 'marking' as a learned form of non-verbal communication in toddlers that develops sometime between the ages of two and three.

In the study, two- and three-year-old toddlers were tested on their recognition of markedness within gestures. The experiment was conducted in a room with an examiner and the test participants, who for the first study were three-year-olds. The examiner sat across from each child individually and allowed them to play with various objects including a purse with a sponge in it and a box with a sponge in it. After allowing the child to play with the objects for three minutes, the examiner told the child it was time to clean up and motioned by pointing to the objects. They measured the responses of the children by first pointing and not marking the gesture (e.g. with facial expression), to see the child's reaction to the request and if they reached for the objects to clean them up. After observing the child's response, the examiner then asked and pointed again, marking the gesture with facial expression, as to lead the child to believe the objects were supposed to be cleaned up. The results showed that three-year-old children were able to recognize the markedness, by responding to the gesture and cleaning the objects up far more than when the gesture was presented without being marked.

In the second study, in which the same experiment was performed on two-year-olds, the results were different. For the most part, the children did not recognize the difference between the marked and unmarked gesture by not responding more prevalently to the marked gesture, unlike the results of the test involving the three-year-olds.

Innate non-verbal cues are 'built-in' features of human behaviour that do not need to be taught. Generally, these innate cues are universally prevalent – that is, they can be found in most cultures. For example, smiling, crying and laughing do not need to be learned.

Reasoning

Reasoning is the capacity for consciously making sense of things, applying logic, for establishing and verifying facts, and changing or justifying beliefs based on new or existing information. It is thus associated with thinking, cognition and intellect. Reasoning helps to generate new knowledge and to organize existing knowledge, so that it is more usable for future mental work. Reasoning is therefore central to many forms of thought such as scientific, critical and creative thinking, argumentation, problem-solving and decision-making.

There are several different types of reasoning, for example deductive and inductive. **Inductive reasoning** makes broad generalizations from specific cases or observations. This is sometimes called bottom–up reasoning. Scientists use inductive reasoning to create theories and hypotheses – to generate new knowledge. However, this reasoning can lead to inferences that may not be true. An example of inductive reasoning would be: all the birds in my garden have wings and fly; thus all birds must have wings and fly. Clearly, this is not true since many birds do have wings but don't fly (e.g. penguins and ostriches).

In contrast, in **deductive reasoning** a person starts with a known claim or a general belief and from there asks what follows from these foundations or how these premises will influence other beliefs. In other words, deduction starts with a hypothesis and examines the possibilities to reach a conclusion. The reasoning goes from the general to the specific. Sometimes this is called the 'top–down' approach because the reasoner starts at the top with a very broad spectrum of information and they work their way down to a specific conclusion. This, too, is subject to false reasoning; for example, 'Fred is a teacher. Fred wears glasses. Therefore all teachers wear glasses.' This is clearly an illogical process of reasoning (although it is deductive).

The development of reasoning skills in children has been extensively outlined by Jean Piaget and this will be covered in Chapter 10.

Problem-solving

Problem-solving is a mental process that involves discovering, analysing and solving difficulties or conundrums. The ultimate goal of problem-solving is to overcome obstacles and find a solution that best resolves the issue. The early behavioural approach to account for how humans solve problems suggested a trial-and-error process as the main drive (see Chapter 5 on the 'Law of Effect'). By contrast, the Gestalt theorists claimed that the process of thinking about a problem enabled individuals to 'restructure' their representation of the problem, leading to a new insight that enabled them to find a solution.

Barriers to effective problem-solving by humans that have been identified by cognitive psychologists include the following:

► **Functional fixedness:** this comes into play when an individual is unable to see all the options available to solve a problem. This is known as a cognitive bias because it limits a person to using an object only in the way it is traditionally used. Karl Duncker (1903–40), a Gestalt psychologist, defined functional fixedness as being a 'mental block against using an object in a new way that is required to solve a problem' (Dunker 1945). This 'block' limits the ability of an individual to use components given to them in different ways in order to complete a task, as they cannot move past the original purpose of those components. Functional fixedness becomes apparent between the ages of five and seven, with younger children well able to use objects creatively, even if not for their intended purpose.

▶ **Mental set:** this refers to an individual wanting to immediately use a problem-solving strategy that they used in the past to solve a problem. While this strategy may be useful, it means that other options (which might be better) are typically ignored. The strategy thus prevents people from thinking up new ways of solving a problem.

Creativity

No discussion of problem-solving would be complete without also talking about creativity; indeed, the two processes go hand in hand. Creativity is the process whereby something new is formed.

THE FOUR PS OF CREATIVITY

Mel Rhodes (1916–76) was a US educational scientist and the originator of the pioneering concept of the Four Ps of Creativity (1961). These are the separate factors that he felt would influence how creative a person might be at any given time. These are Person, Process, Press and Product:

▶ **Person** covers information about personality, intellect, temperament, physique, traits, habits, attitudes, self-concept, value systems and behaviour.

▶ **Process** applies to a person's motivation, perception, learning, thinking and communication.

▶ **Press** refers to the relationship between a person and their environment.

▶ **Product** relates to ideas; when an idea becomes embodied into tangible form it is called a product.

MEASURING CREATIVITY

During the Second World War the psychologist J. P. Guilford developed tests for selecting certain individuals to enter a pilot's training programme. In his psychological model called 'The Structure of Intellect' (Guilford 1950), Guilford used a factor-analytic technique to separate creative thinking skills from other skills; until this point it had been assumed that intelligence was akin to creativity and that the more intelligent you were, the more creative you were, too. Guilford was one of the first psychologists to postulate that IQ and creativity were distinct concepts. As part of his model, Guilford identified two distinct forms of creative skill: divergent and convergent.

Divergent creativity is that skill or ability to access memory to derive unique, multiple and numerous answers to open-ended questions. Convergent thinking means coming up with 'one right answer' for each question, commonly associated with IQ tests. In other words, in divergent creative tasks, there might be many possible answers or solutions, but in convergent there is only one.

An example of a divergent creative task might be to think of a creative use for a pair of plastic cups. Obviously, there are many possible responses. This task was devised by Guilford and is called the 'Alternative Uses Task' (see the 'Spotlight' below).

A convergent task might be to think of a word that goes before each of the following words: bag and held. There is only one answer (hand) but some degree of creative thinking is required to produce it.

Spotlight: Guilford's Test of Divergent Creativity

In 1967 J. P. Guilford developed a test to measure divergent creativity, calling it Guilford's Alternative Uses Task (Guilford et al. 1978).

Test takers list as many possible uses for a common object, such as a cup, a paperclip or a newspaper. Scoring is comprised of four components: originality, fluency, flexibility and elaboration:

Originality is based on each response compared to the total number of responses from a specific group of test takers. Responses given by 5 per cent of the group are unusual (1 point); responses given by only 1 per cent of the group are unique (2 points).

Fluency just totals how many different answers are produced.

Flexibility is based on the number of categories (e.g. weapons, containers, things to wear).

Elaboration is based on the amount of detail given in the response (e.g. saying a cup could be used as a container would get a score of 1 but saying it could be used as a plant pot for seedlings before they are big enough to be replanted in the garden would earn a bigger score).

STAGES OF THE CREATIVE PROCESS

In 1926, at the age of 68, the English social psychologist Graham Wallas (1858–1932), co-founder of the London School of Economics, wrote a book entitled *The Art of Thought*, in which he outlined an account of the creative process that has become a classic approach to describing creativity. In it, Wallas outlines four stages of the process:

1 **Preparation:** this is the conscious stage of investigating a problem and using all resources to try to come up with a solution.

2 **Incubation:** this is followed by an unconscious stage whereby no effort is put into thinking about the problem at all.

3 **Illumination:** this stage is followed by the 'flash of insight' that often comes about when we leave a problem and turn to other matters (during the incubation stage). This is also often at the unconscious level.

4 **Verification:** this final stage is very much conscious again and is a deliberate effort to test the validity of the idea generated.

'In the daily stream of thought these four different stages constantly overlap each other as we explore different problems. An economist reading a Blue Book, a physiologist watching an experiment, or a businessman going through his morning's letters, may at the same time be 'incubating' on a problem which he proposed to himself a few days ago, be accumulating knowledge in 'preparation' for a second problem, and be 'verifying' his conclusions on a third problem. Even in exploring the same problem, the mind may be unconsciously incubating on one aspect of it, while it is consciously employed in preparing for or verifying another aspect.'

Graham Wallas, *The Art of Thought* (London: Jonathan Cape, 1926)

Spotlight: Boredom and creativity

Did you know that boredom can increase creativity? I carried out some groundbreaking research into this myself with my student Rebekah Cadman, at the University of Central Lancashire, UK.

Our research examined the relationship between boredom and creativity on a range of tasks and found that engaging in 'boring activities' such as tedious writing exercises before undertaking creative tasks results in more productive thinking. We believe that the reason for this was that boredom allows daydreaming, which is a key to creativity (since it provides the ability to re-evaluate information and mull over possible solutions).

To measure whether creativity was indeed a result of daydreaming, a subsequent study was conducted based on similar activities but instead focused on reading (which allows daydreaming more easily) instead of writing.

The first study involved participants copying telephone numbers from a phone directory for 15 minutes so that we could explore the impact on subsequent levels of creativity shown in a divergent thinking task (which included coming up with as many uses for a pair of polystyrene cups as possible). Participants provided varied examples such as pencil pots, earrings, drums and plant pots.

We found that the number of creative answers were higher for participants who completed a boredom task followed by the creative task than participants who completed the creative task in isolation. However, in the next study we had people read the phone numbers and found that levels of creativity then to be even higher. This suggests that passive activities, like reading or attending meetings, can lead to more creativity whereas writing, which inherently reduces the scope for daydreaming, lessens the chance to be creative.

Dig deeper

Article on language acquisition:
http://users.ecs.soton.ac.uk/harnad/Papers/Py104/pinker.
langacq.html

Noam Chomsky website:
http://www.chomsky.info/

An excellent TED Talk on creativity by Gerard J. Puccio, chair and
professor of the International Center for Studies in Creativity at
Buffalo State University:
https://www.youtube.com/watch?v=ltPAsp71rmI&list=PLfJZEI22
FEjTrR8HbqGjc9gMK5GvBZSLs

Fact-check

1 Which of the following statements about language acquisition is true?

  ⓐ Speech perception always precedes speech production

  b Speech production always precedes speech perception

  c Speech production and perception occur round about the same time.

  d There are no hard-and-fast rules about the order in which speech production and perception occur

2 What is a phoneme?

  a A measure of vocabulary

  b A rule about grammar

  c A non-verbal communicator

  ⓓ The smallest unit of sound in a language

3 What is a language acquisition device (LAD)?

  a A device used to learn a second language

  b An app for phones to help people learn a second language

  ⓒ An innate mechanism or process that allows children to develop language skills

  d A means by which language and thought are interlinked

4 The linguistic relativity hypothesis:

  a Explains how languages relate to each other

  b Is a theory that opposes the Sapir–Whorf Hypothesis

  ⓒ Claimed that language determines the way people think

  d Claimed that the way people think determines language

5 Which of the following is *not* a primary function of non-verbal communication?

  a To express emotions

  b To perform rituals

  c To express one's personality

  ⓓ To help people with hearing difficulties

6 Functional fixedness is when
   a Only one solution is available to solve a problem
   b An individual is unable to see all the options available to solve a problem
   c An individual cannot see what function an object has
   d An individual is fixated on the function of an object

7 Which of the following is not one of the 'Four Ps of Creativity'?
   a Process
   b Place
   c Person
   d Perfect

8 Which of the following components is *not* used to score Guilford's Test of Divergent Creativity?
   a Originality
   b Fluency
   c Elaboration
   d Depth

9 The incubation stage of the creative process is when:
   a The thinker deliberately thinks about the problem
   b No effort is put into thinking about the problem at all
   c The thinker tests ideas about solutions to the problem
   d Resources are gathered to solve a problem

10 Boredom increases creativity because it:
   a Facilitates daydreaming
   b Inhibits daydreaming
   c Stops you thinking
   d Distracts you

7

Emotion

What exactly is an emotion and how does it occur? And why do we have emotions? Psychologists over the years have been concerned with defining and classifying emotions, as well as trying to work out how (and why) they happen.

> 'An emotion is a complex psychological state that involves three distinct components: a subjective experience, a physiological response, and a behavioral or expressive response.'
>
> D. H. Hockenbury and S. E. Hockenbury, *Discovering Psychology*
> (New York: Worth Publishers, 2007)

Most researchers believe that emotions consist of five distinct components and some believe that to truly experience an emotion, at least four out of five components must exist (there is some doubt about the fifth). These are:

1. **Our feelings:** we label the way we feel as being angry, sad and so on. These feelings are very subjective and also quite personal in that other people cannot always tell how we feel just by looking at us.

2. **Our physiological reactions:** our bodies change when we are emotional (e.g. we might sweat, experience raised heartbeat, clench our fists). This category includes the bodily changes that we cannot see or notice such as chemicals secreted from various glands. Many of the physical reactions experienced during an emotion are controlled by the sympathetic nervous system, a branch of the autonomic nervous system (see Chapter 17). The brain also has a role in these responses; the amygdala, for example, which is part of the limbic system, plays an important role in emotion (especially in fear) – there is more on this in Chapter 17.

3. **Our behaviour:** for example, certain emotions might lead us to run away, hit someone/something, hug someone and so forth.

4. **Our cognitions:** this is what we think – our interpretation of the events that produce the emotion. For example, thinking about a sad event such as a bereavement will make us feel sad.

5. **Expression:** this component doesn't have to be present in that you can feel an emotion without any outward expression, but, often, emotions are accompanied by a distinct change in facial and/or vocal expression (e.g. we blush when we are embarrassed and smile when we are happy). Such expression

can also be used to deliberately convey an emotion (that is either felt or not felt) – there is more on this later in this chapter.

Thus, to experience the phenomenon of an emotion that we are all so familiar with, the emotional trigger or stimulus must penetrate our consciousness (i.e. we must notice the trigger), there must be some kind of reaction in our body (even if we are not aware of it), we produce some kind of behavioural change and we label the whole thing as an 'emotion' (and this emotion may be communicated by our outward expressions).

How many emotions?

According to classic work by Paul Ekman in 1972, there are only six distinct emotions. These are anger, disgust, fear, happiness, sadness and surprise (although in 1999 he expanded this list to include a number of other basic emotions including embarrassment, excitement, contempt, shame, pride, satisfaction and amusement). Later on, in 2002, another well-known emotions expert, Robert Plutchik, agreed that there were a finite number of distinct emotions but suggested that there are eight basic emotions, rather than six, and that these could be grouped into four pairs of opposites:

Joy – Sadness

Trust – Disgust

Anger – Fear

Surprise – Anticipation

He further suggested that these primary emotions could be 'blended' (a bit like primary colours) into more complex emotions. For example, disgust and anger could blend together to form contempt. In Plutchik's view, all emotions are a combination of these basic emotions and many of the emotions that we identify are, in reality, just forms of the above eight. Thus, for example, we might claim that we are elated, thrilled, happy, delighted or even exhilarated, but all these are variations of the basic emotion of 'joy'. Similarly, rage and annoyance are forms of anger.

There are generally two kinds of emotion: those that do not require anyone else to be involved and those that do. The former such as happiness and sadness do not rely on an audience or on anyone else's participation. These emotions tend to be basic and universal emotions; this means that we tend not to need to learn how to feel these emotions – although we might need to learn to be aware of them, or to be able to label them. Babies, for example, do not need to learn to be happy, sad, disgusted, fearful, surprised or angry – and they will feel these whether or not anyone else is involved.

Spotlight: One by one

The basic emotions appear in the first six months of life, but not all at the same time. Joy, sadness and disgust generally appear first, followed by anger then surprise, while fear is a later response.

In contrast, there are other emotions that require a more social environment to be fully experienced. These so-called 'social emotions' include embarrassment, shame, jealousy and pride. In order to feel these, we need to understand the mental states of ourselves and of other people – a skill that doesn't fully develop until early adolescence.

Theories of emotion

But what is the mechanism for experiencing these emotions?

The American psychologist William James first outlined his theory of emotion in *Mind* in 1884. Actually, he only just pipped his fellow physiologist, the Dutchman Carle Lange, to the post as they both postulated the same processes as being involved. Consequently, the resulting theory is referred to as the **James–Lange Theory of Emotion** to acknowledge the input of both parties.

Their theory stated that emotion occurs as a direct result of the physiological changes produced by the autonomic nervous system in our bodies. To experience an emotion, they said, you need to see something (or hear/feel it) and this causes physical changes to occur in your body. You then interpret those changes as an emotion. For example, imagine it's late at night and a stranger approaches you in a dark alleyway. This external stimulus causes your heartbeat to increase and your legs to tremble. You notice these changes in your body and decide that you must be feeling frightened ('I am trembling therefore I am frightened').

This theory turned on its head what was seen as the obvious sequence of events at the time. As James himself said, 'Common sense says, we lose our fortune, are sorry and weep; we meet a bear, are frightened and run; we are insulted by a rival, are angry and strike' (James 1890). This, he claimed, was not the correct order of events and actually, he said, we feel sorry because we cry, we are angry because we hit and we are afraid because we tremble. Without these physical reactions in our bodies, we might still run away from the bear because it is the sensible, rational thing to do – but this would be an unemotional, cognitive decision, devoid of any emotion; we would not actually feel frightened unless we experience the physical changes first.

In the 1920s Walter Cannon (who was later joined by Phillip Bard) disagreed with the James–Lange Theory and put forward four main arguments to discredit it:

1 People can, in fact, experience physiological arousal *without* experiencing emotion, such as when they have been engaged in exercise. In this case, the physiological symptoms, such as increased heart rate, are not indicative of emotions (e.g. fear) but of physiological arousal.

2 Physiological reactions do not occur very rapidly so are unlikely to be the cause of the experiences of emotion since we often experience emotions quickly. For example, if you are alone at night in your house and hear a sudden suspicious noise, you are likely to feel afraid rather quickly, while the physical 'symptoms' of fear generally take longer to materialize.

3 People can experience very different emotions even when they have the same pattern of physiological arousal. For example, a person may have an increased heart rate and feel breathless both when they are angry and when they are excited.

4   Emotion can still be experienced even when the physical changes occurring in the body are prevented from being communicated back to the brain. Cannon conducted experiments on cats in which he disconnected the nerves giving feedback to the brains and these cats still demonstrated 'rage' when provoked (this was called 'sham rage' since, according to Lange, without feedback to the brain, they shouldn't experience real rage at all).

The **Cannon–Bard Theory of Emotion,** as it became known, postulated, then, that, rather than the physical reactions coming first and then producing the emotion, the two processes happen simultaneously (Cannon 1927). Some external stimulus (the sight of that hoody in the dark alleyway) will trigger the thalamus in the brain to send information to both other areas of the brain (specifically the cerebral cortex) and the autonomic nervous system (including the skeletal muscles) at the same time, so that both the awareness of emotion (in the brain) and the physical reaction (e.g. in the muscles) occur at once.

More recent explanations (first put forward by Schachter and Singer in 1962) to account for the emotional experience focus on the role played by our brains in interpreting physical sensations as emotions. It is not enough to just experience the physical reactions in our body; we must also interpret and label these changes as a particular emotion. The actual physical changes we experience may not differ; it is our interpretation of the environment and so on that leads us to label these sensations as a particular emotion. Singer and Schachter's theory became known as the **Two-Factor Theory of Emotion.** From this theory came two main propositions:

1   If a person experiences a state of arousal for which they do not have any immediate explanation, they will look for an explanation of that arousal that may involve attributing it to an emotion.

2   If a person experiences a state of arousal for which they do have an appropriate explanation, then they will be unlikely to look for an alternative means to account for it, and thus be less likely to label it as an emotion.

These propositions were tested with the now-famous Adrenalin Study described in the following case study.

Case study: The Adrenalin Study

In 1962 Stanley Schachter and Jerome E. Singer performed a study that tested how people use clues in their environment to explain physiological changes. At Minnesota University 184 male psychology students were recruited. Each participant was taken to a room by the experimenter and told that the aim of the experiment was to look at the effects of vitamin injections (given the made-up name of Suproxin) on visual skills.

They were given an injection (by a doctor) of either adrenalin (this is called epinephrine when it is manufactured in a lab) or a placebo (a saline solution), both of which the participants believed to be the Suproxin. The effects of adrenalin are an increase in blood pressure, heart rate, blood sugar level and respiration rate, and these are often experienced as palpitations, tremors, flushing and faster breathing. The effects begin after three minutes and last from ten minutes to an hour.

The participants were then put in one of four experimental conditions:

1 **Ignorant:** participants here were given the adrenalin injection (instead of the vitamin they were expecting) and were not told anything about how the injection would make them feel.

2 **Informed:** participants here were given the adrenalin injection but this time they were accurately warned of the side effects of the drug (although they still assumed the drug was Suproxin).

3 **Misinformed:** in this condition, participants were given an adrenalin injection but were told to expect side effects that were completely different from the ones that adrenalin gives (e.g. headache).

4 **Control group:** participants were given a placebo injection that would have no effect and were given no instructions about what to expect.

Participants were then allocated to emotional conditions – either a euphoria condition or an anger condition. In the euphoria situation, a stooge in a waiting room carried out a number of silly tasks designed to entertain and amuse the participant. In the anger situation, a stooge in a waiting room carried out tasks and made comments designed to annoy the participant.

In the euphoria condition, the misinformed participants reported feeling happier than all the others. The second happiest group was the ignorant group. This was because these participants had no plausible explanation of why their bodies felt as they did (due to the effects of the adrenalin injection) – so they looked around and decided it must be because they felt happy. The informed group felt the least happy because they had a perfectly reasonable explanation to account for the physical changes in their bodies.

In the anger condition, the ignorant group felt the angriest. The second angriest group was the placebo group. The least angry group was those who were informed. Again, this shows that participants were more susceptible to picking up on the emotions of the stooge when they had no other readily available explanation of why their body felt as it did.

So, our emotional experiences rely on us noticing physical changes in our bodies and giving them an appropriate emotional label. In other words, appraisal is a key feature and it is this appraisal that explains how different people can experience the same event but feel different emotions. This led to the well-known Wobbly Bridge Study described in the following case study – and explains why you should take your date to a scary film or a white-knuckle roller coaster if you want them to fall in love with you.

Case study: The Wobbly Bridge Study

In 1974 psychologists Donald Dutton and Arthur Aron conducted a study at the Capilano Canyon in Canada which is crossed by two particular bridges. One bridge is a solid wooden one only 3 metres above a shallow part of the canyon below. The other is a more frail-looking suspension bridge that tends to sway, tilt and wobble such that people stepping on it feel that they might be at risk of falling

70 metres into the canyon below. People walking across the rickety bridge thus tended to be quite aroused with fear – their pulse rates would quicken, they may have sweated and their hearts would pound. Indeed, this may be why they chose that bridge. No such arousal was likely on the lower, solid bridge.

The experimenters interviewed men crossing each of the two bridges and tested how attracted they were to a female confederate on the other side of the canyon. What they found was that those men on the swaying suspension bridge were more attracted to the woman than those on the sturdier crossing. The reason given was that the men on the scarier bridge experienced a state of arousal that, in the presence of a woman, they interpreted as attraction for her. The men on the sturdy bridge had no such physical feelings to misinterpret.

The study shows why colleagues at work who have been through some emotional experience together (such as beating a tight deadline or winning a big contract) can end up in a romance – they misinterpret the emotions they are feeling as love.

Facial expression

'Many facial expressions ... occur throughout the world in every human race and culture. The expressions appear to represent, in every culture, the same emotions.'
N. H. Frijda, *The Emotions* (Cambridge: Cambridge University Press, 1986)

In our evolutionary past, using facial expressions and correctly detecting them in others was vital to our survival. Before we were advanced enough to have developed an effective verbal language, we had to use facial expressions to communicate. It was essential that we knew, for example, that someone was angry with us, so that we could run away before they attacked us. Similarly, showing displeasure would have allowed our ancestors to have a better chance of getting what they wanted (e.g. food or resources).

Emotional expressions that were particularly important to our ancestors were angry, fearful or anxious ones and being able to express or read these emotions would have been an essential skill for survival. For example, noticing that another member of our tribe was looking terrified would have alerted us to the danger of an approaching predator, while if we expressed our anger this might have caused others in our tribe to act in order to remove the source of our displeasure. All of this helped ensure that our genes endured.

Some emotional displays are thought to be universal, which means that they are recognized all over the world. The so-called **Facial Expression Universality Theory** is thought by many to have been developed by Charles Darwin, although, in reality, his work followed earlier researchers (such as Charles Bell in 1806) in this field. For an emotional expression to be truly universal, it should meet three criteria:

1 The same pattern of facial display should occur in all human groups wherever they are and even if they are isolated from other groups.

2 People in different societies and cultures should attribute the same emotion to the same expression.

3 Those same facial patterns should, indeed, be indicative of that very emotion in all human societies.

It is thought that the universal facial expressions correspond to the six universal emotions discussed earlier. Psychologist Paul Ekman showed photographs of faces to people in 20 different Western cultures and 11 different isolated and non-literate groups in Africa. He found that 96 per cent of Western respondents and 92 per cent of African respondents identified happy faces. Similar numbers of people could identify disgust and anger, suggesting that humans' facial displays are common across cultures for at least these three emotions. Other studies have shown that surprise achieves 'recognition' ratings of 87.5 per cent in Western cultures (and slightly lower in non-Western). Sadness and fear show slightly lower recognition rates, but are still above 80 per cent (Russell 1994).

Spotlight: Emotional 'dialects'

More recent research disputes this universality of facial expression theory, suggesting instead that there are local 'dialects' in emotional display (Jack et al. 2012).

Functions of emotions

'The primary function is to mobilize the organism to deal quickly with important interpersonal encounters.'
Paul Ekman, 'An Argument for Basic Emotions',
Cognition and Emotion 6 (1992): 171

The role of emotions is to alert us to changes in the environment or in ourselves; many of these would have had evolutionary benefit. Emotions motivate us towards change and reaction. For example, the feeling of disgust alerts us that something is present that could harm us or make us ill. Anger transforms us from calmness to a readiness to fight. Fear alerts us that we are in danger and should run. Even sadness can alert us to make changes in our lives, while anxiety can motivate us to study for that upcoming exam. Emotions also have an important communicative role. They tell others how we feel and thus might cause them to act differently; for example, the target of our anger might do something to stop us feeling angry.

The functions of emotions, then, fall into three categories: the **intrapersonal** (the role they play within each individual), the **interpersonal** (the role they play in maintaining relationships between different individuals), and the **societal and cultural** functions (the role emotions play in helping society at large) of emotions.

Emotion regulation

It is possible to experience emotions without any corresponding facial display – and the other way around: we can present a facial display without the accompanying emotion. Research suggests that there are subtle differences between faked facial display and real ones. Faked smiles, for example, are often assumed to be those that do not reach the eyes, a suggestion that originated in the nineteenth century when the French neuro-anatomist Guillaume-Benjamin-Amand Duchenne de Bologne (1806–75) claimed that the muscle orbiting the eye (orbicularis oculi) is not engaged during faked smiles. Indeed, more than a dozen studies since Duchenne's suggestion have revealed this assertion to be correct; genuine smiles are now even sometimes referred to as 'Duchenne smiles'.

Smiles are not the only facial displays that consist of some muscle action that is hard to fake. Anger, fear and sadness also contain muscular actions that are hard for people to deliberately perform; these emotional displays also contain some that are easier to fake, too. Surprise and disgust, however, contain only 'difficult to make' muscle actions (called 'reliable' actions by Ekman because they are reliable indicators of true emotions), which is why these are the hardest emotions to fake. Those of us who are keen photographers will certainly know this is true of surprise; how many times have we tried to capture the surprise on a loved one's face at a birthday surprise, for example, only to miss the fleeting moment – however much we try to get our subject to emulate that initial expression, it is never quite as convincing as capturing genuine surprise and delight.

Sometimes we use facial expressions in the full knowledge that other people will know they are fake. This is called 'referential' expression and might occur when we are describing a past event; we will refer to something that happened and adopt the appropriate emotional expression as a way of adding emphasis, but everyone is aware that the display is simply referring to that experienced during the event, rather than intending to be a genuine expression of how we feel now during the retelling. The 'reliable' muscles are not used in these referential expressions, but that is considered acceptable, as no one expects them to be reflecting genuine emotion. In fact, the actor is likely to actually want to impress upon their audience that the expression is faked in this instance; they might go to extra lengths to show this perhaps by deliberately exaggerating their expression.

There might be another reason why reliable muscle actions will be deliberately missed out during referential displays: research has consistently shown that arranging our face to show the appropriate emotional expression can actually lead us to genuinely feeling that emotion – something that we don't necessarily want when we are recounting an event. When we arrange our face into the emotion we are attempting to express, the physiological pattern is noticed by the brain and interpreted as reflecting the emotion; my face is smiling so I must be happy. This is why, if we are recounting an emotional experience that involves referential facial displays, we sometimes end up actually feeling the emotion; for example, retelling an event that made you angry can reignite your anger all over again.

This idea – that the facial display can actually produce or enhance the emotion – was first suggested by Darwin in 1872. William James went even further by claiming that, if a person does not express an emotion on their face, they haven't felt it at all. Although modern scientists don't go quite this far, facial expressions are thought to play a big role in how intensely we feel emotions.

In 2011 psychologists at the University of Cardiff in Wales found that people whose ability to frown was limited by cosmetic Botox injections were happier, on average, than people who could frown. This wasn't because the Botoxed people felt any more attractive (they checked that); the emotional effects were not driven by any psychological boost that could have come from the Botox making them look better, but because they were unable to frown – the messages of sadness that a frown produces were simply not being sent to the brain.

An intriguing study reported in the journal *Psychological Science* took this idea one stage further (Kraft and Pressman 2012). Researchers from the University of Kansas had people hold chopsticks in their mouths in such a way that they either produced neutral expressions, fake smiles or Duchenne (genuine) smiles. They were not aware that they were actually mimicking the muscle patterns of a smile with the chopsticks. They then gave all the participants a stressful activity and found that those who had arranged their faces into smiles showed faster recovery from the stress than those who didn't. Those who adopted the genuine Duchenne smile recovered the quickest. This suggests that smiling can help cope with stress, even if we don't actually feel like smiling.

The effect seems to work in the opposite way, too; one study showed that people who frown during an uncomfortable or painful procedure report feel more pain than those who do not. Researchers applied heat to the forearms of participants, who were asked to either make unhappy, neutral or relaxed faces during the procedure. Those who made the negative expressions reported being in more pain than the other two groups. It could well be then that, in order to feel less pain, all we need to do is stop ourselves expressing it our facial displays.

Humans are (we assume) unique among the animals in that we are very able to manage and regulate our emotions and their display. Hiding what we feel and faking what we don't is an important part of our emotional life. Emotion management is about the care we take in presenting the right emotional display at the right time. Humans are able to manage or control the emotions that they display by faking appropriate emotions and suppressing felt ones.

There are thought to be two different methods of faking unfelt emotion or suppressing felt emotions in order to meet display rule expectations (i.e. written or unwritten rules about which displays one should express or suppress in a public space) – surface or deep acting:

▶ **Surface acting** refers to making changes to our external appearance – our surface – in order to match the required persona – putting on a 'face' or mask. This is all about superficial change with no change to actual feeing involved. Thus, for example, if we are required to express concern or interest (that we do not feel), we can simply arrange our facial features into the appropriate expression in order to convey the corresponding emotion. In other words, we don't actually need to feel the emotion we are trying to portray.

▶ **Deep acting,** however, is about changing how we actually feel in order to match the expected emotion and outward expression of that emotion. Thus, we try to genuinely feel interested or concerned, rather than just concerning ourselves with *appearing* to do so. We might have to psych ourselves up (perhaps by imagining that the recipient of our display is a loved relative) to feel the required emotion since simply arranging our face won't do it.

Dig deeper

A book about disgust:

Susan B. Miller, *Disgust: The Gatekeeper Emotion* (London: Routledge, 2004)

Journalistic article about blushing:

Nick Collins. 'Blushing in the Dark: First Experimental Proof', *The Telegraph*, 4 September 2013:
http://www.telegraph.co.uk/science/science-news/10285883/Blushing-in-the-dark-first-experimental-proof.html

Online article about how Botox may prevent young people learning to express and read emotions properly:
http://www.bbc.co.uk/news/health-29174929

Fact-check

1 Which of the following is *not* an essential component of emotion?
- **a** Cognition
- **b** Physical changes
- **c** Expression
- **d** Behaviour

2 How many distinct, basic emotions did Plutchik believe there were?
- **a** 6
- **b** 12
- **c** 4
- **d** 8

3 The Two-Factor Theory of Emotion was developed by:
- **a** James and Lange
- **b** Cannon and Bard
- **c** Schachter and Singer
- **d** Schachter and Lange

4 What is Suproxin?
- **a** A vitamin
- **b** Adrenalin
- **c** Epinephrine
- **d** A placebo

5 For an emotional expression to be truly universal, it should:
- **a** Have the same pattern of facial movement in all human groups
- **b** Be attributed to the same emotion by different observers in different cultural groups
- **c** Be manifestations of that very emotion in all human societies
- **d** All of the above

6 The functions of emotion fall into which of the following categories:
- **a** Interpersonal
- **b** Intrapersonal
- **c** Societal
- **d** All of the above

7 What is a Duchenne smile?
- **a** A fake smile
- **b** A genuine smile
- **c** One in which all the facial muscles are used
- **d** All of the above

8 To decrease the feeling of pain during a painful procedure, one should:
- **a** Frown
- **b** Cry
- **c** Smile
- **d** Close the eyes

9 To control your facial expression so that you present the expression you are expected to, you should:
- **a** Deep-act only
- **b** Surface-act only
- **c** Be genuine
- **d** Surface- or deep-act.

10 What are display rules?
- **a** Rules about which emotions one may express or suppress in public
- **b** Rules about how posters should be displayed at work
- **c** Rules about how you should feel at work
- **d** Unwritten

8

Intelligence

The word 'intelligence' derives from the Latin verb *intelligere*, meaning 'to comprehend' or 'to perceive'. The concept of intelligence, however, is elusive and there are many, varied ways to define it.

Some definitions

Some of the most influential researchers into intelligence have suggested the following definitions:

'Judgment, otherwise called "good sense," "practical sense," "initiative," the faculty of adapting one's self to circumstances ... auto-critique.'
Alfred Binet, pioneering intelligence researcher

'The aggregate or global capacity of the individual to act purposefully, to think rationally, and to deal effectively with his environment.'
David Wechsler, deviser of the Wechsler Adult Intelligent Scale (WAIS), much used in clinical settings

'To my mind, a human intellectual competence must entail a set of skills of problem-solving — enabling the individual to resolve genuine problems or difficulties that he or she encounters and, when appropriate, to create an effective product — and must also entail the potential for finding or creating problems — and thereby laying the groundwork for the acquisition of new knowledge.'
Howard Gardner, developmental psychologist well known for his Theory of Multiple Intelligences

'...all branches of intellectual activity have in common one fundamental function, whereas the remaining or specific elements of the activity seem in every case to be wholly different from that in all the others.'
Charles Spearman, deviser of the single intelligence factor, g

Models and theories of intelligence

A number of theories have been proposed to account for what intelligence actually is; some of the most prominent ones will be outlined here.

SPEARMAN'S TWO-FACTOR THEORY

Charles Spearman (1863–1945) was an English psychologist well known for his work in statistics. His theory of intelligence proposed that there were two elements or factors that make up intelligence: a general factor (which he called g) and one or more specific factors such as verbal, mathematical, and artistic skills. The g factor is an innate and universal ability whereas specific factors are learned.

THURSTONE'S PRIMARY MENTAL ABILITIES

Louis Thurstone (1887–1955) was a US pioneer in the field of psychometrics. Thurstone's work in factor analysis led him to formulate a model of intelligence centred around 'Primary Mental Abilities' (PMAs), which were independent factors of intelligence that different individuals possessed in varying degrees. Unlike Spearman, he opposed the notion of a singular general intelligence and instead focused on seven primary factors:

1 Verbal comprehension

2 Reasoning

3 Perceptual speed

4 Numerical ability

5 Word fluency

6 Associative memory

7 Spatial visualization.

Some intelligence tests, such as the Wechsler Adult Intelligence Scale (WAIS), which will be discussed later in this chapter, have sections that test for these seven factors, although they might have different names (e.g. perceptual speed is called processing speed on the WAIS).

GARDNER'S THEORY OF MULTIPLE INTELLIGENCES

Again, this is a theory that does not see intelligence as a single entity. In his 1983 book, *Frames of Mind: The Theory of Multiple Intelligences,* the US developmental psychologist Howard Gardner (born 1943) articulated seven criteria for a behaviour to be considered an intelligence. These were that the intelligences showed the following traits:

1 Identification in the case of brain damage (i.e. damage to a specific area of the brain isolates that ability from others)

2 An evolutionary purpose

3 Presence of a clear operation or information-processing mechanism that manages specific kinds of input

4 Ability to be encoded (i.e. they showed symbolic expression in outputs such as language, images and music)

5 A distinct developmental progression

6 The existence of giftedness, savants and prodigies in that area

7 Support from various experimental psychology and psychometric findings.

Gardner believed that each individual possesses a unique blend of all the intelligences and he claimed that eight abilities met these criteria:

▶ **Musical–rhythmic:** this is an intelligence that centres around sounds, rhythms, tones and music. People with a high musical intelligence usually sing and play instruments to a high standard, may compose music and generally have a natural flair for all things musical. Many have good or even perfect pitch.

▶ **Visual–spatial:** people with a high visual–spatial intelligence are good at making spatial judgements and at picturing and manipulating objects and scenes in their imagination. They are good at remembering faces and images and tend to notice fine details.

▶ **Verbal–linguistic:** people with high verbal–linguistic intelligence are good with words and languages. They are typically good at reading, writing, telling stories, explaining things to others and so on.

- **Logical–mathematical:** people high in this area are strong at logic, abstractions, reasoning, numbers, pattern detection and critical thinking. Logical reasoning is closely linked to fluid intelligence (see below) and to general intelligence (the g factor).

- **Bodily–kinaesthetic:** people who have high bodily-kinaesthetic intelligence tend to be good at physical activities such as sports, dance, acting, fine motor skills and making things. They are often quite active people with strong motor skills and body awareness.

- **Interpersonal:** individuals who have high interpersonal intelligence have great sensitivity to others' moods, feelings, temperaments and motivations, and are good at working in a team. Because of these skills they are often quite popular and have many friends.

- **Intrapersonal:** this area has to do with introspective and self-reflective capacities. People high in these skills have a clear understanding of themselves, their strengths and weaknesses. They tend to analyse themselves quite deeply, trying to work out their goals and motivations.

- **Naturalistic:** people high in this area tend to be good at working with their sense of touch and they learn by holding, feeling and manipulating. They probably have a natural affinity for plants and the animal kingdom, an ability that was clearly of value in our evolutionary past as hunters, gatherers and farmers.

Fluid vs crystallized intelligence

This is another way to conceptualize intelligence that was originally identified in 1971 by Raymond Cattell (who is well known for his work on individual differences such as personality).

Fluid intelligence (sometimes called 'fluid reasoning') is the ability to think logically and to solve problems in new situations without the need for previous or learned knowledge. Thus, people with good fluid intelligence are good at analysing novel problems by identifying the patterns and relationships that underpin these problems. Fluid reasoning includes inductive reasoning and deductive reasoning (as explained in Chapter 6).

While fluid intelligence is independent of learning, **crystallized intelligence** is the ability to use learned skills, knowledge and experience. It is distinct from memory, though it does rely on accessing information from long-term memory. Crystallized intelligence uses what we have learned and thus involves vocabulary and general knowledge. This is why crystallized intelligence tends to improve with age, as the experiences we have throughout our lives tend to expand our knowledge. Crystallized intelligence is thus the product of both educational and cultural experience but it also interacts with fluid intelligence.

The two intelligences are thus correlated with each other, and most IQ tests attempt to measure both varieties. For example, the Wechsler Adult Intelligence Scale (WAIS) measures fluid intelligence on the performance scale and crystallized intelligence on the verbal scale. The overall IQ score is based on a combination of these two scales.

Fluid intelligence typically peaks in young adulthood and then steadily declines. This decline may be due to local atrophy of the right cerebellum in the brain, though some researchers have suggested that a lack of practice, along with age-related changes in the brain, may contribute to the decline. Crystallized intelligence, on the other hand, typically increases gradually, stays relatively stable across most of adulthood, and then begins to decline after age 65.

Spotlight: *Inteligenz-quotient*

The abbreviation 'IQ' was coined by the psychologist William Stern for the German term *Intelligenz-quotient*, his term for a scoring method for intelligence tests he advocated in a book he published in 1912.

Measuring intelligence

The pioneer of intelligence testing was the French psychologist Alfred Binet (1857–1911). In the early 1900s the French government was reforming education for children and wanted to know which children would benefit the most and which would need extra help. Binet, with his colleague Théodore Simon (1872–1961), attempted to design a battery of questions aimed at separating out the children likely to do well at school from those who were less likely. He focused on those skills not dependent on taught material, such as problem-solving (fluid intelligence). The test they devised was known as the **Binet–Simon Scale** and it is generally recognized as the first effective intelligence test (and it still forms the basis of measures of intelligence today).

Binet realized that some children were able to answer more advanced questions than older children were generally able to answer, while other children of the same age were only able to answer questions that younger children could typically answer. Based on this observation, Binet developed the concept of a **mental age,** or a measure of intelligence based on the average abilities of children of a certain age group. A child's mental age could be higher or lower than their chronological age.

The Binet–Simon Scale was brought to the United States where the psychologist Lewis Terman from Stanford University took Binet's original test and standardized it using a sample of American participants. This version, first published in 1916, was called the **Stanford–Binet Intelligence Scale** and soon became the standard intelligence test used in the United States. It utilized a single measure of intelligence that was known as the **intelligence quotient** (or **IQ**). This score was calculated by dividing the test taker's mental age by their chronological age, and then multiplying this number by 100. For example, a child with a mental age of eight and a chronological age of ten would have an IQ of 80 (8/10 x 100). No matter what the child's chronological age, if the mental age matched the chronological age, then the IQ would equal 100. An IQ of 100 thus indicates a child of average intellectual development.

Spotlight: The deviation method

The old 'ratio method' of computing IQ as described above is no longer used. The currently used method is called the **deviation method,** and is based on the fact that IQ scores tend to closely follow a normal distribution (sometimes known as the 'bell curve' – see below).

To map the IQ scores on to the normal distribution, the test was given to a large sample and the median (average) and standard deviation (a measure of score variability) computed for the group. These statistics were then used in a conversion formula to convert the 'raw' scores from the test into standard IQ scores that have a predetermined mean and standard deviation. When current IQ tests were developed, the mean raw score of the norming sample was defined as IQ 100 (i.e. an average IQ is 100). Approximately 95 per cent of the population have scores within two standard deviations (SD) of the mean. If one SD is 15 points, as is common in almost all modern tests, then 95 per cent of the population are within a range of 70 to 130, and 98 per cent are below 131. Alternatively, two-thirds of the population have IQ scores within one SD of the mean – that is, within the range 85–115.

Spotlight: The bell-shaped curve

IQ, like many attributes, is distributed within the general population in a way that follows a bell, or inverted U shape, with a few scores appearing at the farthest points from the centre and a large bulge of scores at and around the centre. This means that most people will score in the middle bulge with fewer people at either end. The bell curve is sometimes referred to as a **Gaussian distribution,** after the German mathematician and physicist Karl Gauss, who brought the model to the scientific community by using it to show the distribution of astronomical data.

In psychological terms, the bell-shaped curve is referred to as the 'normal distribution' and any attributes that follow this shape are said to have a normal distribution (height is another example of a normally distributed attribute in that most people of a certain age and gender will have an average height, with only a few particularly tall or short people at either ends of the scale).

During the First World War, intelligence testing really took off as the army needed to screen and test thousands of recruits quickly. Special army IQ tests were developed called Army Alpha and Beta and used to screen 2 million recruits. This heralded the arrival of mass IQ testing.

THE WECHSLER INTELLIGENCE SCALES

The next significant development in the history of intelligence testing was the creation of a new measurement instrument by the American psychologist David Wechsler (1896–1981). Like Binet, Wechsler believed that intelligence involved a number of different mental abilities but he felt that the Stanford–Binet Scale suffered from too many limitations (such as a heavy reliance on verbal ability). He thus developed the Wechsler Adult Intelligence Scale (WAIS) in 1955 and this is still in wide use today (although it has been revised several times since that first version – the one currently in use is WAIS-IV). Wechsler also developed two different tests specifically for use with children: the Wechsler Intelligence Scale for Children (WISC) and the Wechsler Preschool and Primary Scale of Intelligence (WPPSI).

Rather than score the test based on chronological age and mental age, as was the case with the original Stanford–Binet, the WAIS is scored by comparing the test taker's score to the scores of others in the same age group. The average score is fixed at 100, with two-thirds of scores lying in the normal range between 85 and 115. This scoring method has become the standard technique in intelligence testing and is also used in the modern revision of the Stanford–Binet test.

The current version of the WAIS was released in 2008 and includes ten core subtests as well as five supplemental subtests. The test provides four major scores:

▶ Verbal comprehension

▶ Perceptual reasoning

▶ Working memory

▶ Processing speed.

Additionally, WAIS-IV provides two overall summary scores:

1 Full Scale IQ

2 General Ability Index.

RAVEN'S TEST OF INTELLIGENCE

It is worth mentioning Raven's Progressive Matrices as a test of intelligence since this is a non-verbal test and as such does not rely on verbal skill. This makes it suitable for young children or for people for whom language skill is an issue that could interfere with ordinary intelligence measures (e.g. where English is not their first language). The tests were originally developed by the English psychologist John Carlyle Raven (1902–71) in 1936, and in each test item the subject is asked to identify the missing element that completes a pattern. Many patterns are presented in the form of a 4 × 4, 3 × 3 or 2 × 2 matrix.

The matrices are available in three different forms for participants of different ability:

▶ **Standard Progressive Matrices:** these were the original form of the matrices, first published in 1938, with items within a set becoming increasingly difficult. All items are presented in black ink on a white background.

▶ **Coloured Progressive Matrices:** these were designed for children aged five through eleven years of age, for the elderly, and for mentally and physically impaired individuals. Most items are presented on a coloured background to make the test visually stimulating for participants.

▶ **Advanced Progressive Matrices:** the advanced form of the matrices contains 48 items and is appropriate for adults and adolescents of above-average intelligence.

WHAT DO IQ TESTS REALLY MEASURE?

Even the modern 'IQ test' is not a perfect measure of intelligence, with many researchers today claiming that all IQ tests really measure is your ability to do IQ tests. An intelligence quotient, or IQ, is a measure of 'fluid and crystallized intelligence'. An IQ test thus measures reasoning and problem-solving abilities. There are different kinds of IQ tests, but most analyse visual, mathematical and language abilities as well as memory and information-processing speed. IQ is really a measure of how well you do in a test compared with other people of your age. However, IQ scores do not measure practical intelligence, creativity, common sense or emotional intelligence (see below) – all factors needed to perform and interact successfully with the world around us. IQs do not always stay stable either; they change slightly as we age and factors such as nutrition, stress and education can all affect them. Taking many IQ tests can also increase your score.

Case study: The 'Termites'

In the early part of the twentieth century the American psychologist Lewis Terman (1877–1956) set up what was known as the Genetic Studies of Genius. Terman believed that IQ was all that was needed to predict future success and he set out to prove this by selecting an elite group of children using IQ tests. This group had an average IQ of 151 (which is very high).

Terman then followed these children (who later called themselves 'Termites') through to adulthood and found that, 35 years later, his expectations appeared to have been proven. They were taller, healthier and more socially adept than average, and had an impressive array of accomplishments: nearly 2,000 scientific and technical papers and articles and some 60 books and monographs in the sciences, literature, arts, and humanities had been published by the Termites. Patents granted to them amounted to at least 230. Thirty-one of them appeared in *Who's Who in America*.

While the evidence certainly sounds impressive, the Termites study is not without its critics. For example, it is argued that the socio-economic status of the Termites was more of a predictor of their success than their IQ. There are also some who argue that even their impressive list of accomplishments is overshadowed by those of non-Termites of the same era: William Shockley, for example, was rejected from the study as not being intelligent enough, yet went to Harvard, earned a doctorate and eventually a Nobel Prize in Physics, an award that not one of the Termites managed to earn.

Over the years more than 100 scientific articles and almost a dozen books have been based on the Terman data.

INTELLIGENCE AND CULTURE

Researchers have long debated whether average differences in IQ scores – such as those between different ethnic groups – reflect differences in intelligence, social and economic factors, or both. The debate intensified in 1994 with the publication of *The Bell Curve* (the book's title comes from the bell-shaped normal distribution of intelligence quotient scores in a population, described above) by Richard Herrnstein and Charles Murray, which suggested that the lower-than-average IQ scores of some ethnic groups, such as African-Americans and Hispanics, were due in large part to genetic differences between them and Caucasian groups.

'It seems highly likely to us that both genes and the environment have something to do with racial differences [in IQ].'
R. Herrnstein and C. Murray, *The Bell Curve* (New York: Free Press, 1994)

That view has been challenged by many scientists. *The Bell Curve* prompted the publication of several multiple-author books responding with a variety of points of view. They include *The Bell Curve Debate* (1995), *Inequality by Design: Cracking the Bell Curve Myth* (1996) and a second edition of *The Mismeasure of Man* (1996) by Steven J. Gould. More recent examples of responses to the arguments in *The Bell Curve* include that of Richard Nisbett, a psychologist at the University of Michigan, in his 2009 book *Intelligence and How to Get It*, in which he argued that differences in IQ scores found were largely as a result of social and economic factors and that, by controlling for these, the differences between ethnic groups largely disappeared.

Incidentally, *The Bell Curve* was also controversial because of its argument that women of low IQ (who, the authors claimed, are disproportionately represented in the lower socio-economic groups) should not be encouraged to reproduce: 'We urge generally that these policies, represented by the extensive network of cash and services for low-income women who have babies, be ended' (p. 548). Unsurprisingly, these and the rest of their assertions were subject to a great deal of criticism by later scholars.

THE FLYNN EFFECT

The Flynn Effect refers to the substantial increase in average scores on intelligence tests over time all over the world. When IQ tests are initially standardized using a standardization sample, the average result is set to 100. By convention, the standard deviation of the results is set to 15 points. When IQ tests are revised they are again standardized using a new standardization sample and the average result set to 100. However, if the new sample is tested using older tests, in almost every case they score substantially above 100. The effect has been observed in most parts of the world at different rates. The Flynn Effect is named for James R. Flynn, Emeritus Professor of Political Studies at the University of Otago in Dunedin, New Zealand, who did much to document it and promote awareness of its implications.

There are several proposed explanations of the Flynn Effect. These include improved nutrition, a trend towards smaller families, better education, greater environmental stimulation (e.g. from pictures on the wall and movies to video games to computers) and heterosis (the occurrence of genetically superior offspring from mixing the genes of its parents). Another explanation is that people are getting more experienced at taking IQ tests. It is unlikely that genetic selection is the cause as the increase has been too rapid to allow for this.

Emotional intelligence

Emotional intelligence (EI) is the ability to monitor one's own and other people's emotions, to discriminate between different emotions and label them appropriately, and to use emotional information to guide thinking and behaviour. The concept was born out of Howard Gardner's Theory of Multiple Intelligences, which included both interpersonal intelligence (the capacity to understand the intentions, motivations and desires of other people) and intrapersonal intelligence (the capacity to understand oneself, to appreciate one's feelings, fears and motivations). The first use of the term 'emotional intelligence' is usually attributed to Wayne Payne's doctoral thesis 'A Study of Emotion: Developing Emotional Intelligence' from 1985, but the term became widely known with the 1996 publication of Daniel Goleman's *Emotional Intelligence: Why It Can Matter More than IQ*.

Some experts believe that EI is more important than IQ because EI incorporates more of the skills that are really necessary to succeed in life. Latterly, however, Goleman has modified these claims in the light of sceptics who refute the suggestion that EI really does count more than IQ. This issue was clarified by Dr Goleman a few years ago when he commented that 'in some life domains emotional intelligence seems to be more highly correlated with a positive outcome than is a measure of IQ. The domains where this can occur are "soft" – those where, e.g., emotional self-regulation or empathy may be more salient skills than are purely cognitive abilities, such as health or marital success.'

Notwithstanding the contention that EI matters more than IQ, Goleman's early work has been criticized for assuming from the beginning that EI is a type of intelligence. For example, in 2000 Michael Eysenck asserted that Goleman's description of EI contained unsubstantiated assumptions about intelligence in general, and that it even runs contrary to what researchers have come to expect when studying types of intelligence. Later, in 2005, Edwin A. Locke claimed that the concept of EI is in itself a misinterpretation of the intelligence construct, and asserted that it is not another form or type of intelligence, but intelligence applied to a particular life domain: emotions. He suggests that the concept should be referred to as a skill rather than a capacity.

Dig deeper

Newspaper article discussing the argument that IQ tests are 'fundamentally flawed':
http://www.independent.co.uk/news/science/iq-tests-are-fundamentally-flawed-and-using-them-alone-to-measure-intelligence-is-a-fallacy-study-finds-8425911.html

Take the IQ test used in the above study:
http://www.cambridgebrainsciences.com/user/login/challenge/2

Daniel Goleman's website:
http://www.danielgoleman.info/topics/emotional-intelligence/

Fact-check

1 Which one of the following is *not* known for their work on intelligence?
  a ~~Howard Gardner~~
  b Alfred Binet
  c David Wechsler
  d Sigmund Freud

2 Spearman's Two-Factor Theory of Intelligence stated that:
  a Intelligence is located in the hypothalamus of the brain
  b Intelligence is a single entity
  c Intelligence is made up of a general factor and specific factors
  d IQ tests cannot measure intelligence

3 For a behaviour to be classed as an intelligence, Gardner stated that it should:
  a Have a clear evolutionary purpose
  b Produce an emotion
  c Be capable of being copied
  d Be observable

4 Fluid intelligence is:
  a The ability to understand liquids
  b Another way of saying crystallized intelligence
  c Also called 'g'
  d About being able to think logically

5 Mental age refers to:
  a Chronological age
  b The age we think we are
  c The age we would like to be
  d The age group that a person's mental capacity equates to

6 Which of the following is not a subscale of the WAIS?
  a Verbal comprehension
  b Short-term memory
  c Perceptual reasoning
  d Working memory

7 Which of the following do IQ tests measure?
  a Creativity
  b Common sense
  c Emotional intelligence
  d Fluid intelligence

8 The Flynn Effect refers to:
  a The fact that intelligence has been decreasing over the years
  b The fact that intelligence has been increasing over the years
  c The fact that intelligence is the same now on average that it was a generation ago
  d None of the above

9 Explanations to account for the Flynn Effect do not include:
  a Genetic selection
  b Nutrition
  c Education
  d Exposure to testing

10 Emotional intelligence refers to:
  a The ability to monitor one's own emotions
  b The ability to read other people's emotions
  c The ability to control one's own emotions
  d All of the above

9

Personality and motivation

We talk of people having a good personality and sometimes we hear of people taking a personality test, but what do we really mean by 'personality' and how does it develop? The word 'personality' derives from the Latin word *persona*, which referred to a theatrical mask worn by performers. According to the American Psychological Association, personality refers to individual differences in characteristic patterns of thinking, feeling and behaving.

Defining personality

> 'Although no single definition is acceptable to all personality theorists, we can say that personality is a pattern of relatively permanent traits and unique characteristics that give both consistency and individuality to a person's behavior.'
>
> J. Feist and G. J. Feist, *Theories of Personality*, 7th edn
> (New York: McGraw-Hill, 2009), p. 4

Personality is made up of a range of factors individual to each person, including thoughts, values and emotions. Personality is thought to have an impact on behaviour and is relatively stable and generalizable in that people would be expected to behave in similar ways across time and across situations. There are many approaches, or theories, that attempt to explain what personality is. These include trait, psychodynamic, behavioural, social-cognitive and humanistic theories.

Theories of personality

TRAIT THEORIES

These approaches view personality as made up of innate characteristics that have a genetic and/or biological basis (hence this is a biologically based approach to personality). Traits are relatively stable characteristics that cause people to behave in certain ways. It is the unique combination of these varied traits that make up an individual's personality.

The German-born psychologist Hans Eysenck (1916–97) was one of the strongest proponents of this approach, arguing that brain systems were directly linked to personality traits. For example, he claimed that introversion was caused by high cortical arousal (leading introverts to avoid any extra stimulation), while extroversion was associated with such low levels of cortical arousal that extroverts feel the need to seek out extra stimulation from the environment. Similarly, Eysenck proposed that individual differences in the limbic system determined where a person lay on the neuroticism dimension (there's more on Eysenck's approach later in this chapter).

Trait theorists are interested in measuring and identifying the different traits that make up an individual's personality. There are three main trait approaches:

▶ Cattell's Sixteen Personality Factors

In 1949 the trait theorist Raymond Cattell (1905–98) identified more than 170 personality traits, which he used to measure a large sample of individuals. Using the statistical technique of factor analysis, he then reduced this list to 16 main dimensions of personality and later developed the 16PF Personality Inventory to measure these in individuals (see below). The 16 dimensions would each involve a scale so that people could see how they scored on that dimension compared with other people in the population. Their personality could then be described according to where they were on each dimension.

▶ Eysenck's Three Dimensions of Personality

Prior to Cattell's approach, Hans Eysenck believed that there were just three main personality traits. These were:

- ▶ **Introversion/extraversion:** introverted individuals tend to be quiet and reserved as they are likely to be preoccupied with directing attention on to their inner experiences, whereas extroverts tend to be more outgoing as they focus their energies more outwardly on to other people and the environment.

- ▶ **Neuroticism/emotional stability:** this dimension of Eysenck's trait theory is concerned with the stability, or otherwise, of an individual's mood. Neuroticism refers to an individual's tendency to become upset or emotional, while stability refers to the tendency to remain more emotionally controlled.

- ▶ **Psychoticism:** Eysenck was influenced by his work with people who had mental health issues and he later added (in the 1970s) this personality dimension to his trait theory. Individuals with high psychoticism tend to have difficulty dealing with reality and may be antisocial, compared with those low on the scale.

Spotlight: The most-cited psychologist

By the time of his death in 1997 at the age of 81, Eysenck had been the living psychologist most frequently cited in science journals. In his lifetime he had written about 80 books and more than 1,600 journal articles.

▶ The Five-Factor Theory of Personality

Many researchers felt that while Cattell focused on too many personality traits, Eysenck focused on too few. This led to the development of a five-factor approach to personality traits, sometimes referred to as the 'Big Five'. The initial five-factor model was advanced by Ernest Tupes and Raymond Christal in 1961 but it did not really make an impact until the 1980s, when Paul Costa and Robert McCrae in 1985 published the NEO Five-Factor Personality Inventory (of which more later).

The five factors are:

▶ **Openness:** this refers to how open a person is to new experiences and new ideas. It also depicts how imaginative and creative they are, and whether they prefer flexible rather than strict routines.

▶ **Conscientiousness:** this refers to how dutiful and disciplined a person is and whether they adopt planned or spontaneous behaviours.

▶ **Extraversion:** this includes the degree to which people are outgoing, sociable and chatty.

▶ **Agreeableness:** this describes the tendency to be compassionate and cooperative rather than hostile and suspicious.

▶ **Neuroticism:** this refers to emotional stability but also to the degree to which people experience the negative emotions such as anger and depression.

It should be noted that these are really dimensions not types, so that people fall somewhere within each pole on a scale, rather than either being one or the other.

PSYCHODYNAMIC THEORIES

These emphasize the influence of the unconscious on the development of personality. The Austrian neurologist Sigmund Freud (1856–1939) was one of the main drivers of this approach.

Spotlight: Sigmund Freud

Sigmund Freud (born Sigismund Schlomo Freud) was an Austrian neurologist born to Jewish parents in 1856. He became known as the founding father of **psychoanalysis**, a clinical method for treating psychopathology through dialogue between a patient and a psychoanalyst. Freud qualified as a doctor of medicine at the University of Vienna in 1881 and in 1886 he resigned his hospital post and entered private practice specializing in 'nervous disorders'. In 1933 the Nazis publicly burned a number of Freud's books and in 1938, shortly after the Nazis annexed Austria, Freud left Vienna for London with his wife and daughter Anna. Freud had been diagnosed with cancer of the jaw in 1923 (related to his heavy smoking), and underwent more than 30 operations. He died of cancer on 23 September 1939.

Freud's theory states that personality is driven by several factors:

▶ Instinctual drives

▶ Unconscious processes

▶ Early childhood influences.

'A child in its greed for love does not enjoy having to share the affection of its parents with its brothers and sisters; and it notices that the whole of their affection is lavished upon it once more whenever it arouses their anxiety by falling ill. It has now discovered a means of enticing out its parents' love and will make use of that means as soon as it has the necessary psychical material at its disposal for producing an illness.'
Sigmund Freud, *Fragments of an Analysis of a Case of Hysteria* (1905 [1901]), Standard Edition, vol. 7, p. 37

These factors interact, especially in the first five years of life, to influence the developing personality. Freud believed that an individual's personality is structured into three parts (which is why his theory is sometimes called the **Tripartite Theory of Personality**) – the id, ego and superego – all developing at different stages in our lives:

▶ The **id** is the primitive and instinctive component of personality and consists of all the inherited (i.e. biological) components of personality. It is driven by the *pleasure principle*, demanding immediate gratification. It is the id, then, that drives us towards food, water, sex and other basic needs.

▶ The **ego** is the decision-making part of personality that tries to control the more instinctive id. It operates not on a pleasure principle like the id, but on a *reality principle* as it tries to work out realistic ways of satisfying the needs of the id without attracting negative consequences; for example by trying to postpone the id's drives to a more socially acceptable time. The ego takes into account the social expectations, norms, etiquette and rules of society.

▶ The **superego** acts like a conscience by incorporating values and morals that are learned from one's parents and others. It acts on the ego through the use of guilt.

Thus, Freud claims, the three components are in constant conflict, each battling to exert their influence on actions and behaviour. To manage these internal conflicts and reduce anxiety, people may use **defence mechanisms,** which are usually automatic and unconscious. In 1936 Anna Freud (daughter of Sigmund) enumerated a total of ten defence mechanisms that appeared in the works of her famous father.

'A defence mechanism is a coping technique that reduces anxiety arising from unacceptable or potentially harmful impulses.'
D. L. Schacter, *Psychology*, 2nd edn (New York: Worth Publishers, 2011), pp. 482–3

These include:

- ▶ **Repression:** this is a subconscious attempt to keep unpleasant thoughts, memories and feelings out of mind and even memory.

- ▶ **Projection:** this is where, instead of acknowledging unacceptable thoughts or feelings, we attribute them to someone else.

- ▶ **Reaction formation:** here a person might attempt to distance themselves from unacceptable thoughts or feelings by behaving in a way that is directly opposite to their real inclinations.

- ▶ **Rationalization:** This is an attempt to use incorrect explanations to justify unacceptable behaviour, thoughts or feelings.

- ▶ **Displacement:** here we might transfer feelings about a person or event on to someone or something else.

- ▶ **Denial:** This is where a person refuses to acknowledge something that is obvious to most other people.

- ▶ **Regression:** here a person might revert back to a more immature state of psychological development that is felt to be safer and less demanding.

- ▶ **Sublimation:** this is the channelling of unacceptable thoughts and feelings into socially acceptable behaviour.

Other influential players in the psychoanalytical approaches to personality were Erik Erikson (1902–94), who emphasized the social elements of personality development, the identity crisis and how personality is shaped over the course of the entire lifespan, and Carl Jung (1875–1961), who focused on the role that concepts such as the **collective unconscious** (the reservoir of all the experience and knowledge of the human species) had on personality development. Jung also developed a theory of psychological types designed to categorize people in terms of various personality patterns. These types were:

- ▶ Extraversion vs Introversion

- ▶ Sensation vs Intuition

- ▶ Thinking vs Feeling
- ▶ Judging vs Perceiving

This theory later led to the development of the now-famous **Myers–Briggs Type Indicator** to measure personality (we will return to this later in the chapter).

BEHAVIOURAL THEORIES

These state that personality develops as a result of an interaction between the individual and the environment. According to this view, individuals develop consistent behaviour patterns because they have learned particular ways of responding. Behaviours that have positive consequences tend to increase, while behaviours that have negative consequences tend to decrease. We can also learn behaviours through modelling or observation (see Chapter 5 for more on behaviourism). Because everyone is exposed to different learning experiences, everyone develops their own unique personality.

Whereas Freud in his psychoanalytical approach felt that personality developed mainly in early childhood, the behavioural approach (led by B. F. Skinner as outlined in Chapter 5) stressed that personality develops across a much longer period of time – even a lifetime – as a person encounters new situations.

Skinner also argued that it is possible to change our personality by changing our environment, since it is the environment that shapes personality. This is in contrast with other views that, to make changes, we must change our inner self first.

Skinner was not the only proponent of the behaviourist approach to personality. The American psychologist Julian Rotter (1916–2014) was also very influential in developing these ideas, emphasizing how social learning leads to the development of personality. In contrast with psychoanalytical theories and with strict behavioural approaches, Rotter argued that humans are not motivated to act simply to avoid punishment, but are motivated by life goals and vision to maximize the rewards they want to receive. It is this set of motivations, then, that shape our behaviours and personality.

SOCIAL-COGNITIVE THEORIES

Cognitive theories are theories of personality that emphasize cognitive processes, such as thinking and judging; the social part comes from the idea that these cognitive processes interact with influences from the environment and other people. Albert Bandura was one of the proponents of social-cognitive approaches to personality; we met him in Chapter 5 in connection with his Bobo doll experiments.

In his social-cognitive theory of personality, Bandura stressed the role of observational learning. He argued that the reinforcement of the behaviourist approach must include cognitive processes, too. Bandura agreed with the behaviourist view that environment causes behaviour, but he also maintained that behaviour can 'cause environment'; a process he called reciprocal determinism. For example, a person may have learned to have an aggressive personality because aggressive behaviour was reinforced at some point in their life by something occurring in their environment. But their aggression then acts on the environment by changing the way others act around him – by perhaps causing people to avoid him or give into him when he becomes aggressive. In this way, the environment has acted on his personality but his personality is also changing the environment.

Bandura later proposed that this two-way process was actually lacking a third factor – the person's psychological or cognitive processes. He said that our capacity to process language, images and other sensory stimuli in our minds has an effect on how we behave, how we develop our personality traits and, thus, how we affect our environment.

HUMANIST THEORIES

These emphasize free will and the individual experience in the development of personality. Psychologists such as Carl Rogers (1902–87) and Abraham Maslow (1908–70) disliked both psychodynamic and behaviourist explanations of personality because they felt that these theories ignored the qualities that make humans unique among animals, such as striving for self-determination and self-realization. In the humanistic view, people are responsible for their own lives and actions and have the freedom and will to change their attitudes and behaviour – they are able to overcome their biological urges and also overcome their past.

Abraham Maslow is best known for his theories on motivation and for developing a ladder of human motives (see later in this chapter). At the top of this ladder is the need for self-actualization, which is something that Maslow said all humans strive for. Self-actualization is the need to fulfil one's potential, and this is something people strive for once they have satisfied their more basic needs.

> 'Musicians must make music, artists must paint, poets must write if they are to be ultimately at peace with themselves. What human beings can be, they must be. They must be true to their own nature. This need we may call self-actualization.'
> Abraham Maslow, *Motivation and Personality* (New York: Harper, 1954)

Maslow believed that only a self-actualizing individual could have a healthy personality and he studied many well-known successful people to establish what made up their personalities. He then outlined several characteristics that self-actualizing people (and thus people with healthy personalities) share:

▶ Awareness and acceptance of themselves

▶ Openness and spontaneity

▶ The ability to enjoy work and see work as a mission to fulfilment

▶ The ability to develop close friendships without being overly dependent on other people

▶ A good sense of humour

▶ The tendency to have peak experiences that are spiritually or emotionally satisfying.

As referred to earlier, another influential humanistic psychologist is the American Carl Rogers, the founder of **Person-Centred Theory**. Like Freud (but unlike Maslow), Rogers drew on clinical case studies to come up with his theory and he emphasized the role of **self-concept** in the development of personality. The self-concept is our image of who we are, what we stand for and who we want to be. It includes all the thoughts, feelings and beliefs people have about themselves.

People tend to be aware of their self-concept, but their self-awareness may be somewhat skewed and not matching reality. He called this state **incongruence**. Incongruence can develop when a person's self-concept is threatened, causing anxiety. To protect themselves from this anxiety, they distort their experiences so that they can hold on to their self-concept. People who have a high degree of incongruence are likely to feel very anxious because reality continually threatens their self-concept (and thus self-esteem). For example, someone may be a successful and respected individual but regard themselves as a failure. The reality is incongruent with their view of themselves. The greater the gap between the self-image and reality, the more likelihood there is of anxiety and emotional disturbances (there is more on this in Chapter 16).

Assessment of personality

Personality tests are used in occupational settings as well as clinical ones, and they can be used to match personality types with those thought to be required in different job roles.

Common personality tests include:

▶ **Occupational Personality Questionnaire** (published by Saville & Holdsworth Ltd, 1984): this measures 32 facets of temperament thought to be relevant in occupational settings. These facets are grouped into three domains: relationships with people, thinking style and feelings/emotions. Each domain is divided into subdomains. For example, relationships with people are grouped in the three subdomains of assertiveness, gregariousness and empathy.

▶ **16PF** (published by OPP): this is widely used and was developed from a statistical analysis that located 16 personality factors from a mass of personality measures. This is based on Cattell's theory as outlined above. It was first created by Cattell in 1949 and is now in its fifth edition.

▶ **Eysenck Personality Questionnaire (EPQ):** this is short; it takes about ten minutes to compete. It was devised by the psychologists Hans Eysenck and his wife, Sybil Eysenck in 1975. It yields scores on psychoticism, extroversion, neuroticism and a lie scale. In 1985 a revised version of EPQ was described – the EPQ-R – in the journal *Personality and Individual Differences*. This version has 100 yes/no questions in its full version and 48 yes/no questions in its short-scale version.

▶ **NEO-FFI Inventory (Neuroticism, Extroversion, Openness, Five-Factor Inventory):** this was produced by Paul Costa and Robert McCrae in 1989 and is based on analyses that identify the 'Big Five' personality factors: neuroticism, extroversion, openness, agreeableness and conscientiousness. The first three of these aspects have subscales to measure these facets. For example, neuroticism is divided into anxiety, hostility, depression, self-consciousness, impulsiveness and vulnerability.

▶ **Minnesota Multiphasic Personality Inventory (MMPI):** this was developed in the 1940s and revised in the 1980s. The revised version is called the MMPI-2. The MMPI-2 contains a list of 567 questions. The MMPI was originally developed to help clinical psychologists diagnose psychological disorders.

▶ **Myer–Briggs Type Indicator (MBTI):** this was also published by OPP and is designed to measure psychological preferences in how people perceive the world and make decisions. These preferences were identified by Katharine Cook Briggs and Isabel Briggs Myers from the type theories proposed by Carl Gustav Jung, first published in his 1921 book *Psychological Types*. The MBTI asks the candidate to answer a series of 'forced-choice' questions, where one choice identifies you as belonging to one of four paired traits. The basic test takes 20 minutes, and at the end you are presented with a precise, multi-dimensional summary of your personality. The MBTI test classifies people into types based on the four bipolar dimensions identified by Carl Jung (see above).

Spotlight: MBTI

'The Myers–Briggs Type Indicator (MBTI) is one of the most popular personality tests in the world. Two-and-a-half million US citizens a year take the Myers–Briggs. Eighty-nine companies out of the US Fortune 100 make use of it, for recruitment and selection or to help employees understand themselves or their co-workers.' (http://www.psychometric-success.com/personality-tests/personality-tests-popular-tests.htm)

Case study: Rorschach inkblots

The Rorschach personality test was developed almost 100 years ago and consists of a series of ten inkblots. Psychologists asked subjects to look at the inkblots and describe what they saw, and the psychologists then used complex scoring systems to interpret the subjects' responses. It was thought that people would project their personality on to the inkblots. In the 1960s the Rorschach was the most widely used projective test of personality.

Using interpretation of 'ambiguous designs' to assess an individual's personality is an idea that goes back to Leonardo da Vinci. The Rorschach is what psychologists call a **projective test**. The basic idea of this is that when a person is shown an ambiguous, meaningless image (i.e. an inkblot) the mind will work hard at imposing meaning on the image by 'projecting' their personality on to it. Hermann Rorschach created the Rorschach inkblot test in 1921 but he never intended the inkblots to be used as a general personality test; he developed them as a tool for the diagnosis of schizophrenia. It was not until 1939 that the test was used as a projective test of personality, a use for which Rorschach had always been sceptical.

This was a view that came to be shared more widely: in the 1959 edition of *Mental Measurement Yearbook*, Lee Cronbach (former President of the Psychometric Society and American Psychological Association) is quoted as stating: 'The test has repeatedly failed as a prediction of practical criteria. There is nothing in the literature to encourage reliance on Rorschach interpretations.' Problems with the Rorschach include the fact that it is possible that the testing psychologist might also project his or her views on to the inkblots when interpreting responses. For example, if the person being tested says that they see a skirt, a male psychologist might classify this as a sexual response, whereas a female psychologist may classify it simply as clothing. Critics have also suggested that the Rorschach lacks reliability; two different testers might come up with two different personality profiles for the same person that they are testing.

A moratorium on its use was finally called in 1999 and very few psychologists would use it now as a personality test.

Motivation

Motivation is what gets us to act or do something and is clearly linked to personality. Motivation is about setting goals and going out to meet them; our personality strongly influences what these goals or drives might be.

Psychologists have proposed a number of different theories to account for motivation, and it is sometimes useful to group the most influential theories into two categories: content and process theories. **Content theories** attempt to explain specific things that motivate people in different situations. They are concerned with identifying people's needs and strengths, looking at what motivates a person. Some of these needs are primary, physical needs that are biologically driven (e.g. food, water, shelter) and some are secondary, psychological needs that vary from person to person but might include power and achievement.

Process theories, on the other hand, try to identify relationships among variables that make up motivation – how motivation is initiated and sustained. These approaches look at the process of motivation rather than the content.

CONTENT THEORIES OF MOTIVATION

There are several content theories that attempt to explain the needs that motivate people, including:

▶ Maslow's Theory of Hierarchical Needs

Abraham Maslow (mentioned earlier in this chapter) believed that needs are physiological or psychological deficiencies that a person feels a compulsion to satisfy (Maslow 1943). These needs create tensions that can influence a person's attitudes and behaviours. Maslow's theory is based on the following two principles:

▶ **The deficit principle:** this states that a satisfied need no longer motivates behaviour.

▶ **The progression principle:** Maslow identified five needs that he believed were arranged in a hierarchy, as shown in the diagram below; the next level only becomes relevant when the previous level has been satisfied (e.g. we are not motivated to satisfy our safety needs until our physiological needs have been met).

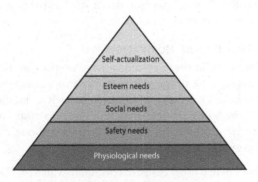

Maslow's Theory of Hierarchical Needs

Maslow's theory has been criticized because little evidence has been found for his hierarchical structure and progression principle.

▶ Herzberg's Two-Factor Theory

The American psychologist Frederick Herzberg (1923–2000) was mainly concerned with workplace motivation. In 1959 he published *The Motivation to Work*, in which he identified certain factors in the workplace that cause job satisfaction (called 'motivators' or 'satisfiers') – while a separate set of factors, if missing, cause dissatisfaction ('hygiene factors' or 'dissatisfiers').

Motivators or satisfiers: these are the things that really motivate people and include achievement, recognition, the work itself and so on.

Hygiene factors or dissatisfiers: although these factors do not motivate people, they can cause dissatisfaction if they are missing. In the workplace they include things such as job security, salary and working conditions. Increasing these factors may not increase satisfaction, but getting rid of them would cause dissatisfaction.

Essentially, hygiene factors are needed to ensure that an employee is not dissatisfied. Motivation factors are needed to motivate an employee to higher performance. The theory has been criticized for being too simplistic: what satisfies one person might be a motivator for another.

PROCESS THEORIES OF MOTIVATION

Whereas the content theories concentrate on the question of 'what' motivates, the process theories are more concerned with how the process works and sustains itself, such as factors that determine how much effort people will put into attaining a goal. There are a number of process theories, although the best known is arguably Vroom's Expectancy Theory.

Expectancy Theory (also called **Expectancy-Valency Theory**) was first proposed by Victor Vroom of the Yale School of Management in 1964. Whereas Maslow and Herzberg look at internal needs, Vroom's expectancy theory separates out effort (which arises from motivation), performance and outcomes. Expectancy theory proposes that the desirability of an outcome determines whether or not someone will be motivated to act to achieve that outcome. In other words, we choose to do things that give us the greatest rewards. This theory is thus concerned with the mental processes regarding that choice.

There are three key elements to the theory:

1 **Expectancy:** this is the belief that effort will lead to a level of performance necessary to obtain rewards ('What are the chances that if I work hard I will reach a certain level of performance?'). A number of factors can contribute to expectancy perceptions:

   ▷ The level of confidence in the skills required for the task

   ▷ The availability of relevant information or resources

   ▷ Previous success at the task.

2 **Instrumentality:** this is the belief that if you reach that level of performance, the reward will be forthcoming ('What are the chances that if I reach that level of performance, I will be rewarded?').

3 **Valence:** this is the importance or value that the individual places upon the reward ('How much do I want that reward?').

Thus, a person will not be motivated to do something if:

▶ They do not think they are capable of doing it; OR

▶ They don't think the rewards associated with doing it are very likely; OR

▶ They don't really care that much about the reward.

Dig deeper

More on the Rorschach inkblot controversy:
http://www.bbc.co.uk/news/magazine-18952667

Take a personality test:
http://www.humanmetrics.com/cgi-win/jtypes1.htm

Application of Maslow's theory to the workplace:
http://www.businessballs.com/maslow.htm

Fact-check

1 Personality traits are:
- **a** Relatively stable characteristics that cause people to behave in certain ways
- **b** Unstable characteristics that cause people to behave in certain ways
- **c** Unconscious processes that affect the development of personality
- **d** Elements of free will that lead to the development of personality

2 Which of the following is *not* one of Cattell's 16 personality factors?
- **a** Dominance
- **b** Warmth
- **c** Liveliness
- **d** Moodiness

3 Which of the following is *not* mentioned as a personality dimension by Eysenck?
- **a** Introversion
- **b** Agreeableness
- **c** Neuroticism
- **d** Emotional stability

4 Which of the following is *not* one of Cattell's Big Five personality factors?
- **a** Psychoticism
- **b** Openness
- **c** Extraversion
- **d** Agreeableness

5 Psychodynamic theories of personality emphasize:
- **a** The influence of traits on the development of personality
- **b** The influence of the unconscious on the development of personality
- **c** The importance of emotional stability in the development of personality
- **d** The need to consider the self in the development of personality

6 Which of the following does Freud *not* claim contributes to the development of personality?

a Instinctual drives

b Unconscious processes

c Early childhood influences

d 'Free will

7 Behavioural theories state that personality develops as a result of:

a An interaction between the individual and the environment

b An interaction between the individual and their unconscious

c The environment and the social situation

d The environment and the id

8 Which of the following is *not* a characteristic of self-actualizing people?

a The ability to speak more than one language.

b Openness and spontaneity

c The ability to develop close friendships without being overly dependent on other people

d Awareness and acceptance of themselves

9 Which of the following is *not* one of Maslow's motivations in his hierarchy of needs?

a Physical needs

b Social needs

c Esteem needs

d Satisfaction needs

10 According to Vroom, a person will only be motivated to do something if:

a They think they are capable of doing it

b They think that doing it will lead to rewards

c They believe those rewards are worth the effort

d All of the above

10

Developmental psychology

Developmental psychology is concerned with, among other areas, cognitive development across the entire lifespan but particularly from birth to adulthood. This involves areas such as problem-solving, moral understanding, conceptual understanding, language acquisition, social development, development of personality, emotional development and self-concept and identity formation. Some of these areas have been addressed in other chapters of this book, and this chapter will concentrate on significant factors that contribute to the development of an emotionally healthy child. For many psychologists, this starts with attachment.

Attachment Theory

Attachment Theory was originally developed by John Bowlby (see the 'Spotlight' below) and focuses on the importance of developing emotionally meaningful relationships with significant others. Attachment is described as a biological system or powerful survival impulse that evolved to ensure the survival of the infant. The theory deals with how early-childhood attachment experiences contribute to the way adult human beings respond within relationships when hurt, being separated from loved ones, or perceiving a threat.

Spotlight: John Bowlby

Born in London in 1907, John Bowlby graduated from the University of Cambridge in 1928. He undertook some work experience in a school that was to set him on his course for life. While at this school, he encountered two different children: one who was remote and affectionless and one who followed Bowlby around everywhere. Both children had poor relationships with their mothers and it was these experiences (and his own, as he was brought up primarily by his nanny who left when he was four, leaving him with an acute sense of loss) that led Bowlby to his now classic work on Attachment Theory. Bowlby died in 1990.

The basic premise of Attachment Theory is that close and early attachment of a baby to its mother is essential for healthy relationships across the child's entire life.

> '[Attachment is] the propensity to make strong emotional bonds to particular individuals [and is] a basic component of human nature.'
> J. Bowlby, *A Secure Base: Parent–Child Attachment and Healthy Human Development* (London: Routledge 1988), p. 3

Bowlby believed that there are four main characteristics of attachment:

▶ **Proximity maintenance:** this is the desire of children to be near their primary caregiver.

- **Safe haven:** this is where the child returns to the attachment figure for comfort and safety when faced with anything that could be perceived as fear, discomfort or threat.

- **Secure base:** the attachment figure acts as a safe base from which the child can explore, comforted in the knowledge that they can return to the base if needed.

- **Separation distress:** this is the anxiety that occurs when the child is away from the primary caregiver.

Bowlby went on to make three key propositions as part of his Attachment Theory:

- When children are raised to have confidence that their primary caregiver will be there for them when they are needed, they will be less fearful than those who are raised without that confidence.

- He believed that there is a critical period (the first three years – see below) in a child's life when that confidence needs to be created and that whatever occurs during that critical period will have long-lasting effects.

- Finally, he pointed out that any expectations that people have about relationships are directly related to the experiences that they have had with their caregivers in the past.

Bowlby believed that there are four stages to the attachment process and that these occur at fairly typical ages in an infant's life – within the sensitive and critical first three years:

Pre-attachment phase (age birth to six weeks): in this stage, the baby uses its innate skills (crying, grasping tightly, gurgling, etc.) to attract and maintain the attention of its caregiver. When this goes according to plan, the baby learns that the caregiver is nearby and will respond when 'asked'. However, at this stage they are not attached to any particular caregiver and will not mind being left with strangers.

Attachment in the making phase (age six weeks to six to eight months): at this point the infant begins to recognize its primary caregiver and responds differently to them than to others. But he or she is still happy to be left with strangers.

Clear-cut attachment phase (age six to eight months to 18–24 months): at this point the infant begins to experience separation anxiety and will be clearly distressed at the primary caregiver's absence. This stage often becomes less acute when Piaget's stage of object permanence begins (see later in this chapter).

Formation of reciprocal relationship (18–24 months and beyond): the child soon learns to understand the nature of its caregiver's comings and goings and that they will return (and even *when* they will return). They often try to negotiate with the caregiver, using language skills and other strategies, to influence the length of the separation.

Case study: Harlow's monkey experiments

The American psychologist Harry Harlow (1905–81) is best known for his maternal-separation experiments on rhesus monkeys. He conducted most of his research at the University of Wisconsin–Madison, where the humanistic psychologist Abraham Maslow (see Chapter 9) worked for a time with him.

Harlow's experiments were controversial since they involved rearing baby monkeys in isolation chambers, apart, not only from their mothers, but also from other monkeys, for up to 24 months; most emerged severely disturbed. So controversial were these animal experiments that some believe that they even led to the rise of the animal liberation movement in the United States.

These controversial monkey studies actually began life as something else entirely and were never intended as the studies in maternal deprivation into which they evolved. Harlow first established a breeding colony of rhesus macaques in 1932 in order to study cognitive processes. It was during these experiments that Harlow noticed effects that he hadn't been expecting; although he and his team soon learned how to care for the physical needs of their infant monkeys, they soon realized that the nursery-reared infants became very different from their mother-reared peers. In fact, these infants seemed slightly strange: they were reclusive and had definite social deficits and they clung to their cloth nappies. This attachment to the soft cloth of their nappies and the psychological deficits seemed to correlate with the absence of their mother, which led Harlow to investigate the mother–infant bond further.

He then embarked on the now famous monkey studies with the aim of discovering whether the attachment that an infant has to its mother is due to the food (milk) she provides – or whether the nourishment is not as important as the comfort and love offered. Harlow tested this by creating an intriguing experiment. Using wire and wood, he built inanimate surrogate mothers for the baby monkeys. Even though the wire 'mothers' could not move or offer warmth or real comfort, each infant became attached to its particular inanimate mother, recognizing its unique face and preferring it above all others.

Harlow next wanted to know what the most important features of these inanimate mothers were: her texture or her provision of milk. For this experiment he presented the infants with a cloth mother and a wire mother under two conditions. In one, the wire mother held a bottle with food and the cloth mother held no food, and in the other, the cloth mother held the bottle and the wire mother had nothing.

Overwhelmingly, the infant primates preferred spending their time clinging to the cloth mother. Even when only the wire mother could provide nourishment, the monkeys visited her only to feed, returning to the milk-less cloth mother the rest of the time. Harlow concluded that there was much more to the mother–infant relationship than milk and that this 'contact comfort' was essential to the psychological development and health of infant monkeys and children. Later experiments showed that the babies used the inanimate mother as a base for exploration and a source of comfort and protection in novel and even frightening situations; for example, in one experiment Harlow presented the infant monkeys with a loud mechanical toy from which they fled to the comfort of the cloth mother (rather than the milk-providing wire one). Thus, he showed that they became attached, in Bowlby's sense, to the warmth and comfort offered by the milk-less cloth 'mother' rather than to the food offered by the cold and hard 'mother'.

Spotlight: Monkey hatred

Despite Harlow being famous for his work with monkeys, he had a strong dislike for the primates and is quoted as saying, 'The only thing I care about is whether a monkey will turn out a property I can publish. I don't have any love for them. Never have. I don't really like animals. I despise cats. I hate dogs. How could you like monkeys?'

THE INFLUENCE OF MARY AINSWORTH

Mary Dinsmore Salter Ainsworth (1913–99) was an American-Canadian developmental psychologist known for her work in early emotional attachment with the **Strange Situation Procedure** in 1965, as well as her work in the development of Attachment Theory. She developed the Strange Situation Procedure as a way of assessing attachment behaviour in young children. The investigative procedure is divided into eight episodes, all of which are observed through a one-way mirror:

1 The infant and his or her caregiver are introduced into a laboratory setting, filled with toys and two chairs. The caregiver interacts and plays with the baby.

2 After a minute the caregiver is asked to withdraw and sits quietly, not interacting as before, leaving the child to explore his or her surroundings.

3 After a further minute, a person unknown to the infant enters the room and at first, just observes, then slowly tries to engage with the child.

4 *The first separation:* the caregiver now leaves the child with the stranger for three minutes; this generally causes the child to become distressed and the stranger attempts to comfort them.

5 *First reunion:* the caregiver returns and is able to comfort the child and the stranger leaves.

6 *Second separation:* the caregiver departs for a second time, leaving the child entirely alone for three minutes, which is again expected to cause some anxiety.

7 It is then the stranger who enters and offers to comfort the infant.

8 Finally, the caregiver returns, and is instructed to pick up the child.

The reunions and separations are of particular interest to observers. On the basis of their behaviours, the 26 children in Ainsworth's original Baltimore study were placed into one of three classifications. Each of these groups reflects a different kind of attachment relationship with the caregiver, and implies different ways of responding to perceived threats.

▶ **Secure attachment:** a child who is securely attached to its mother will explore freely while the caregiver is present, using her as a 'safe base' from which to explore. The child will engage with the stranger when the caregiver is present, and will be visibly upset when the caregiver departs but happy to see the caregiver on his or her return.

▶ **Avoidant insecure attachment:** a child with the anxious-avoidant insecure attachment style will avoid or ignore the caregiver – showing little emotion when the caregiver departs or returns. The child will not explore very much regardless of who is there. There is not much emotional range regardless of who is in the room or if it is empty.

▶ **Resistant insecure attachment:** children classified as anxious–ambivalent/resistant showed distress even before separation, and were clingy and difficult to comfort on the caregiver's return.

A fourth category was added later:

▶ **Disorganized/disoriented attachment:** this is when there is no clear (or mixed) attachment between the child and his caregiver, probably because the parent acts as an apprehensive caregiver and a reassuring one at different times. The child may look away when the parent tries to hold them or engage with them.

Piaget's Theory of Cognitive Development

If Bowlby and Ainsworth were concerned with the development of secure attachments, the French developmental psychologist Jean Piaget (1896–1980) was more occupied with how cognitive and intellectual skill develops in children. Children, he claimed, were like scientists, actively trying to understand and make sense of their world. He proposed that children progress through a series of four key stages of cognitive development, each stage being marked by a shift in understanding. This process of understanding and change involves two basic functions: assimilation and accommodation.

Assimilation is when children adapt new information into pre-existing cognitive schemas. This occurs when children are faced with new or unfamiliar information, which they try to make sense of by fitting it into what they already know. In contrast, **accommodation** is the process of altering pre-existing schemas in order to fit in the new information. This happens when they try to accommodate (i.e., fit the new knowledge into existing schemas) but this attempt does not work so they need to change pre-existing schemas to fit the new information they have. Using accommodation and assimilation, the child progresses through Piaget's four stages of cognitive development:

THE SENSORIMOTOR STAGE

This is the first stage that begins at birth and extends into the period of language acquisition. During this stage (which has six sub-stages), infants and toddlers acquire knowledge through sensory experiences and manipulating objects; they learn about their world, primarily, via their senses and physical actions that they take in their environment. There is no use of symbols. The child begins to learn that she is separate from the environment and that this environment continues to exist, even when she cannot see or hear it (this realization is termed **object permanence**); thus they learn that Mum will return or that an object hidden under a blanket is still there even though they can't see it.

THE PREOPERATIONAL STAGE

This stage (which has two sub-stages) starts around age two and lasts until the age of around seven. Children learn through pretend and symbolic play (e.g. a box is a car), which increases during this stage, but they still struggle with logic and taking the point of view of other people (i.e. they are still what Piaget termed 'egocentric').

THE CONCRETE OPERATIONAL STAGE

This happens at around the age of seven and lasts until the age of about eleven. Children at this point of development begin to think more logically, but their thinking can also be very rigid. They tend to struggle with abstract and hypothetical concepts; they can only solve problems that apply to concrete events or objects. 'Concrete' means based on actual people, places and things that children have observed in their environment. Their representations are limited to the tangible, touchable and concrete and thus they find it hard to understand events that require imagination or abstract thought.

The primary milestones of a child's concrete operational stage include the ability to distinguish between their own thoughts and perceptions and those of others (and to know that these might be different), the ability to think logically about objects and events and the ability to *conserve* (this is the ability to understand when the amount of something remains constant across two or more situations despite its appearance changing across those situations). There are seven types of 'conservation' including number, length, liquid, mass, weight, area and volume. An example of conservation is when a child recognizes that a thin, tall beaker can hold the same amount of liquid as a short, fat one.

THE FORMAL OPERATIONAL STAGE

The final stage of Piaget's theory begins at adolescence (roughly from age 11) and continues into early adulthood (around 15–20 years old). It involves an increase in logic, the ability to use deductive reasoning, and an understanding of abstract ideas such as freedom or religiosity.

Vygotsky's Development Theory

While Piaget's ideas and observations about the cognitive development of children have stood up very well to research scrutiny, there are aspects that have been criticized strongly by the psychological community. Piaget's view was that children develop almost entirely on their own, without the need for much adult input at all. Newer research suggests that this is not the whole picture and it takes more than a child's private experiments for them to develop so completely. More recent research suggests that aspects of the social world that the child lives in are just as important for their cognitive development. Lev Vygotsky (1896–1934), a Soviet psychologist born in Belarus, emphasized the important contribution of social, interpersonal and other dimensions in facilitating children's cognitive development.

At the core of Vygotsky's approach, then, is that learning takes place as a result of a child's interactions with his environment – with peers, siblings, parents, caregivers, school and so on. These interactions also involve objects such as toys or books, or even junk. Vygotsky noted how useful older children and adults are to a child's development and coined the term **Zones of Proximal Development** (ZPD) to describe the gap between what a child can do alone and what they need assistance with to accomplish.

'[The Zone of Proximal Development is] the distance between the actual developmental level as determined by independent problem solving and the level of potential development as determined through problem solving under adult guidance, or in collaboration with more capable peers.'

L. S. Vygotsky, *Mind in Society: Development of Higher Psychological Processes*, p. 86

There are two levels of attainment for the ZPD:

▶ **Level 1 – the 'current level of development':** this describes what the child is capable of doing now, without the input of anyone else.

- Level 2 – the 'potential level of development': this means what the child could potentially achieve with help from other people, such as older children or adults.

The 'zone' is the gap between levels 1 and 2. To help a child cross the gap between what they can accomplish on their own, adults or older children use '**scaffolding**', whereby their instruction and help lessen as the child becomes more capable.

Stages of moral development

Morality is our understanding of what is right and wrong and is subject to the morality of the culture and society we live in. Morality does not develop in a vacuum but is greatly influenced by parents and others that a child interacts with. Between the ages of two and five, many children start to show some basic morally based behaviours and beliefs; they might tell the teacher if someone is being 'mean' to another child, for example. They become aware of moral codes and show guilt if they break them.

Piaget's view of moral development was that children between the ages of five and ten see the world through a **heteronomous morality.** This means that they think that rules are simply what teachers and adults tell children to follow. They see these rules as absolutes and not open to negotiation or to being changed. As they grow older and develop more abstract thinking, they begin to see that rules can be more flexible and open to discussion.

The American developmental psychologist Lawrence Kohlberg (1927–87) built on Piaget's work to develop his theory of the **stages of moral development.** His theory proposed that morality is developed across three stages, each of which is further subdivided into two more stages. This process occurs across a lifetime and is not restricted to childhood development.

Kohlberg gave people moral dilemmas like the Heinz story (see the 'Spotlight' below) and was interested in the reasoning behind whatever response they gave.

Spotlight: The Heinz dilemma

Kohlberg used a series of moral dilemmas to test how people would make and justify moral decisions. An example of such a dilemma is the 'Heinz' dilemma:

> 'A woman was near death from a special kind of cancer. There was one drug that the doctors thought might save her. It was a form of radium that a druggist in the same town had recently discovered. The drug was expensive to make, but the druggist was charging ten times what the drug cost him to produce. He paid $200 for the radium and charged $2,000 for a small dose of the drug. The sick woman's husband, Heinz, went to everyone he knew to borrow the money, but he could only get together about $1,000 which is half of what it cost. He told the druggist that his wife was dying and asked him to sell it cheaper or let him pay later. But the druggist said: "No, I discovered the drug and I'm going to make money from it." So Heinz got desperate and broke into the man's store to steal the drug for his wife. Should Heinz have broken into the laboratory to steal the drug for his wife? Why or why not?'

Lawrence Kohlberg, *Essays on Moral Development, Vol. I: The Philosophy of Moral Development* (San Francisco: Harper & Row, 1981)

He then classified the responses according to the six stages of moral development that he identified:

LEVEL 1: PRE-CONVENTIONAL

▶ Stage 1: Obedience and punishment

This earliest stage of moral development is most common in young children, but adults are not immune from expressing this type of reasoning. This is where rules are seen as fixed and absolute and rules are obeyed simply to avoid punishment. The worse the punishment, the more 'bad' an act is judged to be.

▶ Stage 2: Individualism and exchange

Children in this stage are able to account for individual points of view but take a 'What's in it for me?' approach. In the Heinz dilemma, children at this stage of moral development argued that the best course of action was the choice that best served Heinz's needs. They are not interested in the greater good of society or other complex issues that come at later stages.

LEVEL 2: CONVENTIONAL

▶ Stage 3: Interpersonal relationships

This stage of moral development (together with Stage 4) is typical of adolescents as well as some adults. It is focused on doing things in order to live up to social expectations and roles. Conformity is very important at this stage and moral decisions will reflect this. They will be 'good' because they think that is what society expects and thus it will make them gain more approval.

▶ Stage 4: Maintaining social order

Here, people begin to consider society more generally when making judgements. The focus is on maintaining law and order by following the rules.

LEVEL 3: POST-CONVENTIONAL

▶ Stage 5: Social contract and individual rights

At this stage, people begin to account for the differing values, opinions and beliefs of other people. Decisions will be based on what is best for society as a whole rather than individuals.

▶ Stage 6: Universal principles

Kohlberg's final level of moral reasoning is based upon universal ethical principles and abstract reasoning (e.g. imagining being in someone else's shoes). At this stage, people follow these internalized principles of justice, even if they conflict with laws and rules. Not all adults reach this level.

Stages of play

Play is an important part of how a child develops. Stages of play is a theory and classification of children's participation in play developed by Mildred Parten (1902–after 1932) in 1932. Parten observed American preschool age children (ages two to five) at free play and identified six stages of play:

LEVEL 1: NON-SOCIAL PLAY

1 **Unoccupied** (play): here the child is not actually playing, just observing. She may be standing in one spot or performing random movements. She is not observing anything or anyone in particular. Technically, this is not play, but just some attempt at amusing the self.

2 **Onlooker play:** here the child watches others at play but does not engage in it. The child may engage in forms of social interaction, such as conversation about the play, without actually joining in the activity.

3 **Solitary (independent) play:** at this stage the child is alone and maintains focus on his activity. Such a child is uninterested in or unaware of what others are doing.

4 **Parallel play:** at this stage the child plays separately from others but close to them and mimicking their actions The toys might be the same as those the other children have but they are not playing with them together. There might be limited communication or none at all. This type of play is seen as a transitory stage from a socially immature solitary and onlooker type of play to a more socially mature associative and cooperative type of play.

LEVEL 2: SOCIAL PLAY

5 **Associative play:** the child here is interested in the people playing but not in coordinating his activities with those people. There is a substantial amount of interaction involved, but the activities are not in sync. He may talk and share toys but is still essentially playing alone.

6 **Cooperative play:** at this stage the child is interested both in the people playing and in the activity they are engaged in. In cooperative play, the activity is organized and participants have assigned roles (e.g. in role play where they might act out adult situations or in a game where each person has a role).

According to Parten, as children became older, improving their communication skills, and as opportunities for peer interaction become more frequent, the non-social (solitary and parallel) types of play become less common and the social (associative and cooperative) types of play more common.

Dig deeper

Harlow's monkey experiments:
http://www.youtube.com/watch?v=OrNBEhzjg8I

Strange Situation:
http://www.simplypsychology.org/mary-ainsworth.html

Piaget's stages of development:
https://www.youtube.com/watch?v=TRF27F2bn-A

Fact-check

1 Attachment Theory was originally developed by:
   a Jean Piaget
   b John Bowlby
   c Mary Ainsworth
   d Lawrence Kohlberg

2 Which of the following is *not* a characteristic of Bowlby's Attachment Theory?
   a Proximity maintenance
   b Safe haven
   c Separation distress
   d Resistant insecure attachment

3 Which of the following is *not* one of Ainsworth's Strange Situations classifications?
   a Secure attachment
   b Avoidant insecure attachment
   c Proximity maintenance
   d Disorganized/disoriented attachment

4 Assimilation is where:
   a Children adapt new information into pre-existing cognitive schemas
   b Children alter pre-existing schemas in order to fit in the new information
   c Infants and toddlers acquire knowledge through sensory experiences and manipulating objects
   d Children learn through pretend and symbolic play

5 Which of the following is *not* one of Piaget's Stages of Cognitive Development?
   a Pre-operational
   b Concrete
   c Operational
   d Object permanence

6 Piaget used the term 'egocentric' to describe:

   a When a child does not have the maturity to see other people's viewpoints

   b People who are selfish and think only of their own needs

   c Narcissistic personality types

   d The stage when children do not understand that an object is still there even if it is covered up

7 What is meant by Vygotsky's Zone of Proximal Development?

   a It is the gap between what a child can do alone and what they need assistance with to accomplish

   b It is the ideal distance that an adult should have when working alongside a child

   c It is a description of the stages of a child's moral development

   d It describes the relationship between a child and its siblings

8 Heteronomous morality is:

   a The age at which children develop morals

   b Morality that people develop when they become adults

   c A description of the way morality develops

   d The way children view rules

9 Which of the following is *not* one of Kohlberg's Stages of Moral Development?

   a Obedience and punishment

   b Heteronomous morality

   c Interpersonal relationships

   d Maintaining social order

10 Which of the following expresses Parten's Stages of Play in the correct order?

   a Solitary, associative, cooperative, parallel

   b Solitary, parallel, cooperative, associative

   c Solitary, cooperative, parallel, associative

   d Solitary, parallel, associative, cooperative

11

Gender and sexuality

Arguably, the first thing we notice when we first encounter someone is their gender. Knowing whether they are male or female influences how we interact with them and the expectations we have of them. Gender is one of the key pieces of information gathered in application forms and there is not a culture in the world that does not distinguish people in some way based on their gender. Our gender also plays an important part in our own self-identity and we generally expect others to correctly identify our own gender (and we may be deeply offended if they get it wrong). Much of this distinction is tied in with the expectation that the two genders are different in varying ways. But how different are they really? And what accounts for these differences? This chapter will explore these issues.

Sexual identity

It would seem that gender and sexual identity might be one and the same; after all, if you are male, surely you can assume you will have a male sexual identity? However, researchers nowadays distinguish between biological gender (made up of genetic and reproductive anatomy) and gender identity – which do not always coincide. Even biological gender is not as simple to determine as you might expect. There are in fact four factors that can determine one's gender, and while in most cases these correspond (i.e. all four will point to male or female characteristics), in some cases they do not.

The four biological gender-determining categories are:

► **Chromosomes:** normal females will have XX chromosomes (one inherited from each parent) while a normal male will be XY (X from the mother and Y from the father).

► **Reproductive organs:** for example, ovaries in females and testes in males.

► **Hormones:** testosterone is secreted by the testes in men and oestrogen and progesterone are secreted by the ovaries in women. In fact, we all secrete all three hormones, but men usually have far more testosterone and women far more of the 'female' hormones. Testosterone, when released in the womb, causes the development of male sex organs (at seven weeks) and acts upon the hypothalamus, which results in the masculinization of the brain. For example, the language centre in the male brain is usually in the dominant (usually left) hemisphere, whereas females use both hemispheres of the brain to process language. This may explain why females seem to have stronger communication skills and relish interpersonal communication more than males and why, on average, girls learn to speak and read earlier than boys.

► **Genitalia:** the external organs (penis, vagina, etc.).

Spotlight: Hormones and gender roles

Researchers have shown how important hormones are in the developing gender roles of animals; for example, Quadagno et al. (1977) found that female monkeys who were deliberately exposed to testosterone during prenatal development later engaged in more rough-and-tumble play than other females.

Young (1966) changed the sexual behaviour of both male and female rats by manipulating the amount of male and female hormones that the rats received during their early development.

Sometimes some of these biological factors are atypical, which can result in disparities between sex and gender identity. Studying people who have such abnormalities, for example those found in Turner's syndrome and Klinefelter's syndrome, and comparing their development with those of typical people, helps us understand which elements of gender are determined by which biological factors (and, indeed, the role of other factors such as nurture and upbringing).

▶ **Turner syndrome:** this condition, affecting 1 in every 2,000 baby girls, occurs when females develop with only one X chromosome instead of two. Turner syndrome is named after Dr Henry Turner who first described it in 1938 and refers to the absence (or partial absence) of the second X chromosome, which results in a child with a female external appearance but whose ovaries have failed to develop. This means that the hormones normally secreted by the ovaries fail to appear at puberty so the child does not develop mature female characteristics. They also have differences in behaviour and abilities compared to most XX females.

▶ **Klinefelter's syndrome:** This is a condition affecting between 1 in 500–1,000 males, who are born with an extra X chromosome, making them XXY instead of XY. Dr Harry F. Klinefelter first described this syndrome in the USA in 1942. Physically affected boys appear male, although the effect of the additional X chromosome causes a relative lack of body hair and underdeveloped genitals. Because they have small testes, they do not produce enough of the male hormone testosterone before birth and during puberty. This lack of testosterone means that during puberty the normal male sexual characteristics do not develop fully. There is reduced facial and pubic hair, and some breast tissue often develops. The lack of testosterone is also responsible for other symptoms, including infertility. However, the main difference between them and XY males is in their behaviour: as well as poor language skills, they are generally shy and passive, suggesting that male aggression may have biological (rather than environmental) roots.

The biological or evolutionary approach to gender concurs with what studies of chromosomally atypical men and women show: that males and females develop different characteristics as a result of biological programming. These different characteristics are designed to help the genders carry out their separate roles of survival, reproduction, rearing and caring for their young, and so on. This biological approach to gender assumes that these gender roles are instinctive and thus cannot easily be overcome by nurture and the environment.

However, other approaches (such as the biosocial approach) suggest that humans are not simply controlled by their biology and that other factors are important, too. For example, the biosocial approach to gender (Money and Ehrhardt 1972) argues that gender development is an interaction between nature and nurture; social labelling and differential treatment of boys and girls interact with biological factors to influence gender development.

Gender socialization: do we treat boys and girls differently?

The biosocial model suggests that many of the differences between how men and women behave are due to environmental factors – that is, the different ways in which males and females are treated from birth by their families, their school and their environment. Of course, much of this is culture-specific, with different gender roles assigned more or less strongly in different cultures. Parents may well follow the unwritten guidelines set by their own culture that govern how they speak to, interact with, play, dress and educate their child. For example, in many Western cultures, it is traditional to differentiate even newborn babies by the pink/blue code: pink if they are a girl and blue if they are a boy. Why is it considered so important in these cultures to indicate a baby's gender to others? And does this early gendering affect how others interact with them?

Spotlight: Pink wasn't always a feminine colour

As recently as the early 1900s, pink was seen by many as a boy colour and blue as a girl colour. In 1914 one paper advised readers to 'use pink for the boy and blue for the girl, if you are a follower of convention'. Another paper, the *Ladies Home Journal*, in 1918 reported that 'the generally accepted rule is pink for the boy and blue for the girl'. This was because pink was seen as a bold colour, close to red, whereas blue was seen as more delicate and appropriate for girls. Men happily wore pink: in the 1925 novel *The Great Gatsby*, a male character shows up to lunch with his mistress and her husband in a pink suit – a colour that was not considered feminine but 'working class'. However, by the 1950s pink became more associated with girls in the United States and the UK – although it is not entirely clear why it went that way.

There is plenty of evidence to suggest that people do treat babies differently when they are aware of their gender. Baby girls are treated as if they are more delicate than baby boys, and baby boys attract more attention for gross motor skills (e.g. waving their arms or kicking their legs). Baby boys are more likely to be encouraged in rougher play, bounced in the air and tickled, while girls are more likely to be stroked and spoken to softly. Parents talk to girl babies more, they spend longer comforting female children and they let boys play farther away from them than girls.

Gender-related stereotypes also affect how we view a baby's behaviour. A classic study by Condry and Condry (1976) involved showing college students a video recording of a baby reacting strongly to a jack-in-the-box. If told the baby was a boy, the students were more likely to label the baby's reaction anger; if told the baby was a girl, they were more likely to label it fear. And our gender stereotypes also affect the views we have of babies' abilities; in one recent study, mothers of 11-month-old infants with identical crawling and risk-taking ability were shown an adjustable sloping walkway and asked to estimate what steepness of slope their baby could manage and would attempt. The mothers underestimated girls and overestimated boys, both in crawling ability and crawling attempts.

Gender socialization carries on in this vein, perpetuating the stereotypes of how males and females should behave in society. Children receive gender-segregated toys, clothes and even furniture and tableware, all of which promote the image of girls as nurturing, caring and delicate, and boys as assertive, aggressive and competitive. It is this socialization that biosocial theorists believe is responsible for many of the differences between men and women.

The rise of non-gendered parenting

Gender-neutral parenting is a fairly new phenomenon that has arisen in response to the perceptions that gender roles are determined more by socialization than by biology. Some parents feel that this socialization limits their children by forcing them to conform to gender stereotypes that can even affect their career choices. They attempt to limit these influences for as long as possible by endeavouring to bring up their child as 'gender-neutral'; some go so far as to give the child a gender-neutral name, referring to them as 'it' rather than 'he' or 'she'.

Spotlight: *Hen*

The Swedish unisex personal pronoun, *hen*, is sometimes used to replace *han* (he) or *hon* (she). Sweden has gone to extraordinary lengths to impose gender neutrality in classrooms, regularly filming teachers' interactions with children and analysing them for gender bias.

The gender-neutral movement is certainly growing. Toca Boca makes gender-neutral game apps for children and is second only to Disney for children's downloads in Apple's App Store.

(Interestingly, Apple is one of the few retailers to organize children's apps by age instead of boy and girl categories.) Tootsa MacGinty is a unisex children's clothing label stocked in Selfridges, Fenwick and independent boutiques across the UK, as is the unisex Swedish brand Polarn O Pyret (which is stocked by Mothercare and John Lewis). And the movement against gender-segregated toys is spearheaded by the movement Let Toys Be Toys, which campaigns to remove signs in toyshops advertising 'girls' toys' and 'boys' toys'.

But is such a gender-neutral upbringing likely to have negative effects on a child's developing sexual identity and development? Critics of one couple's decision to raise their child, Storm, as gender-neutral accused them of conducting a social experiment on their child, with some even going so far as calling what they were doing child abuse. The parents outline their story in their book *Chasing Rainbows: Exploring Gender Fluid Parenting Practices*. It is probably too early to know whether such practices are helpful or harmful to the developing sexual identity of a child.

Sexual orientation

Sexual orientation refers to the gender towards which a person directs their attraction or sexual interest. People who prefer their own gender are referred to as homosexual ('gay') and those who prefer the opposite as heterosexual ('straight'). Many researchers believe that the distinction is not clear-cut and that a continuum best describes sexual orientation, with some people definitely gay, others straight, but some in the middle who are bisexual. Researchers estimate that between 2 to 10 per cent of adults in the United States identify themselves as gay, lesbian or bisexual.

What determines sexual orientation is not clear. There are two main approaches: one is that a homosexual orientation is essentially dictated by genetic and/or biological factors – put simply, that people are 'born gay'. The other theory is that homosexual attractions develop primarily as a result of psychological and environmental influences and early experiences. The former theory has gained in popularity over the years.

Most research into the causes of sexual orientation has focused on male homosexuality. A recent study of gay men in the United States found evidence that male sexual orientation is influenced by genes. Scientists tested the DNA of 400 gay men and found that genes on at least two chromosomes affected whether a man was gay or straight. The study confirms the findings of a smaller study that sparked widespread controversy in 1993, when Dean Hamer, a scientist at the US National Cancer Institute, investigated the family histories of more than 100 gay men and found that homosexuality tended to be inherited. More than 10 per cent of brothers of gay men were gay themselves, compared to around 3 per cent of the general population. Uncles and male cousins on the mother's side had a greater than average chance of being gay, too.

However, while genes are likely to contribute to sexual orientation, this is unlikely to be the only factor, since homosexual people tend to have fewer children than heterosexuals – and yet the number of homosexuals in a population does not seem to change. Other multiple factors may well play a greater role, perhaps including the levels of hormones a baby is exposed to in the womb. For example, girls exposed to higher-than-normal prenatal levels of androgens (male hormones) tend to show traits and preferences more typical of males, and males exposed to lower-than-normal-levels of androgens show more female-typical patterns and choices.

Spotlight: Animals can be gay, too

Some biologists claim 'gay' animal behaviour has been spotted in 1,500 different species and reliably recorded in a third of these cases. In some cases there are reproductive reasons: for example, male Goodeid fish mimic females to dupe rivals and male dung flies appear to mate with other males with the aim of exhausting them and thereby reducing the competition for females. Long-term preference for same-sex mates is rarer in the animal kingdom, but 6 per cent of male bighorn sheep are effectively 'gay'. A study of an albatross colony at the University of Hawaii revealed that one-third of the 'couples' who commit to each other for life, consist of two females who, after mating with a male, nest with their female companion.

Other approaches that appear to lend support to biological theories are those that study brain structure. For example, a handful of studies published during the 1990s claimed to offer evidence in favour of a biological cause for homosexuality, one of the most popular being that conducted in 1991 by the former Salk Institute researcher Simon LeVay. LeVay studied the brains of cadavers, including 18 men known to have been homosexual and one known to have been bisexual. He compared them with the brains of another 16 men and six women whom he presumed to have been heterosexual. He found that there was a cluster in the brain termed the INAH 3 that was more than twice as large in the heterosexual men as in the women. It was also, however, more than twice as large in the heterosexual men as in the homosexual men. This, he claimed, indicated that INAH is 'dimorphic with sexual orientation [i.e. it shows a difference in structure between homosexuals and heterosexuals], at least in men, and suggests that sexual orientation has a biological substrate.'

His approach was, however, heavily criticized because of its serious methodological errors; for example, LeVay made questionable assumptions regarding the orientation of the 'heterosexual' cadavers. He assumed that they were all heterosexual, even though a number of the allegedly 'heterosexual' subjects had died of AIDS, a disease that remains far more common among homosexual men than among heterosexuals. All 19 of his homosexual subjects had died of AIDS, and LeVay noted that another 'problem' was 'the possibility that AIDS patients constitute an unrepresentative subset of gay men, characterized, for example, by a tendency to engage in sexual relations with large numbers of different partners or by a strong preference for the receptive role in anal intercourse.'

Many researchers today ascribe to the view that sexual orientation is the result of both biological and environmental factors. One interesting theory, referred to as 'exotic becomes erotic theory', developed by Bern (1996), tries to integrate the findings on biological and environmental influences. The theory suggests that children who grow up feeling different from their own gender for whatever reason (e.g. they are more aggressive or more passive) tend to view the other members of their gender as different (exotic) and thus undesirable; these perceptions will cause arousal that they interpret as dislike, discomfort or sometimes even anger or fear. Once the child reaches puberty, this arousal is cognitively reinterpreted as attraction.

Transgender and transsexual

Transgender is the state of one's gender identity or gender expression not matching one's assigned sex. Transgender is independent of sexual orientation: transgender people may identify as heterosexual, homosexual, bisexual and so on. The term 'transgender' was first mooted in 1965 in *Sexual Hygiene and Pathology* by the psychiatrist John F. Oliven of Columbia University. By 1984 the concept of a 'transgender community' had developed, in which transgender was used as an umbrella term. A 2010 study of 121 transgender people found that 38 per cent of them had realized that they had gender variance by age five.

Transsexual is often used interchangeably with transgender, but transgender is the umbrella term for people who feel they do not identify with their biological gender but who may not feel the need to have gender realignment surgery to change genders. Transsexual refers to a person who does not identify with the sex they were assigned at birth and wishes to realign their gender and their sex through medical intervention.
The American 'bible' of psychiatric conditions, *Diagnostic and Statistical Manual of Mental Disorders DSM-V*, labels transsexual people as 'gender dysphoric', to describe the emotional distress that can result from 'a marked incongruence between one's experienced/expressed gender and assigned gender' – a label contested by many 'trans' people, who say the problem is physical, not mental (in 1973 homosexuality was similarly declassified as a mental disorder in the USA).

Case study: Jazz Jennings

Jazz Jennings, a Florida teen, was born a boy and 'longed to be a girl' from age three when she was diagnosed with gender identity disorder. In 2014 Jazz was named one of *TIME* magazine's 25 most influential teenagers – alongside Taliban victim and Nobel Peace Prize-winner Malala Yousafzai. She started to live as a female at the age of five and plans to undergo gender realignment surgery when she is 18. Jennings's story has been covered by national television shows *20/20* and *The Rosie Show*. In 2014 Jennings published a children's book titled *I Am Jazz*, with writer Jessica Herthel, about herself and her life as a transgender child.

Many theories abound to try to explain what makes a person transgender or transsexual. Research in 2011 found that differences in the brain's white matter that clash with a person's genetic sex may hold the key to identifying transsexual people before puberty. A team at the National University of Distance Education in Madrid, Spain, ran MRI scans on the brains of 18 female-to-male transsexual people who had not had treatment and compared them with those of 24 males and 19 females. They found significant differences between male and female brains in four regions of white matter – and the female-to-male transsexual people had white matter in these regions that resembled a male brain.

In a separate study, the team used the same technique to compare white matter in 18 male-to-female transsexual people with that in 19 males and 19 females. Surprisingly, in each transsexual person's brain the structure of the white matter in the four regions was halfway between that of the males and females; in other words, the brains of the male-to-female transsexuals were not completely masculinized but not completely feminized – but the individual still felt female.

Case study: David Reimer

David Peter Reimer (1965–2004) was a Canadian man born in Winnipeg, Manitoba – biologically male and initially named Bruce. At the age of six months, after concern was raised about how he and his twin brother urinated, the boys were diagnosed with phimosis (a condition where the foreskin is too tight to be pulled back over the head of the penis). They were referred for circumcision at the age of seven months but this left Bruce with such a damaged penis that it was beyond repair (following the disaster, his twin did not go through the procedure and his phimosis eventually cleared up on its own).

His parents, naturally worried about their son's future, took him to see John Money at Johns Hopkins Hospital in Baltimore. Money was a psychologist whose work with intersex patients (whose genitals are ambiguous or missing) was gaining him a reputation as a pioneer in the field of sexual development and gender identity. Money's view was that gender identity developed primarily as a result of social learning from early childhood and that it could be changed with the appropriate behavioural interventions; he called this the 'Theory of Gender Neutrality'. Money thus persuaded the baby's parents that sex reassignment surgery would be in Reimer's best interest. And so, at the age of 22 months, baby Bruce underwent surgery to reassign him to be raised as female and he was given the name Brenda.

When, early in his life, it was considered that his gender reassignment surgery had been successful, this was presented as evidence that gender identity is primarily learned – especially as Brenda had a twin brother who was a perfect control in this experiment. However, Reimer failed to identify as female after the age of nine and transitioned to living as a male at age 15. He went public with his story in a book, *As Nature Made Him: The Boy Who Was Raised as a Girl*, in order to tell the world just how wrong the theories that had led to his transition were. His story influenced several medical practices and even current understanding of the biology of gender. The case accelerated the decline of sex reassignment and surgery for ambiguous XY male infants with unclear genitals, various other rare congenital malformations and penile loss in infancy.

Tragically, in 2004 David committed suicide after suffering years of severe depression. His twin brother, Brian, had earlier died of an overdose of anti-depressants.

Dig deeper

Read Lise Eliot's book *Pink Brain, Blue Brain: How Small Differences Grow into Troublesome Gaps and What We Can Do about It* (London: Oneworld Publishing, 2012)

BBC radio programme (transcript) about David Reimer: http://www.bbc.co.uk/sn/tvradio/programmes/horizon/dr_money_prog_summary.shtml

Homosexuality: nature or nurture?: http://allpsych.com/journal/homosexuality/#.VQl27Y7kdL8

Fact-check

1 Which of the following does *not* determine one's gender?
   a Hormones
   b Chromosomes
   c Brain structure
   d Genitalia

2 Which of the following statements about chromosomes of men and women is true?
   a Men are usually XX
   b Women are usually XY
   c Klinefelter's syndrome is when men are XXY
   d Turner's syndrome is when men are YYX

3 'Gender-neutral' parenting involves:
   a Bringing up an intersex child
   b Parenting children whose sexual identity is confused
   c Activities that usually produce homosexual adults
   d Allowing boys to play with 'girls' toys'

4 Which of the following is *not* a sexual orientation?
   a Homosexual
   b Heterosexual
   c Transsexual
   d Bisexual

5 Which of the following statements about the causes of sexual orientation is correct?
   a The causes of homosexuality are likely to be a mix of both biology and environment
   b Homosexuality is a genetic condition
   c If your brother is gay, you are likely to be, too
   d Homosexuality is caused by traumatic childhood experiences

6 The 'exotic becomes erotic theory' of sexual orientation states that:
   a Children become attracted to the same gender due to a poor relationship with their same-gendered parent
   b Children with homosexual parents are likely to be homosexual too
   c Children who grow up feeling different from their peers may be more likely to become homosexual
   d Heterosexual and homosexual people have different brain structures

7 Transgender is:
   a When you don't identify with your aligned gender
   b When you wish to change genders
   c When you are attracted to both genders
   d When you are attracted to the same gender

8 Transsexual is:
   a When you don't identify with your aligned gender
   b When you wish to change genders
   c When you are attracted to both genders
   d When you are attracted to the same gender

9 The David Reimer case shows that:
   a Gender is entirely dependent on genitalia
   b Gender can be changed by altering genitalia
   c Gender is determined by more than genitalia
   d Gender identity is primarily learned

10 The Theory of Gender Neutrality explains that:
   a Gender identity can be changed with the appropriate behavioural interventions
   b Bringing up children in a gender neutral way is best
   c Giving children gender-neutral names limits the influence of gender socialization
   d Homosexual orientation is genetically influenced

12

Social influence

Our emotions, opinions and behaviours are often affected by others; this is termed social influence. Examples of the impact of social influence include conformity, socialization, peer pressure, obedience, leadership, persuasion, and sales and marketing. Most of us behave differently when there are others around us than when we are alone, and this chapter will examine some of the impacts that social influence can have.

The Bystander Effect

One of the best-known phenomena in terms of how people react differently in and out of the presence of other people was first demonstrated in the laboratory by John Darley and Bibb Latané in 1968 after they became interested in the topic following the murder of Kitty Genovese in 1964 (see the case study below).

Case study: The tragic case of Kitty Genovese

Catherine Susan 'Kitty' Genovese (born 1935), of New York City, was stabbed to death by Winston Moseley near her home on 13 March 1964. What was notable about this senseless murder was how many neighbours witnessed the attack – but did nothing to help her. Arriving home at about 3:15 a.m., she parked about 30 metres from her apartment's door, located in an alleyway at the rear of the building. As she walked towards the building, she was approached by Moseley. Frightened, Genovese began to run across the parking lot and towards the front of her building but Moseley ran after her, quickly overtook her, and stabbed her twice in the back. Several neighbours heard her cry but, on a cold night with the windows closed, only a few of them recognized the sound as a cry for help. At one point a neighbour did shout out and Moseley ran away, leaving Kitty seriously injured, but alive. He then returned and stabbed her several more times, killing her.

Later investigation by police and prosecutors revealed that approximately a dozen individuals nearby had heard or observed portions of the attack – although the number 37 was cited in a *New York Times* article published two weeks after the murder, which bore the headline 'Thirty-Seven Who Saw Murder Didn't Call the Police'.

The alleged lack of reaction (this was disputed in later accounts – see 'Dig deeper') by numerous neighbours watching the scene prompted research into diffusion of responsibility and the so-called 'Bystander Effect'. Social psychologists John Darley and Bibb Latané started this line of research, showing that contrary to common expectations, larger numbers of bystanders decrease the likelihood that someone will step forward and help a victim. The reasons include the fact that onlookers see that others are

Darley and Latané tried to replicate the sort of situation Kitty's neighbours found themselves in, with and without other people around. In a typical experiment, the participant was either alone or among a group of other participants, or confederates. An emergency situation was staged and the researchers measured how long it took the participants to intervene (if, indeed, they did intervene). These experiments revealed that, contrary to the common feeling at the time that the more people there were around, the more likely it would be that help would be summoned, the presence of others actually inhibited helping (this is known as **diffusion of responsibility**). For example, Bibb Latané and Judith Rodin (1969) staged an experiment around a woman in distress. Seventy per cent of people who thought they were alone alone called out or went to help the woman after they believed she had fallen and was hurt, but when there were other people in the room only 40 per cent offered to help.

In trying to account for the way other people inhibit helping behaviours, Darley and Latané note that there are five stages that a bystander goes through when faced with an emergency situation:

1 Bystanders first have to notice that something is going on. People are usually more aware of their surroundings when they are on their own, perhaps because they think it is considered rude or odd to be gazing around too much when they are with other people. In one study, Latané and Darley wanted to see how quickly people would react to the presence of smoke. They took participants to a room to complete a questionnaire – either alone or with a confederate – then released smoke through a vent. Seventy-five per cent of participants working alone reported smoke (half within two minutes), while 62 per cent in the group never reported the smoke at all – even when it was difficult to see (at which point the experiment was stopped).

2   Bystanders then need to interpret the situation as an emergency. According to the principle of social influence, bystanders look to other people in an emergency situation to see how they are behaving. If others are not reacting, then they probably won't perceive the situation as an emergency either. This is why, when fire alarms go off, so many people stay where they are rather than evacuate. Often, a situation is ambiguous, so we look at how others are interpreting it to decide whether it is a genuine emergency.

3   The bystander then assesses the degree of responsibility they feel. This depends on three things: 1) whether or not they feel the person is deserving of help; 2) their perceived competence ('Do I have the skills to help?'); and 3) their relationship with the victim (we are less likely to help people we don't know). The term 'diffusion of responsibility' is used to explain how this responsibility is shared among all the people present – and can thus explain why other people can inhibit helping.

4   The bystander will then consider what form of assistance is required. This might be either **direct intervention** (directly assisting) or **detour intervention** (such as reporting elsewhere). Sometimes the bystander will simply not know what to do.

5   At this point, they can implement the action choice – or perhaps social embarrassment or other concerns will prevent them from acting.

Not all these stages are connected with the presence of others but enough of them are for us to understand how the presence of other people can inhibit helping.

Social facilitation

Related to the Bystander Effect is the broader concept of social facilitation. This is the tendency for people to do better on simple tasks that they are already good at when in the presence of other people. Even the imagined presence of others can have this effect. The Indiana University psychologist Norman Triplett (1861–1931) pioneered research on social facilitation in 1898 when he found that cyclists had faster race times when in the presence of other cyclists. Triplett theorized that the faster times came about because the presence of others made individuals more competitive. Further research led Triplett to theorize that the presence of others increases individuals' performances in other situations as well. However, in situations where people are less skilled, the presence of others can decrease performance.

The role of social facilitation is important to consider in social situations because it implies that people's performance does not rely solely on their abilities, but also on their awareness that they are being monitored and evaluated by others; this means that other people can influence how an individual behaves. Researchers since Triplett have tried to account for why and how the presence of others can affect people. For example, in 1965 Robert Zajonc proposed the first **activation theory** to explain social facilitation. Zajonc argued that the presence of others is arousing, and heightened arousal increases the likelihood of doing well at something that is familiar or that we are skilled at. Thus, arousal improves performance in simple (well-learned) tasks, but impairs performance in complex (not well-learned) tasks.

Spotlight: Cockroaches are subject to social facilitation, too

Zajonc discovered that humans are not unique when it comes to social facilitation; he found that cockroaches ran through an easy maze faster when other cockroaches were watching them or were with them, compared to when the cockroaches ran through the maze alone. In contrast, cockroaches ran more slowly through a difficult maze when there were other cockroaches present than when they ran through it alone.

Other possible 'activation' explanations for the social facilitation effect are:

▶ **The alertness hypothesis:** this suggests that people are uncertain of how other people will act, so they become more alert in the presence of others and it is this heightened alertness which causes them to perform better on tasks.

- ▶ **The challenge and threat hypothesis:** this states that people perform worse in complex tasks and better in simple tasks when in the presence of others because of their perceptions of threat. This is shown by physiological responses; when performing a simple task in the presence of others, people show a normal cardiovascular response but, when performing a complex task in the presence of others, the cardiovascular response is similar to that of a person being threatened.

- ▶ **The evaluation apprehension hypothesis:** this suggests that it is not the mere presence of others that increases individual activation/arousal, but rather the fear of being evaluated.

In the 1980s explanations shifted from activation theories to attention theories. Attention theories that attempt to explain social facilitation include:

- ▶ **The distraction-conflict hypothesis:** this states that in the presence of others there is a conflict between attending to the person and attending to the task. This conflict leads to arousal. As with Zajonc's theory, this arousal will help simple tasks but may hinder complex tasks because there is too much conflict and thus too much arousal. This relates to the next theory.

- ▶ **The overload hypothesis:** here it is postulated that distracters do not lead to increased arousal, but rather to cognitive overload (when an individual is bombarded with excessive information in their working memory) and while in cognitive overload individuals will do worse in complex tasks and better in more simple tasks.

The feedback-loop model suggests that when people feel they are being observed, they focus attention on themselves. While in this state, individuals become aware of the differences between their actual behaviour and anticipated behaviour – and thus work harder to match them on tasks where they feel they could do better.

Compliance and weapons of influence

While social facilitation refers to the changes in performance as a mere result of being observed, compliance refers to changes in behaviour as a result of others requesting that change. Compliance is a form of social influence that is different from obedience (see below), which involves a powerful other person: with compliance the other person doesn't have power to make someone else comply. Psychologists have long been interested in what makes someone compliant and what techniques persuasive people might use to increase compliance (and why these techniques work).

> 'Compliance refers to a change in behavior that is requested by another person or group; the individual acted in some way because others asked him or her to do so (but it was possible to refuse or decline).'
> Steven Breckler, James Olson and Elizabeth Wiggins,
> *Social Psychology Alive* (Belmont, CA: Thomson Wadsworth, 2006)

One of the psychologists best known for insights on what influences compliance and persuasion is Robert Cialdini, Regents' Professor Emeritus of Psychology and Marketing at Arizona State University. He published a book in 1984 entitled *Influence: The Psychology of Persuasion* in which he outlined **Six Principles of Influence** (also known as the **Six Weapons of Influence**) that he believed were used by those skilled in the art of persuading, convincing and influencing others.

The six principles are as follows:

1 **Reciprocity:** according to the idea of reciprocity, we feel obliged to return favours that have been bestowed on us. This is because we are uncomfortable with feeling indebted to others. So, if we help someone else, or do something nice for them, or give them a gift, they feel obliged to pay it back. This is why advertisers will give free samples and why charities give free pens and so on – in the hope that we will feel obliged to return the favour by purchasing their goods or making a donation.

2 **Commitment (and consistency):** Cialdini maintains that we have a deep psychological need to be consistent. Thus, once we've committed to something, or we feel as if we have, we are then more inclined to go through with it. So, if you are trying to persuade someone to lend you money, if you can first persuade them that they agree that the venture you wish to spend the money on is worth while, it is then harder for them not to follow through with that by then refusing the loan.

3 **Social proof:** this relates to the ideas expressed earlier that we look to others to see how we should behave. For example, if other people are buying a certain new phone, watching a particular programme, wearing a type of fashion or eating a certain food, we feel that they must be right and we are more likely to follow the crowd. This is particularly the case when we are feeling uncertain, and we are even more likely to be influenced if the people we see seem to be similar to us. That's why adverts often use mums, not celebrities, to advertise food products – and why social media advertising is so effective, since, if we see our friend using a product, we are more likely to want one as well.

4 **Liking:** we are more likely to be influenced by people we like. Again, this is what makes social media advertising so powerful and why, when we buy a product online, we are urged to share this choice with our friends.

5 **Authority:** we are more influenced and persuaded by people in positions of authority. This is why skincare products are often advertised by 'clinicians' or by using scientific terminology.

6 **Scarcity:** things are more attractive when their availability is limited – hence marketing that relies on the 'limited offer' concept.

Spotlight: A bestseller

Influence: The Psychology of Persuasion has sold over 2 million copies and been translated into 26 languages. It has been listed on the *New York Times* business bestseller list. *Fortune Magazine* lists *Influence* on their '75 Smartest Business Books'.

Obedience

Unlike compliance, obedience is an act of social influence whereby someone simply orders others to do something rather than trying to persuade them. One of the most important studies on obedience was conducted by Stanley Milgram (see the case study below) and it shows that there are a number of factors that increase the likelihood of obedience. For example, someone who has visible signs of their power and status (e.g. a white lab coat or a suit) is more successful at instilling obedience than someone without. Obedience can also be more successful when commands start off quite reasonable and gentle and only gradually become more extreme and authoritarian – which might go some way to explaining the horrors of Nazi Germany, where the systematic murder of the Jews began with far less severe measures such as segregation.

Case study: The Milgram Experiment

The now-infamous Milgram Experiment was conducted by the Yale University psychologist Stanley Milgram (1933–84) and was set up to measure how willing people would be to obey an authority figure who instructed them to perform acts that would appear to cause pain to others. The experiments began in July 1961, three months after the start of the trial of German Nazi war criminal Adolf Eichmann in Jerusalem. Milgram devised his psychological study to answer the popular question at that particular time: 'Could it be that Eichmann and his million accomplices in the Holocaust were just following orders?' Milgram wondered whether anyone could be ordered to do unspeakable things if they were told to with enough authority.

The study involved three participants in each scenario: the 'teacher' (the subject in the study), who was given a list of word pairs that he was to teach the 'learner' (who was actually a confederate). The third person involved was the white-coated experimenter (Milgram) who was leading the study and who told the 'teacher' and 'learner' what to do. The 'teacher' was instructed to read the first word of each pair and read four possible answers. The 'learner' would then press a button to indicate his response. If the answer was incorrect, the 'teacher' was told to administer a 'shock' to the 'learner', with the voltage increasing in 15-volt increments for each wrong answer. If the answer was correct, the 'teacher' would read the next word pair.

The subjects believed that for each wrong answer the 'learner' was receiving actual shocks. In reality, there were no shocks. After a number of voltage-level increases, the 'learner' started to bang on the wall that separated him from the subject. After several times banging on the wall and complaining about his heart condition, all responses by the 'learner' would cease.

At this point, many of the 'teachers', the test subjects, indicated their desire to stop the experiment and check on the learner. Some of the test subjects paused at 135 volts and began to question the purpose of the experiment. However, most continued after being assured that they would not be held responsible – and many by simply being told that they must continue.

Before conducting the experiment, Milgram had polled Yale University senior-year psychology majors, psychiatrists from a medical school and his colleagues to predict the behaviour of the 'teachers'. Most believed that only a very small fraction of them would be prepared to inflict the maximum voltage. However, 65 per cent of the subjects of the experiment administered the experiment's final massive 450-volt shock, although many were clearly very uncomfortable doing so.

Spotlight: Preserved for posterity

The original Simulated Shock Generator and Event Recorder, or *shock box*, is located in the Archives of the History of American Psychology at the University of Akron, in Akron, Ohio.

'Stark authority was pitted against the subjects' [participants'] strongest moral imperatives against hurting others, and, with the subjects' [participants'] ears ringing with the screams of the victims, authority won more often than not.'
Stanley Milgram, 'The Perils of Obedience', *Harper's Magazine* (1974)

Although Milgram's experiments were meant to add weight to our understanding of how the Nazis could carry out their murderous and sadistic acts during the Holocaust, many have criticized the idea that the research can shed much light on the Nazi regime, and for various reasons. For example, Professor James Waller, Chair of Holocaust and Genocide Studies at Keene State College, pointed out that:

'While the participants in Milgram's experiments were assured in advance that no permanent physical damage would result from their actions, the Nazis were clearly fully aware of their hands-on killing and torture of their victims and could not have been unaware that the pain they inflicted was real.

'While the Milgram experiments were relatively brief, lasting for just an hour, with no time for the subjects to really consider the implications of their behaviour, the Holocaust lasted for years with ample time for participants in the atrocities to realize what they were doing and the implications of it.'

James Waller, *Becoming Evil: How Ordinary People Commit Genocide and Mass Killing* (Oxford: Oxford University Press, 2002), pp. 111–13

The other classical study on obedience was conducted at Stanford University during the 1970s by Phillip Zimbardo (see the case study below). It showed how easily people can abuse their authority by demanding excessive obedience when given the opportunity.

Case study: The Stanford Prison Experiment

The Stanford Prison Experiment (SPE) was a study to investigate brutality and sadistic behaviours within prison systems by guards and hoped to answer the question of whether it was inherent personality that made people act that way – or whether there was some aspect of the environment that caused them to change. Twenty-four male students were selected to take on randomly assigned roles of prisoners and guards in a mock prison situated in the basement of the Stanford psychology building for a period of 7–14 days. The researchers provided the 'guards' (who had been screened for personalities that might favour brutal actions) with wooden batons to establish their status, clothing similar to that of an actual prison guard (khaki shirt and pants) and mirrored sunglasses to prevent eye contact. 'Prisoners' wore uncomfortable ill-fitting smocks and stocking caps, as well as a chain around one ankle. 'Guards' were instructed to call 'prisoners' by their assigned numbers, sewn on their uniforms, instead of by name.

The participants adapted to their roles well beyond Zimbardo's expectations, as the guards enforced authoritarian measures and ultimately subjected some of the prisoners to psychological torture. Many of the 'prisoners' passively accepted psychological abuse and, at the request of the guards, readily harassed other prisoners who attempted to prevent it. The experiment even affected Zimbardo himself, who, in his role as the superintendent, permitted the abuse to continue. Zimbardo aborted the experiment early when Christina Maslach, a graduate student in psychology (who later became an eminent psychologist in her own right), whom he was dating (and later married), objected to the conditions of the prison.

The study showed that the environment can greatly influence how people act and that they take on stereotypical role expectations independent of their own personalities.

'The most apparent thing that I noticed was how most of the people in this study derive their sense of identity and well-being from their immediate surroundings rather than from within themselves, and that's why they broke down – just couldn't stand the pressure – they had nothing within them to hold up against all of this.'

P. G. Zimbardo, *The Lucifer Effect: Understanding How Good People Turn Evil* (New York: Rider, 2007)

Conformity

Conformity is when we are influenced by others because we want to fit in by behaving in ways that are acceptable to them. All groups and societies have their social norms that govern the range of acceptable behaviours within that group, and, if we wish to conform, we will obey these rules. The strength of the urge to conform was nicely demonstrated by a classic study involving the autokinetic effect; this is a visual phenomenon whereby if you have a single stationary source of light in an otherwise pitch-dark room, that light source will appear to move. In 1936 Muzafer Sherif (1906–88), a Turkish-American social psychologist, used this phenomenon to study how people are influenced by other people's opinions. He put participants in a dark room, first on their own and then with others, and told them to watch a pinpoint of light and report how far it moved (they were not told that this was an illusion so they believed that the light really did move).

On their own, the participants soon established their own individual *norms* for the judgement of how much the light had moved – usually 5 to 15 cm. In groups, however, Sherif noted a tendency to compromise. People who usually made an estimate like 15 cm soon made smaller judgements like 10 cm. Those who saw less movement, such as 5 cm, soon increased their judgements to about 10 cm. People changed their judgement to resemble more the others in the group. They began to conform to the group norms.

This work was later developed by American psychologist Solomon Asch (1907–96) who, in 1956, conducted the now-classic conformity studies that have helped shape our understanding of the factors that contribute towards conformity and minority influence. College students participated in a 'perceptual' task where all but one of the participants were confederates (i.e. actors), and the true focus of the study was about how the remaining student (i.e. the real participant) would react to the confederates' behaviours.

Each participant was placed in a room with seven 'confederates'. Participants were shown a card with a line on it, followed by a card with three lines on it (lines labelled A, B and C, respectively). Participants were then asked to say aloud which line (i.e. A, B or C) matched the line on the first card in length. Prior to the experiment, all confederates were told to unanimously give the incorrect response. The group was arranged so that the participant was always the last to respond. Would the participant change his answer and respond in the same way as the confederates, despite it obviously being the wrong answer?

Overall, in the experimental group, 75 per cent of the participants gave an incorrect answer to at least one question.

In follow-ups to this study, Asch found that the subjects conformed much less if they had an 'ally' – one other person who gave the correct answer. There were several reasons for these findings. First, the real subject was reassured that the others did not ridicule the dissenter for his answer. Secondly, the dissenter's answers gave the participant more confidence in his own answer. This 'ally effect' increased with the number of allies – until two or three, whereby there was no further increase in the number of subjects prepared to give the correct answers.

Other factors affecting conformity were later examined and include group cohesiveness such that the more we are attracted to a group and want to belong to it the more we conform.

Minority influence

Discussion of conformity and ally effects leads nicely on to the role of minority influence, a form of social influence that takes place when a member of a minority group, like an individual, influences a majority to accept the minority's beliefs or behaviour. Whereas majority influence occurs when people conform to certain beliefs and behaviours in order to be accepted by others or to fit in, minority influence does not influence others through this normative social influence (i.e. where we are influenced by social norms) because most people are less concerned with fitting in with a minority.

To influence the majority, then, the minority would be better taking an informational social influence approach whereby they convince others that they are correct (rather than trying to work on their need to fit in). In 1969 the Romanian-born French psychologist Serge Moscovici (1925–2014) used a variation of the Asch paradigm (using coloured slides rather than lines, which Moscovici felt were more ambiguous and thus a better test) and identified a number of factors as being important for a minority to have an influence over a majority. These include:

▶ **Consistency:** the minority must be consistent and unchanging in their opinion if they are to exert the most influence. This is important because it shows that the minority is committed to their viewpoint, even in the face of opposition from many others, and creates doubt in the minds of the majority about their own view.

▶ **Flexibility:** Researchers have questioned whether consistency on its own is enough for a minority to influence a majority. If the consistent minority is viewed by the majority as inflexible, rigid, uncompromising and dogmatic, they will have less influence. However, if they appear flexible and compromising, they are likely to be seen as less extreme, as more moderate, cooperative and reasonable. As a result, they will have a better chance of changing majority views.

▶ **Identification:** People tend to identify with people they see as similar to themselves. Research indicates that, if the majority identifies with the minority, they are more likely to take the views of the minority seriously and change their own views in line with those of the minority.

Dig deeper

Debunking the myth of Kitty Genovese:
http://nypost.com/2014/02/16/book-reveals-real-story-behind-the-kitty-genovese-murder/

Stanford Prison Experiment website:
http://www.prisonexp.org/

Asch conformity experiments:
https://www.youtube.com/watch?v=NyDDyT1lDhA

Fact-check

1 Which of the following is *not* a form of social influence?
   a Conformity
   b Generalized anxiety
   c Socialization
   d Obedience

2 In the Bystander Effect, which of the following influences their decision to act or not?
   a How anxious they feel about what they have seen
   b Whether they know the person needing help
   c Whether other people persuade them to help
   d Whether they have helped in the past

3 What is social facilitation?
   a The tendency for people to do better on simple tasks that they are already good at when in the presence of other people
   b The tendency for people to do better on complex tasks when in the presence of other people
   c The tendency for people to do better on simple and complex tasks when in the presence of other people
   d The tendency for people to do worse on simple tasks that they are already good at when in the presence of other people

4 Possible explanations for the social facilitation effect do *not* include:
   a The alertness hypothesis
   b The challenge and threat hypothesis
   c The evaluation apprehension hypothesis
   d The reciprocity hypothesis

5 Which one of the following is *not* one of Cialdini's Six Weapons of Influence?
   a Cohesion
   b Social proof
   c Liking
   d Scarcity

6 Obedience is likely to be increased when the person instilling authority:
   a Is wearing a lab coat
   b Talks in a higher pitch
   c Speaks faster than usual
   d Wears a hat

7 The autokinetic effect is:
   a When a light source in a dark room moves
   b When people agree that matching lines don't match
   c When a light source in a dark room appears to move
   d When people over-estimate the amount of movement of a light in the presence of others

8 Both Sherif and Asch's studies show that:
   a Optical illusions are common
   b People can't trust their own judgements
   c We conform to the view of others around us
   d We obey authority when faced with uncertainty

9 Subjects conform much less if they have an ally because:
   a They want to obey the ally
   b The ally gives them confidence in their own judgement
   c The ally is an authoritarian figure
   d The ally allows social facilitation to occur

10 Which of the following does not have an impact on the influence a minority can have on the majority?
   a Consistency
   b Flexibility
   c Identification
   d Social proof

13

Social and group processes

Humans are inherently social creatures who rely on interpersonal relationships to sustain many elements of their existence. We prefer to live in groups, not alone, and our behaviour towards others affects how well those groups function and how well we fit in. Social processes are the ways in which individuals and groups interact and establish relationships with one other. These patterns of behaviour are modified and adapted through social interactions. This chapter examines a range of social interactions and processes that influence and create our social existence.

Stereotypes, prejudice and discrimination

We encounter many people in our day-to-day lives and, like many stimuli, the range and sheer numbers can sometimes lead to cognitive overload. We cope with this overload by making cognitive short cuts that help us simplify and classify the stimuli we encounter. One such short cut is the use of stereotypes; employing this technique probably gave us a selective advantage in our evolutionary past as it would have allowed us to establish very quickly who was friend (a member of our own in-group) and who was foe (a member of the out-group). Stereotypes can thus help us make sense of the world. They are a form of categorization that helps to simplify and systematize information. Thus, information is more easily identified, recalled, predicted and reacted to.

Spotlight: A 'small brain'

As recently as 1964, the *Encyclopædia Britannica* entry for 'Races of Mankind' described 'woolly-haired groups' as having: 'dark skin sometimes almost black, broad noses, usually a rather small brain in relation to their size'.

Stereotypes, then, are beliefs about people based on their membership of a particular group and they can be positive or negative. They allow us to quickly process new information about an event or a person without having to think too deeply. They help us to assess differences between individuals and groups at speed and to make apparently useful predictions about other people's behaviour. The problem with stereotypes, of course, is that they are often wrong because they are based on broad characteristics – and may sometimes even be simply the result of *prejudice*. **Prejudice** is a negative belief or feeling about a particular group of individuals and is a phenomenon that has benefit for the individual holding it; for example, it provides scapegoats in times of trouble, can boost self-esteem (by putting others down), it allows them to strengthen their own group bonds by being negative about other groups, and it legitimizes discrimination because it apparently justifies one group's dominance over another.

> *'The killing of Americans and their civilian and military allies is a religious duty for each and every Muslim... We – with God's help – call on every Muslim who believes in God and wishes to be rewarded to comply with God's order to kill Americans and plunder their money whenever and wherever they find it.'*
> Osama Bin Laden, in a videotaped statement in the autumn of 2001

Stereotypes can thus lead to distortions of reality since they can cause people to exaggerate or even create differences among groups, and they also lead to a tendency to see groups of people as being overly homogenous instead of made up of individuals.

Unfortunately, stereotypes are often quite stable attributions that can be resistant to change. This is because of **confirmatory bias**: when we encounter someone who conforms to our stereotype, we use that as confirmation of our beliefs – and when we encounter members of the group who do not conform to our stereotypes, we simply discount those as 'atypical'. We also selectively recall instances that confirm our stereotypes and forget about disconfirming instances.

Spotlight: Stereotype

The term 'stereotype' derives from the Greek words *stereos* ('firm, solid') and *typos* ('impression', hence 'solid impression').

The term was first adopted in 1798 to describe a printing plate that duplicated any typography. The duplicate printing plate, or the stereotype, is used for printing instead of the original.

Outside printing, the first reference to 'stereotype' was in 1850, as a noun that meant 'image perpetuated without change'. However, it was not until 1922 that 'stereotype' was first used in the modern psychological sense by the American journalist Walter Lippmann in his work *Public Opinion*.

Holding stereotypes, which may result from prejudice, can lead to discrimination. Stereotypes are regarded as the cognitive component and often occurs without conscious awareness, whereas prejudice is the affective component of stereotyping;

people are prejudiced when they react in an emotional way to seeing or hearing a group that they hold stereotypes about. **Discrimination** is the behavioural component of prejudicial reactions and is where we treat people differently simply because they are a member of a particular group. Prejudice, stereotyping and discrimination do often coexist, but it is also possible to have one without the others. For example, an ethnic group might be stereotyped with a neutral or positive attribute such as 'family-oriented' and thus might not invoke prejudice and discrimination. Similarly, a generalized prejudice against 'foreigners' may not include specific stereotypes or acts of discrimination.

Spotlight: The origins of research into prejudice

According to John Duckitt (1992), psychological research on prejudice first emerged in the 1920s and was based upon American and European race theories that attempted to prove white superiority.

Case study: Blue eyes / brown eyes

On 4 April 1968 the American teacher Jane Elliott (born 1933) learned of Martin Luther King Jr's assassination. This led to a discussion the following day with her class about racism. However, she felt that she was not really getting through to the eight-year-old students, who were, like her, born and raised in the small town of Riceville, Iowa and were not normally exposed to black people. She felt that simply talking about racism would not allow her all-white class to fully comprehend racism's meaning and effects.

She then devised an exercise, based on eye colour rather than skin colour, to allow the children to feel what it would be like to be treated the way a person of colour is treated in America. She designated the blue-eyed children in the class as the superior group and gave them extra privileges, such as extra helpings at lunch, access to the new playground equipment, and extra playtime at break. The blue-eyed children sat in the front of the classroom, whereas the brown-eyed children were sent to sit at the back. The blue-eyed children were encouraged to play only with other blue-eyed children and to ignore those with brown eyes. Elliott also forbade the brown-eyed and blue-eyed children from drinking from the same water fountain.

At first, the children in the minority group were resistant to the idea that blue-eyed children were better than brown-eyed children. So, Elliott lied to the children by explaining that melanin is responsible for making children blue-eyed and that this was also linked to their higher intelligence and learning ability.

The effect of her intervention was stark. Those who were deemed 'superior' became arrogant, bossy and rather nasty to their 'inferior' classmates. Their grades were better, and they even completed mathematical and reading tasks that had seemed outside their ability before. The 'inferior' classmates also changed – they became more and subservient and did less well in tests.

As news of the exercise spread, Jane began to appear on television shows and started to repeat the exercise in professional training days for adults. In 1971 the American Broadcasting Company (ABC) aired a documentary about her called *The Eye of the Storm* and made her even more nationally known. Subsequently, William Peters wrote two books – *A Class Divided* and *A Class Divided: Then and Now* –about her and the exercise.

A Class Divided was turned into a PBS Frontline documentary in 1985 and included a reunion of the schoolchildren featured in *The Eye of the Storm*, for which Elliott received The Hillman Prize. A televised edition of the exercise was shown in the United Kingdom on 29 October 2009 on Channel 4 and entitled *The Event: How Racist Are You?*

Attributional bias

One possible cause of prejudice and stereotyping could be attributional bias, a process that forms many of our perceptions about other people as well as events. People make attributions in order to understand their own experiences and these attributions strongly influence the way we interact with others. We are constantly making attributions, or guesses, regarding the cause of our own and others' behaviours but these attributions do not always accurately reflect reality. For example, if we perform poorly in a test, we might blame ourselves for not having studied the material well enough, or our teacher for not having taught it well enough. When our friend does well in the same test, we might attribute their superior performance to luck – completely ignoring the fact that they may have worked hard or be very bright.

Attributional bias, then, is a cognitive bias that refers to the systematic errors made when people evaluate or try to find reasons for their own and others' behaviours; humans are prone to perceptual errors that lead to biased interpretations of their social world.

Research on attribution biases is founded **in Attribution Theory,** which was proposed to explain why and how we create meaning about others' and our own behaviour. Attribution Theory focuses on identifying how someone uses information from their social environment in order to create a causal explanation for what has occurred and why. Attribution Theory also provides explanations for why different people can interpret the same event in different ways and what factors contribute to attribution biases.

Attribution Theory proposes that the attributions people make about events and behaviour can be classed as either internal or external. In **internal attribution,** people infer that a person's behaviour is due to personal factors such as traits, abilities or feelings. In an **external,** or **situational, attribution,** people infer that a person's behaviour is due to situational factors.

Attributional biases then are the systematic biases people can hold which can lead them to make incorrect guesses about why someone may have acted the way they did. These biases include the fundamental attribution error and the self-serving bias:

▶ The **fundamental attribution error** is the tendency to attribute *other people's* behaviour to internal factors such as personality traits, abilities and feelings – while ignoring possible external causes. This can lead to blaming of the victim so that, should something bad happen, we look for reasons they may have been responsible – and thus why such a calamity would not happen to us, which can be a self-protecting mechanism. Thus, for example, when we learn that someone has been the victim of a crime, we seek to reassure ourselves that we won't become a victim by blaming them for what they were wearing, the route they took or how ostentatious they were with their possessions.

▶ The **self-serving bias** is the tendency to attribute successes to internal factors and failures to situational factors. This allows us to protect our self-esteem. For example, if I do well in a test, it is due to my working hard, but if I do badly, it is because the teacher didn't teach me well enough. Depressed people may have the reverse bias: they attribute positive events to chance or external help, and negative events to their own character.

Attitudes and attitude change

Our attributional biases contribute to how we understand the social world and our place in it and may lead to prejudice, which is clearly a biased way of thinking. Psychologists have long been interested in how such views of others or of the world, or attitudes, can be changed.

'[An attitude is] a relatively enduring organization of beliefs, feelings, and behavioral tendencies towards socially significant objects, groups, events or symbols.'
Michael Hogg and Graham Vaughan, *Social Psychology* (Eaglewood Cliffs: Prentice-Hall, 2005), p. 150

Attitudes are thought to be made up of three components:

▶ **Affective component:** this involves a person's feelings/emotions about the attitude object (e.g. 'I dislike foreigners'). The affective components are assessed by monitoring physiological signs such as heart rate.

▶ **Behavioural component:** the way the attitude we have influences how we act or behave (e.g. 'I will not employ a foreigner'). Behaviour may be assessed by direct observation.

- **Cognitive component:** this involves a person's belief/ knowledge about an attitude object (e.g. 'Foreigners are not trustworthy'). The cognitive aspects of attitude are generally measured by surveys, interviews and other reporting methods.

These three elements do not always concur – it is possible to feel one way about something but act in another. Expressed attitudes do not always reflect behaviour, perhaps because of competing attitudes or because of a need to suppress true views. After all, plenty of people support a particular candidate or political party and yet fail vote for them.

Sometimes, when behaviour does not match attitudes, people may actually change their attitudes to fit with their behaviour. In 1957 the American psychologist Leon Festinger (1919–89) identified the phenomenon of **cognitive dissonance,** in which a person experiences psychological discomfort due to holding beliefs or attitudes that conflict with behaviour; in order to reduce this tension, they may change their attitudes. For example, a heavy smoker holds two conflicting cognitions – that smoking is unhealthy yet they smoke. To reconcile these two conflicting views, they might convince themselves that smoking is not so bad, or that they smoke less harmful brands.

Attitudes can serve various functions for the individual. Daniel Katz (1960) outlined four main functions:

- **Knowledge:** we all have a need for a world that is consistent and relatively stable so that we can predict, to some extent, what is likely to happen; this gives us some semblance of control. Thus, having an attitude about someone or a group of people gives us knowledge about them that might help us predict how they will behave in a given situation.

- **Ego-defensive:** the attitudes we express help communicate who we are and may enhance our own self-esteem. This is because our attitudes are shaped by our feelings, beliefs and values.

- **Adaptive/adjustment:** attitudes can help us fit in and adapt to our social world. We seek out those who share our attitudes and may develop attitudes that are similar to those held by people we like and admire. When we express attitudes that others share, they are likely to reward us with approval and acceptance. We are thus pushed towards holding attitudes that reward us and avoiding those that punish us.

▶ **Utilitarian:** people adopt attitudes that are rewarding and that help them avoid punishment. In other words, any attitude that is adopted in a person's own self-interest is considered to serve a utilitarian function; for example, you may have a particular attitude towards higher taxes because you know your family would be affected.

Attitudes are formed in different ways. Children acquire many of their attitudes by modelling their parents' attitudes or via classical or operant conditioning (see Chapter 5). Attitudes are also formed through direct experience and are influenced by social norms. Attitudes are not always stable and can be changed; psychologists are particularly interested in how to change attitudes, especially when such attitudes might be harmful or based on prejudice.

Researchers have identified a number of dimensions of an attitude that can effect how stable and resistant to change attitudes are. For example, strong attitudes that are firmly held and that highly influence behaviour are harder to change. Attitudes that are important to a person or in which we have a vested interest tend to be strong. We tend to have stronger, and thus more stable attitudes about things, events, ideas or people we have considerable knowledge and information about. In addition, attitudes that are highly accessible – that is, come to mind more easily – tend to be stronger and more resistant to change.

Attitudes can, of course, be changed, even when they are stable. The **Elaboration Likelihood Theory of Attitude Change** developed by Richard E. Petty and John Cacioppo in the mid-1970s describes how attitudes form and change. The model explains different ways of processing stimuli, why they are used, and their outcomes on attitude change. The ELM proposes two major routes to persuasion that can lead to changes in attitude or beliefs: the central route and the peripheral route.

When the **central route** is utilized, persuasion is most likely to occur through careful and thoughtful weighing up of the merits of the information in the persuasive message. Any resulting attitude change will be relatively long lasting, resistant to further attempts to change, and predictive of behaviour in relation to that attitude. The central route is used when the message recipient is motivated to change or to listen to the message and they are able to think about the message and its topic.

Under the **peripheral route,** however, persuasion results from a person's association with positive or negative cues in the stimulus or how it makes them feel, rather than deep processing. Thus, factors such as the credibility or attractiveness of the sources of the message, or the quality of the message, can have greater influence than the actual quality of the arguments (as in the central route). The peripheral route is used when the receiver of the message has little or no interest in the subject and/or has less ability to process the message. Advertisers use the ELM to influence people into buying their products either with persuasive arguments or with peripheral factors (such as celebrity endorsements).

Group polarization

Attitudes are an important influence on many processes, one of which is decision-making. And, if attitudes are shaped by other people, then the decision-making process is also greatly influenced by the presence or otherwise of others. Researchers have long been fascinated by the impact that being with other people can have on the quality of decision-making. Until the 1960s it was generally thought that a group opinion corresponded roughly to the average of the opinions of its constituent members. This view was influenced by the research on conformity that suggested that group members were likely to converge on some normative position when asked to make a collective judgement.

However, in 1961 the psychologist James Stoner changed all that. He asked individuals to make some judgements about a number of hypothetical social dilemmas. Each dilemma involved someone having to make the choice between two courses of action, one of which (with the more desirable outcome) involved a higher degree of risk than the other. The individuals were then put into groups and asked to reach a unanimous decision on each of the dilemmas they had considered individually. The group decisions were nearly always riskier on average than the average of the individual group-member pre-discussion decisions (Stoner 1968).

In many studies that followed, it became clear that the so-called 'shift to risk' was actually a 'shift to extremity'. Groups can actually also make more cautious or conservative choices than individuals. Therefore it became better known as a polarization phenomenon. Where pre-discussion decisions are to the left of the notional midpoint of the scale, groups shifted further to the left; where the individuals were initially cautious, the groups shifted even further in that direction.

There are three main explanations for group polarization:

FESTINGER'S SOCIAL COMPARISON THEORY (1954)

Associated with any issue on which a group must make a decision are likely to be a number of social values (e.g. caring for others, being adventurous, not taking risks with one's health). Taken together, these values will result in an initial social preference towards one decision outcome rather then another. Each person, prior to group discussion, will probably perceive him/herself as being somewhat further towards this socially desirable outcome than their peers. Once the group discussion gets under way – thereby heightening the importance of the relevant social values – some of these individuals realize that there are others who endorse positions further towards the socially valued pole than they do. The outcome of this social comparison is that they will then shift further in that direction in order to present themselves in an even more socially desirable light. The net result is that the collective decision is more extreme than the average of the individual positions.

PERSUASIVE ARGUMENTS THEORY (BURNSTEIN AND VINOKUR 1977)

The idea here is that the main causal factor underlying group polarization is the exchange of information and arguments that precedes the collective decision. The basic premise is that in any discussion there are unlikely to be exactly the same number of arguments for and against a decision. There is likely to be a bias in one direction. Each individual may not, at first, have access to all these arguments and nor will all the individuals be aware of the same arguments. Once the discussion gets under way, all this different information comes out into the open; each person becomes more acquainted with more of the arguments supporting the dominant view (and perhaps one or two extra arguments against). The group members then act as rational 'information processors' and respond to the additional arguments and evidence by shifting their opinion even further in that direction.

SOCIAL IDENTIFICATION THEORY (WETHERELL 1987)

According to this view, what is happening when a group polarizes is that the group members are attempting to conform more closely to the normative position that they see as prototypical for their in-group. When a situation occurs to make their in-group identity more important, then the relevant in-group norms become more extreme so as to clearly differentiate them from those of the out-group – hence polarization is enhanced.

Groupthink

The discussion so far has been concerned with the outcomes of group decisions in terms of their level of risk. This section now discusses the quality of the group decision-making process that leads to the outcomes. It might be intuitively thought that groups would make better decisions than individuals because individuals are subject to attitude biases, prejudice and other processes that being with others might be expected to cancel out. However, research shows that groups are subject to other problems that can actually mean that group decision-making results in poorer-quality decisions than those made by individuals.

Spotlight: Group formation

A model of group development, first proposed by Bruce Tuckman in 1965, maintained that all groups go through four stages when they develop: **Forming** (the initiation stage when individuals are learning about each other and the tasks), **Storming** (when conflict is at its most intense), **Norming** (when group norms start to emerge) and **Performing** (when the group is at its most functional).

Groupthink is a term coined by the social psychologist Irving Janis in 1972, to describe faulty decisions caused by group pressures. Janis analysed a number of American foreign-policy decisions made between 1940 and 1970 (the attempted invasion of Cuba at the Bay of Pigs in 1961, the bombing of North Vietnam in 1965 and the lack of defence of Pearl Harbor in 1941) and came to the conclusion that when these turned out badly (i.e. where US interests were damaged) the decision-making process was marked by five features:

1 The group was very cohesive.

2 It was typically isolated and insulated from information outside the group.

3 The decision-makers rarely searched systematically through alternative options.

4 The group was under pressure to make a decision.

5 The group was dominated by a very directive leader.

These five conditions lead to defective decision-making, which Janis calls 'groupthink'. The symptoms of groupthink are as follows:

▶ A cohesive group that is likely to exert pressures on dissenters to conform to the majority view

▶ An illusion of unanimity and correctness: since everyone gives the impression of total agreement, this inhibits any search for alternatives and leads to rejection of other views

▶ The negative stereotyping of out-groups, since they are the likely sources of alternative ideas or options

▶ An illusion of invulnerability – the group feels invincible and that it can do no wrong.

The results are that the group fails to consider alternatives to a preferred decision or action, it fails to examine the risks attached to the favoured decision and it does not engage in a very thorough information search about other possible options. Finally, groupthink means that there is a failure to develop contingency plans. All of this makes for the likelihood of poor-quality and risky decisions being made by groups, when compared with individuals.

Dig deeper

The website of Jane Elliot (of the Blue Eye / Brown Eye Experiment):
http://www.janeelliott.com/

More on groupthink: 'Sinister Groupthink Powers the Modern World', *The Telegraph*:
http://www.telegraph.co.uk/news/earth/environment/10853279/Sinister-groupthink-powers-the-modern-world.html

Fact-check

1 The advantage of stereotypes is that they:
   a Provide shortcuts to enable us to classify the world
   b Allow us to discriminate against people we don't like
   c Help us to select the right person for a job
   d Allow people who are similar to stay together

2 The confirmatory bias is:
   a When we are biased towards other people's beliefs
   b When our biases lead to prejudice
   c When we seek out people to confirm what we believe
   d When we encounter someone who conforms to our stereotype and use that as confirmation of our beliefs

3 Which of the following statements is correct?
   a People are prejudiced when they react in an emotional way to seeing or hearing a group that they hold stereotypes about
   b Discrimination is where we feel uncomfortable about someone simply because they are a member of a particular group
   c Discrimination allows us to make sense of the world
   d Everyone who holds a stereotype is prejudiced

4 Attributional bias is when we:
   a Attribute negative motives to someone else's behaviour
   b Make assumptions about our own and/or other people's behaviour and motives
   c Attribute negative motives to our own behaviour
   d Are prejudiced against someone of a different racial group

5 In internal attribution:
   a People infer that a person's behaviour is due to personal factors
   b People infer that a person's behaviour is due to external factors
   c People make a confirmatory bias
   d People reveal their prejudices

6 The fundamental attribution error is:

   a The tendency to attribute *our own* behaviour to internal factors

   b The tendency to attribute *other people's* behaviour to internal factors

   c The tendency to attribute other people's behaviour to external factors

   d The tendency to attribute someone's behaviour to the colour of their skin

7 Which of the following is *not* part of an attitude?

   a Beliefs

   b Values

   c Behaviours

   d Skills

8 Group polarization occurs when:

   a Groups make riskier or more extreme decisions than individuals

   b Groups fail to consider alternative plans

   c Groups are afraid to take risks

   d Groups make poor-quality decisions

9 Groupthink occurs when:

   a A group is not very cohesive

   b A group is well integrated with the outside world

   c A group has plenty of time to make a decision

   d There is a very directive leader

10 Which of the following is *not* a result of groupthink?

   a The group fails to consider alternatives to a preferred decision or action

   b It fails to examine the risks attached to the favoured decision

   c There is a failure to develop contingency plans

   d The group is very cohesive

14

Stress and mental health

Mental health issues are a serious cause for concern and the statistics speak for themselves: one in four people experience some kind of mental health problem in the course of a year. This chapter examines some of the most common mental health issues that affect people of different ages and looks at some of the causes, symptoms and treatments.

Stress

While many mental illnesses are hard to understand by those who have not experienced them, stress is one condition that most people understand only too well.

Spotlight: Stress as a psychological term

The term 'stress' is derived from the Latin word *stringere*, meaning 'to draw tight'. The word has long been in use in physics to refer to the internal distribution of a force exerted on a material body, resulting in strain. It first became associated with mental health in the 1920s and 1930s, when psychologists began to use the term to refer to a mental strain or to a harmful environmental agent that could cause illness.

Stress is, in fact, a perfectly normal reaction to events around us and it performed valued functions in our evolutionary past. For our ancestors, the stress reaction was essential for survival since it provided extra reserves of strength and energy so they could escape from predators or other threats.

In 1935 the psychologist Walter Cannon developed the idea of the 'flight or fight' mechanism that is associated with the stress response today. This theory states that animals react to threats with a general discharge of the sympathetic nervous system, priming the animal for fighting or fleeing. Hormones are the main players in the stress reaction, and when we are stressed they are released from our adrenal glands (near the pancreas) into the bloodstream with one aim: to prepare the body for flight or to fight. Both fighting and fleeing require extra strength in the arms and legs and more energy in the muscles. The goal is thus to divert as much oxygen-(and thus energy-)carrying blood as possible to the arm and leg muscles. To do this, the body stops concentrating on non-essential functions such as digestion that can wait until later. Blood is thus diverted from the stomach, skin and internal organs to other more important areas.

Adrenalin is one hormone that is released from the adrenal glands (part of the endocrine system – see Chapter 17) to the bloodstream, and it leads to a faster heart rate and raised blood pressure as the heart works harder to pump blood around the body. Cortisol is another hormone released from the adrenal glands and its job is to act on the liver to convert protein (glycogen) to glucose (sugar), which is a major source of energy for us. This glucose thus provides the energy for blood to be pumped faster and for us to be able to run or fight with extra strength. If the body is repeatedly exposed to stress, the result is the repeated liberation of energy stores, which, by the very nature of modern-day stressors, are not usually utilized. This excess glucose (and the free fatty acids released from stored fat) clogs up the blood vessels contributing to the formation of plaques, which can lead to coronary heart disease.

Spotlight

Typically, it takes 20–30 minutes for cortisol levels to rise following an acute stressor.

Another vital chemical is released from the hypothalamus in the brain (see Chapter 17). These are endorphins and they act as natural painkillers so that we feel less pain that would otherwise stop us being able to concentrate on fighting or fleeing.

'It is how people respond to stress that determines whether they will profit from misfortune or be miserable.'
M. Csikszentmihalyi, *Flow: The Psychology of Optimal Experience* (New York: Harper & Row, 1990)

All these reactions were ideal for our ancestors but are not so good for today when our threat is more likely to be a deadline, an angry boss or our demanding children than a predator. What was a valuable adaptive response to threat early in our evolutionary history is not much use in the face of the modern stresses of the twenty-first century. Furthermore, historically, the stress response was designed to combat relatively infrequent and life-threatening events whereas the stressors that we encounter now tend to be more frequent and rarely life-threatening. Consequently, the human stress response system is repeatedly activated. This leaves us with extra glucose surging through our muscles, which can result in the following symptoms:

- ▶ **Aching limbs:** the build-up of glucose in the limbs can make our arms and legs feel heavy and tired. In addition, we tend to tense our muscles in preparation for flight or fight and this tension causes pain.

- ▶ **Neck ache:** we tend to tense our neck muscles when stressed, which causes pain.

- ▶ **Tiredness:** we feel tired because we have been burning up so much extra energy. This rapid mobilization of energy gives short-term benefits but longer-term exhaustion.

- ▶ **Dry mouth:** the flow of saliva is reduced to the mouth as this is part of the non-essential digestive process.

- ▶ **Stomach-ache:** blood is diverted away from this area so digestive mechanisms are reduced – this can lead to digestive problems and discomfort. Poor digestion for long periods can result in more serious stomach problems such as ulcers.

- ▶ **Dizziness:** although we breathe more quickly when we are stressed, we tend to take more shallow breaths and thus we do not breathe in as much oxygen as deeply as when we are not stressed. This can lead to a slightly reduced supply to the brain, causing dizziness.

- ▶ **Illnesses:** stress can also result in a lowered immune system, making the stressed person more vulnerable to illnesses such as colds and flu.

When we remain stressed for long periods of time, or our stress levels rise frequently, we may experience more serious effects such as hypertension (raised blood pressure), which is the result of the heart continually working hard at pumping blood around the body extra quickly. This can escalate into cardiovascular disease as the increase in blood pressure can cause physical damage to the delicate lining of some blood vessels; the points where vessels branch into two (branch points) are particularly vulnerable and, if the smooth vessel lining is torn, the fatty acids and glucose released during the stress response cause further damage, as a result of a build-up of these fatty nutrients underneath the tear in the walls of the vessels. This process gives rise to plaques lining the blood vessels. Plaques occurring in arteries supplying the heart can lead to heart attacks. If they obstruct the flow of blood to the brain, they can cause strokes.

Anxiety

Related to stress is the condition labelled anxiety (sometimes called **generalized anxiety disorder – GAD**). Anxiety is a stress response that is normal in certain threatening situations. It is normal and even helpful to become anxious at times – for example, when faced with someone who is aggressive towards you or when approaching an important examination. Without anxiety, we would be less motivated to do something about the threatening situation, such as run away or study hard. Anxiety has special evolutionary value in that it would have helped our ancestors cope with anxiety-provoking situations (like an advancing predator or food shortage). This is because anxiety like stress and other powerful emotions can have a profound effect on the body. As our anxiety rises, the **hypothalamus** in the brain stimulates the **pituitary gland** at the base of the skull to release a range of hormones that affect every part of our body in one way or another (see Chapter 17). These hormones are similar to those released when we are stressed.

People with GAD tend to feel generally anxious without there necessarily being a specific event or situation that is causing the anxiety. It is thought that GAD affects about 1 in 20 adults in the UK and the US. Slightly more women are affected than men, and the condition is most common in people in their 20s. GAD can cause both psychological and physical symptoms. Psychological symptoms include:

▶ feeling restless

▶ having a constant sense of dread or of impending doom

▶ feeling constantly 'on edge'

▶ having problems concentrating on matters other than the worries

- being easily distracted by worries or concerns
- an inability to work effectively
- feeling depressed or worthless.

Physical symptoms include dizziness, tiredness, irregular heartbeat (palpitations), muscle aches, dry mouth, excessive sweating, shortness of breath, stomach-ache, nausea, diarrhoea, headache, irregular periods, difficulty falling or staying asleep (insomnia).

There are various theories to explain why some people suffer from GAD, including:

- **Life events theory:** people often develop anxiety following a series of stressful life events such as moving house, divorce, bereavement and redundancy. If a few stressful life events happen close together, it is perhaps not surprising that sufferers can become every tense and anxious; they might have been able to bounce back from one event, but two or more can use up their coping resources. Life events can have another impact, too; people can learn to be anxious based on their life experiences. For example, if they have had a health scare in the past, or a close friend has, they may become excessively anxious when reading about health issues.

- **Thinking styles theory:** some people may have a thinking style that lends itself to experiencing greater anxiety. For example, anxious people have a tendency to expect that the worst possible scenario will always occur and that they must constantly be on their guard in case something bad happens. Anxious people often think that, by thinking about the worse-case scenario, they are protecting themselves in some way from that event happening; either because they will be better prepared or because they superstitiously believe that worrying will prevent it actually happening. If they let their guard down, the terrible scenario might be 'allowed' to occur.

Anxiety can be so severe that panic attacks can ensue; this is a sudden 'rush of fear' that peaks very quickly. This fear is accompanied by a range of quite debilitating physical and emotional symptoms and the whole experience is usually extremely frightening for the sufferer. The attack is often so frightening that the sufferer will do almost anything to avoid another one. It is thought that between 1 and 3.5 per cent of the population suffer from panic disorder (i.e. recurrent panic attacks) and they appear to be most common among adolescents and young adults.

Phobias

A phobia is an extreme form of anxiety that is directed towards a particular object. A severe phobic reaction is a classic 'stress' reaction. To call something a 'phobia', most practitioners follow the diagnostic guidelines set in the *Diagnostic and Statistical Manual* (known in the trade as *DSM-V*, to designate the fifth edition of the manual), which is published by the American Psychiatric Association. These guidelines point out that, in order to be classified as a phobia, four conditions must be met:

1 There must be a marked and persistent fear that is excessive or unreasonable, cued by the presence or anticipation of a specific object or situation.

2 Exposure to this stimulus almost invariably provokes an immediate anxiety response, which may take the form of a panic attack.

3 The person recognizes that the fear is excessive or unreasonable.

4 The phobic response interferes significantly with the person's normal routine or social activities.

Phobias can be classified into two broad types:

▶ Specific or simple phobias

▶ Complex phobias (e.g. social phobia or agoraphobia).

Specific phobias can be further classified into four main categories:

▶ Animal phobias (fear of animals or creatures)

▶ Environmental phobias (fear of environmental events such as thunder, lightening, heights and the dark)

- Medical phobias (fear of blood, injections, vomiting, injury, etc.)

- Situational phobias (fear of certain situations such as crowded places, public transport, flying, driving, etc.).

There are a range of reasons why people might develop a phobia:

CONDITIONING

It is possible to induce a phobia, especially in children (see the case study on Little Albert below), by simply pairing a harmless stimulus with one that naturally instils fear. For example, if we were to present a cuddly teddy bear to a small child while at the same time screaming at them, they would most likely become fearful of the teddy. That fear might *generalize* to other soft toys, too.

LEARNING FROM OTHER PEOPLE

So-called vicarious learning means that we can also learn to be phobic. Thus, phobias are often transmitted from parent to child. Studies have shown that parents who show their fear more often to their children have more fearful children than those who hide their fears. This happens because children 1) use the information given to them by parents to develop their own fear and 2) they learn to copy or model their parent's behaviours. In addition, 3) observing someone else's fear can also induce fear.

THE THEORY OF PREPAREDNESS

In 1971 the psychologist Martin Seligman suggested that some things or stimuli are 'evolutionally predisposed' to evoke fear. This goes some way to explaining why some phobias are more common than others, such as spider phobia (one of the most common phobias). Presumably, in our evolutionary past, our ancestors would have encountered deadly spiders so a healthy fear of them might have saved their lives. This, though, doesn't explain why not everyone is phobic of spiders. The Theory of Preparedness goes further, then, by suggesting that some people are more biologically 'prepared' to have phobias than others. It is even possible that this 'preparedness' trait gave an evolutionary advantage, in that more fearful people may have had better survival rates as they avoided more of the dangerous stimuli in life. Indeed, most specific phobias do involve situations that might have posed a threat in some way at some point in our evolutionary past.

FIRST CONTACT THEORY
This theory is related to the above in that it builds on evolutionary principles. Many people have not any traumatic episode that can account for their phobia, neither have they learned it from their parents. These sufferers often report having 'always' been phobic since they were small children, without an obvious cause. The theory goes that it is in our best interests of survival to be afraid of something the first time we meet it (or contact it). This makes us wary until we know whether the new object is safe. This explains why children are often scared of new things or experiences, such as water, thunder and dogs. While most children overcome their fear, some get 'stuck' and remain fearful for life.

Case study: Little Albert

In 1920 the behavioural psychologist John B. Watson carried out a (highly unethical, by today's standards) experiment to show that a child can learn a phobia. Nine-month-old 'Albert' was an emotionally stable child with no history of fearful reactions. A white laboratory rat was placed near Albert and he was allowed to play with it. At this point, the child showed no fear of the rat. Later, however, Watson and his colleague Rosalie Rayner made a loud sound behind Albert's back when the baby touched the rat. Little Albert responded to the noise by crying and showing fear. After several such pairings of the two stimuli, Albert was again presented with only the rat. Now, however, he became very distressed as the rat appeared in the room; he had learned to associate the white rat (originally a neutral stimulus, now a conditioned stimulus) with the loud noise (an unconditioned stimulus) and was producing the fearful or emotional response of crying (originally the unconditioned response to the noise, now the conditioned response to the rat) – see Chapter 5 for more on conditioning.

Little Albert seemed to generalize his fear response to furry objects so that when Watson sent a non-white rabbit into the room 17 days after the original experiment, Albert also became distressed. He showed similar reactions when presented with a furry dog, a sealskin coat, and even when Watson appeared in front of him wearing a Santa Claus beard.

No attempts were made to cure poor Little Albert of the phobias that had been experimentally induced.

Spotlight: Who was Little Albert?

In 2009 the psychologist Hall P. Beck and colleagues published the results of their efforts to solve the mystery of the boy's true identity in *American Psychologist*. There, Beck et al. presented compelling evidence that Little Albert was a little boy named Douglas Merritte, the son of a wet-nurse, Arvilla Merritte, who was employed at the paediatric hospital at John Hopkins University where Watson also worked.

Sadly, the researchers discovered that the child had died at age six of hydrocephalus after contracting meningitis.

Obsessive–compulsive disorder (OCD)

Obsessive–compulsive disorder (OCD) is an anxiety disorder characterized by intrusive thoughts that produce discomfort, apprehension, fear or worry; the sufferer often performs repetitive behaviours aimed at reducing the associated anxiety. According to OCD-UK, it affects about 1.2 per cent of the population and it can be so debilitating and disabling that the World Health Organization (WHO) ranked OCD in the top ten of the most disabling illnesses of any kind, in terms of lost earnings and diminished quality of life.

Obsessions are involuntary, seemingly uncontrollable thoughts, images or impulses that occur over and over again in the sufferer's mind. Sufferers do not want to have these ideas but they cannot stop them. These obsessive thoughts are often disturbing and distracting.

Compulsions are behaviours or rituals that the sufferer feels driven to act out again and again, and often these compulsions are performed in an attempt to make the obsessions go away or become more manageable. For example, if a person is afraid of contamination with germs and fears catching something, they might develop obsessive hand-washing rituals in order to reduce their ongoing worries that they have not washed their hands. However, the relief from washing the hands never lasts, and, in fact, the obsessive thoughts may even come back more strongly. In order to cope with the obsessional thoughts and to reduce the associated anxiety, the hand-washer has to then repeat the hand-washing ritual – and the cycle continues.

The compulsive behaviours often end up causing anxiety themselves as they become more demanding and time-consuming. If the sufferer simply does not 'obey' their thoughts (by carrying out compulsions), they will also get more and more anxious, leaving them in a no-win situation, trapped by the cycle of obsessions and compulsions.

Post-traumatic stress disorder (PTSD)

Post-traumatic stress disorder (PTSD) is a severe anxiety disorder that can develop after exposure to any event that results in psychological trauma. This event may involve the threat of death to oneself or to someone else, or to one's own or someone else's physical, sexual or psychological well-being, overwhelming the ability to cope. According to NHS Direct, PTSD affects up to 30 per cent of people who experience a traumatic event. It affects around 5 per cent of men and 10 per cent of women at some point during their life. PTSD can occur at any age, including during childhood.

The diagnostic criteria for PTSD, stipulated in the *Diagnostic and Statistical Manual of Mental Disorders IV (Text Revision) (DSM-IV-TR)*, suggest that in order to be diagnosed with PTSD, the sufferer should:

1 **have had exposure to a traumatic event:** this must have involved *both* (a) loss of 'physical integrity' or risk of serious injury or death, to self or others, and (b) a response to the event that involved intense fear, horror, or helplessness

2 **persistently replay the event in their mind:** for example flashback memories, recurring distressing dreams, subjective re-experiencing of the traumatic event(s), or an intense negative psychological or physiological response to any objective or subjective reminder of the traumatic event(s)

3 **suffer persistent avoidance and emotional numbing following the event.** This involves a sufficient level of:

  ▷ avoidance of stimuli associated with the trauma, such as certain thoughts or feelings, or talking about the event(s)

  ▷ avoidance of behaviours, places, or people that might lead to distressing memories as well as the disturbing memories, dreams, flashbacks, and intense psychological or physiological distress

  ▷ inability to recall major parts of the trauma(s), or decreased involvement in significant activities

  ▷ decreased capacity (down to complete inability) to feel certain feelings

  ▷ an expectation that one's future will be somehow constrained in ways not normal to other people.

4 **experience persistent symptoms of increased arousal not present before:** these include difficulty falling or staying asleep, or problems with anger, concentration or hyper-vigilance

5 **have symptoms lasting for more than one month**

6 **show significant impairment:** the symptoms reported must lead to 'clinically significant distress or impairment' of major domains of life activity, such as social relations, occupational activities, or other 'important areas of functioning'.

Depression

According to the Royal College of Psychiatrists, one in five people become depressed at some point in their lives and it is thought to be the number-one psychological disorder in the Western world. Ten times more people suffer from major (or clinical) depression now than in 1945 (suggesting that most causes of depression are not biological) and the average age of first onset of major depression is 25–29. Up to 80 per cent of suicide deaths are among sufferers of major depression.

There are four main groups of depressive symptoms:

▶ Those to do with feelings: e.g. feeling sad and miserable

▶ Physical symptoms: e.g. lack of appetite or sleeping difficulties

▶ Thoughts/cognitions: e.g. 'I am worthless', 'No one likes me'

▶ Those to do with behaviour: e.g. staying in bed.

Only around 10 per cent of depressive cases are caused by biological factors; clinical depression is often said to be caused by a chemical imbalance in the brain, and, indeed, this is what most drug treatments are based on. Certainly, in many cases, the amount of certain neurotransmitters (such as serotonin and norepinephrine) is reduced in depressed people (see Chapter 17). However, low serotonin levels may simply be another symptom of depression, not a cause. Depressed people tend to engage in fewer pleasure-seeking activities and this lowers serotonin levels in the brain.

Most depression is caused by unhelpful thinking styles or cognitive distortions (which can be learned from other family members) rather than other factors such as genetics or hormone imbalance (although people may have a genetic predisposition to depression). This table shows examples of these patterns of thinking.

Unhelpful thinking style	Example
Predicting the future	Depressed people tend to spend a lot of time thinking about the future and predicting what could go wrong.
Mindreading	Here, assumptions are made about what other people are thinking, e.g. 'They must think I am so stupid', 'Everyone will think I am an idiot.'
Catastrophizing	Depressed people often blow things out of all proportion. Things are always 'terrible', rather than just 'not very good'. They also assume that catastrophes will result from minor mistakes.
'Should'-ing	'Should' statements are commonly used by depressed people to refer to how badly things have gone and to take the blame for what happened: 'I should have done this or that.' All this serves to make the person feel even worse about themselves and adds to their depressed state.
Over-generalizing	This is where one incident that didn't go well is used as a basis for assuming everything else will follow a similar pattern.
Ignoring the positives	Depressed people often ignore or don't notice when things go well and only focus on when things go badly.
Labelling	Finally, depressed people are more likely to label themselves as 'rubbish', 'a failure', 'boring', etc. Labelling like this can add to their feelings of poor self-worth.

Eating disorders

Eating disorders are psychological illnesses defined by abnormal eating habits that may involve either insufficient or excessive food intake. Bulimia nervosa and anorexia nervosa are the most common specific forms of eating disorders. Bulimia nervosa is a disorder characterized by binge eating and purging (e.g. self-induced vomiting, over-exercising and the use of laxatives). Anorexia nervosa is characterized by extreme food restriction to the point of self-starvation and excessive weight loss.

There are many possible causes of eating disorders, including biological, psychological and/or environmental:

▶ **Genetic:** individuals with a first-degree relative who has a history of an eating disorder are more likely than individuals without such a relative, to themselves develop an eating disorder, suggesting that there may be a genetic link (though this could be learned behaviour, too).

▶ **Family/home influence:** research shows that mothers who diet or worry excessively about their weight may trigger their child to develop an abnormal attitude towards food, as may a father or sibling (or even classmate) who teases an individual about their weight or shape.

▶ **Personality:** people with eating disorders tend to have low self-esteem, a high need for perfectionism and for the approval of others, and other characteristics.

▶ **Psychological factors:** psychological conditions such as post-traumatic stress disorder, anxiety, phobias and depression have all been associated with eating disorders, as have life stressors such as job loss, divorce, or coping with bullying or a learning difficulty such as dyslexia.

▶ **Body image disorders:** many people with eating disorders suffer also from body dysmorphic disorder, which is an altered way of a person seeing him or herself. Studies have found that 15 per cent of individuals diagnosed with body dysmorphic disorder also have either anorexia nervosa or bulimia nervosa.

▶ **Biological factors:** abnormalities of chemical messengers such as serotonin and norepinephrine that help control appetite, anxiety and reward systems may play a role in eating disorders.

Dig deeper

Watch the 'Little Albert' experiments:
http://www.bing.com/videos/search?q=little+albert+experiment&qpvt=little+albert+experiment&FORM=VDRE#view=detail&mid=A47FD8E6F5C2332BA6ACA47FD8E6F5C2332BA6AC

Anxiety website:
https://anxietyuk.org.uk/

Depression self-help guide:
http://www.moodjuice.scot.nhs.uk/depression.asp

Fact-check

1 Which of the following statements about stress is *not* true?
- **a** Stress is an adaptive response designed to save our lives
- **b** Stress makes us ill by lowering our immunity
- **c** Stress can cause heart attacks
- **d** Stress is never good for us any more

2 Which of the following is not a symptom of anxiety?
- **a** Palpitations
- **b** Heart attack
- **c** Dizziness
- **d** Dry mouth

3 Which of these theories might explain how GAD develops?
- **a** Life Events Theory
- **b** Cognitive Behavioural Theory
- **c** First Contact Theory
- **d** Preparedness Theory

4 Which of the following statements about phobias is *not* true?
- **a** To be a phobia, it must interfere significantly with the person's normal routine or social activities
- **b** To be classed as a phobia, the sufferer must recognize that the fear is excessive or unreasonable
- **c** To be classed as a phobia, the sufferer need not recognize that the fear is excessive or unreasonable
- **d** In a phobic response, exposure to the stimulus almost invariably provokes an immediate anxiety response

5 Which of the following is *not* a category of phobias?
- **a** Animal phobias
- **b** Environmental phobias
- **c** Medical phobias
- **d** Exam phobias

6 Which of these theories might explain how phobias develop?
- **a** Life Events Theory
- **b** Cognitive Behavioural Theory
- **c** First Contact Theory
- **d** Elaboration Likelihood Theory

7 Which of the following statements about OCD is true?
  a It is good to reassure OCD sufferers
  b OCD sufferers will feel better by acting out their compulsions
  c Reassuring OCD sufferers only brings temporary relief
  d OCD sufferers usually have depression, too

8 Which one of the following statements about PTSD is true?
  a Sufferers show little or no avoidance of stimuli associated with the trauma
  b Sufferers rarely experience flashbacks about the traumatic incident
  c PTSD can be diagnosed immediately following a traumatic event
  d Symptoms must lead to some kind of impairment of normal functioning to be classed as PTSD

9 Which of the following is *not* an unhelpful pattern of thinking characteristic of depression?
  a 'Should'-ing
  b Mindreading
  c Ruminating
  d Catastrophizing

10 Which of the following statements about eating disorders is true?
  a People with eating disorders tend to have low self-esteem
  b Individuals with a first-degree relative who has a history of an eating disorder are less likely than individuals without such a relative, to themselves develop an eating disorder
  c There are no biological factors associated with eating disorders.
  d Mothers who diet or worry excessively about their weight are no more at risk of having their children develop eating disorders than those who do not diet or worry about their weight

15

Psychological disorders

Chapter 14 began to examine some mental health conditions such as anxiety and depressive disorders that often occur in response to events (although sufferers may have an underlying predisposition towards the condition). This chapter concerns itself with psychological disorders that are caused by biological or physiological factors and that develop largely independently of external circumstances. These include mood disorders such as bipolar disorder, psychotic disorders such as schizophrenia, personality disorders such as multiple personality and developmental disorders such as autism and ADHD. Not every psychological disorder can be covered here but this chapter gives an overview of the more common ones.

Bipolar disorder

Bipolar disorder is sometimes referred to as 'manic depression' but, unlike clinical depression, discussed in Chapter 14, bipolar disorder is a distinct condition. What makes bipolar disorder different from depression is that it includes not only periods of depression but also periods of elation. It combines episodes of mania with episodes of depression, alternating in cycles.

The depressive symptoms of bipolar disorder are similar to those outlined in Chapter 14 and include:

▶ depressed mood

▶ no interest or pleasure in all, or almost all, activities previously enjoyed

▶ insomnia (inability to sleep) or hypersomnia (sleeping too much)

▶ fatigue or lack of energy

▶ feelings of worthlessness or excessive or inappropriate guilt

▶ diminished ability to think or concentrate

▶ recurrent thoughts of death (not just fear of dying)

▶ suicidal ideation.

With bipolar disorder, the depression tends to lift and give way to manic symptoms. After a period of time, this mania also wanes and the sufferer sinks into depression once more. During the manic phase, which lasts for at least a week (for it to be classified as such) and often three to six months, the sufferer may experience three or more of the following symptoms:

▶ Excessive happiness or energy

▶ Inflated self-esteem or grandiosity (at its worst, sufferers may even lose touch with reality and become psychotic – e.g. imagining they have been chosen for a special mission)

▶ Decreased need for sleep (e.g. the sufferer feels rested after only three hours of sleep)

▶ Very talkative, often speaking excessively fast

- Easily distracted
- Impulsivity, which can lead to taking actions without thoughts of the consequences (e.g. expensive shopping sprees or poor business investments).

Around half of sufferers also experience hallucinations or delusions.

Spotlight: Some statistics

About 3 per cent of people in the United States have bipolar disorder at some point in their life. It usually starts between the ages of 15 to 19; it rarely starts after the age of 40. Rates appear to be similar in males and females.

The causes of bipolar disorder probably vary between individuals and the exact mechanism underlying the disorder remains unclear. Genetic influences are believed to account for 60–80 per cent of the risk of developing the disorder; the risk of bipolar disorder is nearly tenfold higher in first-degree relatives (e.g. a parent or sibling) of those affected with bipolar disorder compared to the general population. Other causes might include abnormalities in the structure and/or function of certain brain circuits; structural MRI studies report an increase in the volume of the lateral ventricles and other parts of the brain. Functional MRI findings suggest that abnormalities within the amygdala are likely to contribute to poor emotional regulation and mood symptoms.

Environmental factors are also likely to play a part for those susceptible to the disorder. Thus, for example, traumatic events or stressful experiences might lead to onset of a bipolar episode for those at risk. There may also be neuro-endocrinological factors; for example, dopamine, a known neurotransmitter responsible for mood, has been shown to increase during the manic phase.

A number of medications are used to treat bipolar disorder. The medication with the best evidence is lithium, which is effective in treating acute manic episodes and preventing relapses. There are also other medications that can be used to help; it is possible that sodium valproate, an anti-convulsant, works just as well as lithium. Carbamazepine and lamotrigine are also effective for some people.

Schizophrenia

Schizophrenia is probably the best-known disorder that comes under the category of 'psychoses'; these are mental health conditions where the sufferer is, at times, unable to distinguish between what is real and what is not. For example, people with schizophrenia may see or hear things that don't exist, speak in strange or confusing ways, believe that others are trying to harm them, or feel as if they're being constantly watched. Most cases of schizophrenia appear in the late teens or early adulthood. However, schizophrenia can appear for the first time in middle age or even later. Around 1 per cent of the population suffers from schizophrenia (and this is similar for most countries). About 25 per cent of people who suffer an episode of schizophrenia will go on to recover completely without any further problems in the future.

The symptoms of schizophrenia include those described as 'positive' and those described as 'negative'. Positive symptoms are those that are more 'active' as opposed to the more inactive negative symptoms (which tend to imply an absence of 'normal' thought processes or emotions). Positive symptoms include:

▶ **Delusions:** this is where you believe something totally even there is clear evidence that you are wrong. Delusions occur in more than 90 per cent of those who have the disorder. Often, these delusions involve illogical or bizarre ideas or fantasies. Common schizophrenic delusions include:

  ▷ *Delusions of persecution:* belief that others, often a vague 'they', are out to get him or her

  ▷ *Delusions of control:* belief that one's thoughts or actions are being controlled by other people (e.g. the police)

  ▷ *Delusions of reference:* a particular object is believed to have a special and personal meaning. For example, a person with schizophrenia might believe a certain colour car or a person on TV is sending a message meant specifically for them

▷ *Delusions of grandeur:* belief that one is a famous or important figure, such as Jesus Christ or Elvis Presley. Alternately, delusions of grandeur may involve the belief that one has unusual powers that no one else has (e.g. the ability to make oneself invisible).

▶ **Hallucinations:** these are sounds or sights that seem real to the sufferer but do not in fact exist outside their own mind. The most common hallucination is hearing voices; these voices may provide a commentary on the patient's activities, carry on a conversation with them, warn of impending dangers, or even issue orders. The voices are very real to the sufferer and during calmer periods they might be able to control or manage them – or simply learn to ignore them. But during severe or 'acute' phases, these voices can take over, becoming very controlling and sometimes menacing.

▶ **Disorganized speech:** people with schizophrenia often have trouble concentrating and maintaining a train of thought; this can lead them to start sentences on one topic and then veer completely into an unrelated area, or to say illogical or incoherent things that make little sense to anyone else. Their speech is often punctuated by loose associations (where thoughts or sentences have only loose connections with previous ones), neologisms (made-up words or phrases) and perseveration (repetition of words and statements).

▶ **Chaotic behaviour:** people with schizophrenia can quickly lose the ability to behave within the range of acceptable parameters. Their behaviour might become unpredictable or bizarre, with inappropriate reactions. They might lose their inhibitions and be unable to control their impulses. They might experience sudden and extreme mood swings and stop taking care of their personal hygiene. They are likely to become socially withdrawn as they struggle to cope with social interactions.

Often, the negative symptoms of schizophrenia contribute more to poor functional outcomes and quality of life for individuals with schizophrenia than do positive symptoms. Negative symptoms often persist longer than positive ones and may be more difficult to treat. Negative symptoms, which are to do with the absence of normal functioning, include:

▶ **Lack of emotional expression:** the patient may not display any emotions, either facially or with their voice. For example, they may not smile or make eye contact and may speak in a flat monotone.

▶ **Lack of interest or enthusiasm:** they may display little interest in the world, in hobbies or even in day-to-day activities like eating or personal hygiene.

▶ **Social withdrawal:** they tend to stop interacting with the world around them.

The causes of schizophrenia are not fully known. However, it appears that schizophrenia usually results from a complex interaction between genetic, physiological and environmental factors. Schizophrenia has a strong hereditary component; people with a first-degree relative (parent or sibling) who has schizophrenia have a 10-per-cent chance of developing the disorder, compared with 1-per-cent chance within the general population. But genetics are not the only explanation for the onset of the condition; about 60 per cent of schizophrenics have no family members with the disorder.

It could be that genetics give a person susceptibility to the illness, and that environmental circumstances then trigger it in some people. Stress is one such environmental factor that could trigger schizophrenia in susceptible people, perhaps due to the high levels of cortisol that stress produces. Examples of stressful events include prenatal exposure to a viral infection, low oxygen levels during birth, exposure to a virus during infancy, early parental loss or separation, bereavement or other trauma.

Abnormalities in the brain might also play a role in the development of the illness. Schizophrenic patients have sometimes been shown to have enlarged ventricles (fluid-filled cavities), which might suggest some lack in density of brain tissue in these areas. There may also be low activity in the frontal lobe, while some studies also suggest that abnormalities in the temporal lobes, hippocampus and amygdala correlate with some of schizophrenia's positive symptoms.

Research also suggests that schizophrenia may be caused by a change in the level of two neurotransmitters (see Chapter 17 for more on neurotransmitters): dopamine and serotonin. Indeed, drugs that alter the levels of neurotransmitters in the brain can relieve some of the symptoms of schizophrenia. Certain drugs, particularly cannabis, cocaine, LSD and amphetamines, may trigger symptoms of schizophrenia in people who are susceptible.

Spotlight: Cannabis and schizophrenia

Studies have shown that teenagers under 15 who use cannabis regularly, especially 'skunk' and other more potent forms of the drug, are up to four times more likely to develop schizophrenia by the age of 26.

The most common treatment options for schizophrenia involve medication, although psychological therapies can be used, too.

Personality disorders

Personality develops throughout childhood and everyone has some aspect of their personality that may cause them difficulties at times. However, people with personality disorders (PDs) have more severe problems such that their personality traits cause them significant difficulties in a range of ways; for example, they may find it hard to maintain close relationships, to get on with people, to control their feelings, to keep out of trouble and so on. There are thought to be ten main types of personality disorder that can be grouped into three categories, as shown in the following table.

Suspicious	Emotional/impulsive	Anxious
Paranoid: suspicious, finds it hard to trust others, always looking for signs of betrayal, feels easily rejected, tends to hold grudges, etc.	**Borderline:** very impulsive, hard to control emotions, makes friends easily but hard to maintain those friendships, suffers mood swings, may self-harm, clings to damaging relationships due to fear of being alone.	**Avoidant:** worries a lot, very anxious and tense, very sensitive, insecure, avoids close relationships because of fear of rejection, reluctant to try new activities.
Schizoid: emotionally 'cold', prefers not to have close relationships with others, has little interest in intimacy.	**Histrionic:** self-centred, over-dramatizes events, strong emotions that change quickly, craves excitement, easily influenced, tries to be centre of attention.	**Dependent:** passive, relies on others to make decisions, feels helpless, needy, low in confidence.
Antisocial: uninterested in how others feel, likely to commit crimes, acts impulsively, feels no guilt, acts in ways that hurt others, aggressive, doesn't learn from experience.	**Narcissistic:** strong sense of own importance, believes they will achieve great things, craves admiration from others, uses other people for own ends, fragile self-esteem.	**Obsessive-compulsive:** has unrealistically high standards, likes everything to be just so, worries about making mistakes, wants everything to be perfect, may hang on to items with no obvious value, likes routines, preoccupied with detail.
Schizotypal: eccentric behaviour sometimes related to schizophrenia, odd ideas, may think they have special powers like reading peoples' minds.		

It should be noted that the diagnosis of PD remains controversial as there is no definitive test for any particular type of PD. Like many mental health conditions, the causes of PD are unclear and there are likely to be a variety of factors, such as environmental influences and genetics, contributing to the development of the condition. For example, the role of the family and upbringing may have an impact in the development of some personality traits associated with PD; a family environment where a child's understanding and experience of their own mind and feelings are constantly undermined might, for example, harm the development of social skills that are key to the process of 'mentalization'. Mentalization is akin to empathy and is the ability to make sense of other people's actions by thinking through what is going on in their minds. Parents who constantly belittle a child's opinions and thoughts may thus hinder the development of this trait – and this could be a factor leading to a PD. Even verbal abuse can have an impact on the development of PD. In a study of 793 mothers and children, researchers asked the mothers whether they had told their children that they didn't love them or threatened to send them away. Children who had experienced such verbal abuse were three times as likely as other children to have borderline, narcissistic, obsessive–compulsive or paranoid personality disorders in adulthood.

Other studies have shown a link between the number and type of childhood traumas and the development of personality disorders. People with **borderline personality disorder** (BPD), for example, had especially high rates of childhood sexual trauma (although this does not mean that all BPD patients have experienced sexual abuse or that all victims of sexual abuse will develop BPD).

Some researchers suggest that abnormalities with the neurotransmitters (the chemicals that act as messengers between different parts of the brain) may cause the development of some PDs – particularly serotonin, norepinephrine and dopamine.

Treatment of PDs usually involves psychological therapies rather than medication, although drugs can be used for conditions that may occur alongside the PD (such as depression).

Spotlight: Some statistics

Borderline personality disorder, also known as emotionally unstable or emotional regulation personality disorder, affects around 1 per cent of the population, but 75 per cent of those with the diagnosis are women.

Autism spectrum disorder (ASD)

This is a pervasive developmental disorder in that symptoms are present from an early developmental stage (usually within the first two years of life) and cause significant impairment in functioning. Deficits tend to fall within two main areas:

▶ **Social impairment:** this includes difficulties with social communication caused by lack of eye contact, 'flat' monotone voice, lack of understanding about turn-taking, inability to empathize, narrow range of interests and inability to read social cues.

▶ **Repetitive and stereotyped behaviours:** for example, children may repeatedly flap their arms or wave their fingers in front of their faces. These repetitive actions are sometimes called 'stereotypy', 'stereotyped behaviours' or 'stims'. They might also be obsessed with certain objects or places.

It should be noted that ASD is a 'spectrum', which means that it varies in severity and symptomology. Some children, for example, are very keen to socialize and make friends even though they find it hard to do so, while others are less interested in other people. Sometimes the term Asperger's Syndrome is used to describe those less severely affected (also referred to as high-functioning); unlike the more severe 'autism', people with Asperger's Syndrome have no significant delay in language development. There is also a unique (and rather rare) form of autism called autistic savantism, where a child can actually display outstanding skills in music, art or numbers, as illustrated so well by the character played by Dustin Hoffman in the 1988 film *Rain Man* (see the case study below).

'Savant syndrome is a rare, but extraordinary, condition in which persons with severe mental disabilities, including autistic disorder, have some kind of "islands of genius".'
Darold Treffert, 'The Savant Syndrome: An Extraordinary Condition', *Philosophical Transactions of the Royal Society B: Biological Sciences* 364(1522): 1351–7

Around one in 100 people has ASD. Around half of people with an ASD also have a learning disability. Boys are more likely to be diagnosed with an ASD than girls. Because there is no specific test for ASD, diagnosing the condition can be difficult and usually involves a mix of observation, questionnaires and interview techniques. One psychological test that helps with diagnosis is called ADOS – the Autism Diagnostic Observation Schedule. This is a semi-structured assessment of communication, social interaction and play (or imaginative use of materials) and consists of four modules containing standardized activities that allow the examiner to observe the occurrence or non-occurrence of behaviours that have been identified as important to the diagnosis of autism.

Case study: Savants

An estimated 10 per cent of the autistic population – and an estimated 1 per cent of the non-autistic population – have savant abilities.

Stephen Wiltshire is one such 'savant'. Born in London, England, in 1974 to West Indian parents, he was diagnosed as autistic at the age of three. When he was about seven, Stephen became fascinated with sketching landmark London buildings. After being shown a book of photos depicting the devastation wrought by earthquakes, he began to create detailed architectural drawings of imaginary cityscapes. Wiltshire's amazing skill was that he could look at a subject once and then draw an accurate and detailed picture of it. He frequently draws entire cities from memory, based on brief helicopter rides. For example, he produced a detailed drawing of four square miles of London after a single helicopter ride above that city. His 19-foot (5.8-m)-long drawing of 305 square miles (790 sq. km) of New York City is based on a single 20-minute helicopter ride.

In May 2005 Stephen produced his longest ever panoramic memory drawing of Tokyo on a 32.8-foot (10.0-m)-long canvas within seven days following a helicopter ride over the city. A 2011 project in New York City involved Wiltshire's creation of a 250-foot (76-m)-long panoramic memory drawing of New York, which is now displayed on a giant billboard at JFK Airport. Wiltshire's work has been the subject of many TV documentaries. The renowned neurologist Oliver Sacks writes about him in the chapter 'Prodigies' in his 2009 book *An Anthropologist on Mars*.

In 2006 Wiltshire was appointed a Member of the Order of the British Empire (MBE) for services to art. In September 2006 Stephen opened his permanent gallery in the Royal Opera Arcade, Pall Mall, London (http://www.stephenwiltshire.co.uk/).

Daniel Tammet is another autistic savant. Since the age of three when he suffered an epileptic fit, he has been obsessed with counting (as a child he eschewed football in favour of spending his playtimes counting leaves on the trees) and can perform mind-boggling mathematical calculations at breakneck speeds. He achieves this by feeling and seeing shapes rather than actually calculating them – he sees numbers as colours, shapes and textures. He recently broke the European record for recalling pi, the mathematical constant, to the furthest decimal point (which took five hours); to him, pi isn't an abstract set of numbers but more of a highly visual story.

His incredible abilities can get in the way of everyday life, however: for example, a trip to the supermarket involves high levels of 'mental stimulus' as he feels obliged to count, calculate and work out everything from prices to arrangements of fruit and veg (http://www.danieltammet.net/).

Spotlight: Famous people alleged to have had ASD

Isaac Newton, Albert Einstein, George Orwell, H.G. Wells, Beethoven, Mozart, Hans Christian Andersen and Ludwig Wittgenstein are thought to have shown signs of ASD, according to Michael Fitzgerald, Professor of Psychiatry at Trinity College, Dublin. 'Psychiatric disorders can also have positive dimensions. I'm arguing the genes for autism/Asperger's and creativity are essentially the same,' he said in 2008 at a Royal College of Psychiatrists' Academic Psychiatry conference in London.

There is no clear explanation for what causes ASD. However, family studies have shown that genes play a role; for example, if one identical twin has autism then the other has around a

75-per-cent chance of also having autism. One of the greatest controversies about ASD is centred on whether a link exists between ASD and certain childhood vaccines, particularly the measles–mumps–rubella (MMR) vaccine (see the 'Spotlight' below). Despite extensive research, no reliable study has shown a link between ASD and the MMR vaccine.

Spotlight: The MMR vaccine controversy

In 1998 Dr Andrew Wakefield published a research paper in the medical journal *The Lancet* that lent support to the later discredited claim that colitis and autism spectrum disorders are linked to the combined measles, mumps and rubella (MMR) vaccine. This paper was widely published in the media and directly led to a massive drop in vaccination rates in the UK and Ireland which was followed by a significantly increased incidence of measles and mumps, resulting in deaths and severe and permanent injuries.

Wakefield's research began to unravel when an investigation by the *Sunday Times* journalist Brian Deer discovered that Wakefield had multiple undeclared conflicts of interest, had manipulated evidence, and had broken other ethical codes. *The Lancet* paper was partially retracted in 2004, and fully retracted in 2010, when *The Lancet*'s editor-in-chief Richard Horton described it as 'utterly false' and said that the journal had been 'deceived'. Wakefield was found guilty by the General Medical Council of serious professional misconduct in May 2010 and was struck off the Medical Register, meaning he could no longer practise as a doctor in the UK.

The scientific consensus today is that, despite many studies across the world since 1988, no evidence links the MMR vaccine to the development of autism, and that this vaccine's benefits greatly outweigh its risks. A 2011 journal article described the vaccine–autism connection as 'the most damaging medical hoax of the last 100 years'.

There is no single treatment for autism; treatments generally address behavioural and learning skills. Treatments can include intensive skill-building and educational sessions, known as **applied behaviour analysis** (ABA).

Attention deficit hyperactivity disorder (ADHD)

ADHD is another developmental condition and was first recognized in 1902 by the British paediatrician George Frederic Still. Since Still's day, the disorder has been called various things such as hyperkinetic syndrome, attention-deficit disorder (ADD) and now ADHD. The American Psychiatric Association's *Diagnostic and Statistical Manual of Mental Disorders*, fifth edition, the *DSM-V* (the 'bible' for diagnosing all mental health conditions), outlines indicators for ADHD that include:

▶ **Inattention:** being easily distracted, missing details, forgetting things, frequently switching from one activity to another, having difficulty maintaining focus on one task, becoming bored with a task after only a few minutes (unless doing something enjoyable), having difficulty focusing attention on completing a task or learning something new, having trouble completing homework assignments, often losing things (e.g. pencils, toys, assignments), not seeming to listen when spoken to, daydreaming, becoming easily confused, and struggling to follow instructions.

▶ **Hyperactivity:** fidgets and squirms in their seat, talks nonstop, rushes around, touching or playing with anything and everything in sight, has trouble sitting still, is constantly in motion, has difficulty doing quiet tasks or activities.

▶ **Impulsivity:** being very impatient, blurting out inappropriate comments, acting without regard for consequences, having difficulty waiting their turn in games and often interrupting conversations or others' activities.

Based on the DSM criteria, there are three subtypes of ADHD:

▶ ADHD, predominantly inattentive

▶ ADHD, predominantly hyperactive–impulsive

▶ ADHD, combined type that is a combination of the first two subtypes.

There is no sure-fire way of diagnosing ADHD and the phenomenal rise in children being given this label has led some to believe that it is being diagnosed far too readily. Incidence rates vary according to the diagnostic criteria used but the statistics suggest a massive increase in people with the condition; the Center for Disease Control's national survey of Children's Health in the United States reported an 830-per-cent increase in children diagnosed with ADD or ADHD from 1985 to 2011. An article in the *New York Times* in 2013 reported that, in 24 years, the number of children on medication for ADHD in the United States had soared from 600,000 to 3.5 million. This means that nearly one in five high-school-age boys in the United States and 11 per cent of school-age children overall have received a medical diagnosis of ADHD. The disorder is now the second most frequent long-term diagnosis made in children, narrowly trailing asthma.

As in ASD, there are likely to be a number of factors contributing to the causes of ADHD, including genetic and environmental. Brain imaging studies have revealed that, in young people with ADHD, brain development appears to be delayed, on average, by about three years and this delay is most pronounced in brain regions involved in thinking, paying attention and planning. More recent studies have found that the cortex – the outermost layer of the brain – also shows delayed maturation.

'The symptoms of ADHD can cause significant suffering in children, families, and schools and significant costs to the health care system, education system, juvenile justice system, and employers through parental work loss.'
Erik Parens and Josephine Johnston, 'Facts, Values, and Attention-Deficit Hyperactivity Disorder (ADHD): An Update on the Controversies', *Child and Adolescent Psychiatry and Mental Health* 3/1 (2009)

There is no cure for ADHD but medication is often used to manage the symptoms when these are severe. Stimulants such as methylphenidate ('Ritalin' or 'Concerta') and amphetamines ('Adderall') are the most common type of medication used;

this might seem odd given that hyperactivity is often a major symptom of ADHD but these medications work by stimulating brain circuits that help maintain attention. Non-stimulant medications, such as atomoxetine ('Strattera'), guanfacine and clonidine are also effective for some.

Oppositional defiant disorder (ODD)

ODD is a developmental behavioural disorder thought to be characterized by uncooperative, defiant, negative, irritable and annoying behaviours towards parents, peers, teachers and other authority figures. The condition is somewhat controversial in that some would argue that most children can be oppositional, even very oppositional, at times – something that used to be simply labelled as naughty. Where ODD differs, however, is that the 'naughtiness' persists despite appropriate parenting or other inputs. The condition is defined in the *DSM-V*, which says that four of the following should be exhibited for at least six months to reach a diagnosis. The child:

► actively refuses to comply with authority figure's requests or consensus-supported rules

► performs actions deliberately to annoy others

► is angry and resentful of others

► argues often

► blames others for their own mistakes

► frequently loses temper

► is spiteful or seeks revenge

► is touchy or easily annoyed.

Behaviours must cause considerable distress for the family or interfere significantly with academic or social functioning. Treatment tends to be non-pharmaceutical such as social skills training, training for parents and family therapy.

Dig deeper

Emergence: personality disorder website:
http://www.emergenceplus.org.uk/

Article about Andrew Wakefield:
http://www.nytimes.com/2011/04/24/magazine/mag-24Autism-t.
html?pagewanted=all&_r=0

Fact-check

1 Which of the following is *not* normally a feature of bipolar disorder?
   a Excessive happiness or energy
   b Decreased need for sleep
   c Disorganized speech
   d No interest or pleasure in all, or almost all, activities previously enjoyed

2 What might be the causes of bipolar disorder?
   a Genetic factors
   b Abnormalities in brain structure
   c Environmental factors
   d All of the above

3 Schizophrenic patients often suffer from delusions. These are:
   a Where you hear voices
   b Where you believe something totally even there is clear evidence that you are wrong
   c Where you see things that are not there
   d Where other people don't believe you

4 Negative symptoms of schizophrenia include:
   a Lack of emotional expression
   b Lack of interest or enthusiasm
   c Social withdrawal
   d All of the above

5 Which of the following is an 'anxious' personality disorder?
   a Avoidant
   b Schizoid
   c Narcissistic
   d Borderline

6 Diagnosis of personality disorder remains controversial because:
   a No one knows what it really is
   b The rates have increased so much
   c There is no real test for it
   d It is an insulting term

7 People with autistic spectrum disorder tend to:
   a Suffer delusions
   b Experience hallucinations
   c Hear voices
   d Have difficulty in social situations

8 Autistic savantism is:
   a What most people with ASD experience
   b Where people with ASD have islands of exceptional skill
   c When people with ASD are good at maths
   d When people with ASD are good at art

9 Which of the following is not a sub-type of ADHD?
   a ADHD, predominantly inattentive
   b ADHD, predominantly hyperactive–impulsive
   c ADHD, combined type that is a combination of the first two subtypes
   d ADHD, predominantly autistic

10 People with ADHD are:
   a Usually of below average intelligence
   b Children – adults grow out of it
   c Often psychotic too
   d Often easily distracted

16

Psychological therapies

Psychological therapies are processes designed by psychologists to modify the feelings or change the behaviours of people who are experiencing difficulties that affect their mental health and well-being. They 'encompass a range of interventions, based on psychological theory and evidence, which help people to alter their thinking, behaviours and relationships in the present, and process trauma and disturbance from the past, in order to alleviate emotional distress and improve psychosocial functioning'. Such therapies might be provided to adults or children with mental health issues, to those with learning disabilities or to people with physical and neurological disabilities. There is a wide range of therapies available, many of which are discussed in this chapter.

Behaviour therapy

As its name implies, behaviour therapy (or behaviour modification) aims to change human behaviour that is inappropriate or unhelpful in that it is causing problems or difficulties for the patient. Examples of conditions that respond well to behaviour therapy include addictions, anxiety, phobias and obsessive–compulsive disorder (OCD).

The theoretical approach behind behaviour therapy is that maladaptive behaviours are learned and thus can be unlearned by examining the thoughts and feelings that lead to that behaviour occurring or continuing to occur. Unlike some other therapies that focus on the past, behaviour therapy is much more concerned with the present and how behaviour in the future can be changed or modified. (That is not to say that the past is unimportant in this kind of approach, as it can help to explain present problems, but the focus is very much on moving forward rather than delving into the past.) Behaviour therapy usually focuses on some aspect of behaviour that is easily measurable.

Behaviour therapy is based on the theories of conditioning, which were discussed in Chapter 5. Based on these theoretical underpinnings, various therapeutic approaches are identified that include those based on either classical or operant conditioning.

Examples of therapies based on classical conditioning include:

▶ **Systematic desensitization:** this is a gradual exposure to a feared stimulus (such as spiders if the client has a phobia of arachnoids) so that the patient can unlearn conditioned responses to those stimuli. By teaching the client relaxation skills that can be used at the same time as exposure to the arousing stimulus, pairing of the fear-inducing item and newly learned relaxation behaviour aims to eliminate the conditioned response of fear to the stimulus. This technique is used successfully when treating phobias and panic attacks.

▶ **Aversion therapy:** this is the opposite of systematic desensitization in that it does not try to break the link between a stimulus and a negative response – rather, it tries to create such a link. Aversion therapy pairs undesirable behaviour with some form of aversive stimulus with the aim of reducing that unwanted behaviour. For example, a patient with OCD might snap an elastic band against their wrist whenever an unwanted thought intrudes into their minds.

Therapies based on operant conditioning include:

▶ **Token economies:** using positive reinforcement approaches, this is where individuals are offered 'tokens' that can be exchanged for privileges or goods when desired behaviour occurs. This is commonly used with people who have learning difficulties to help 'shape' desirable behaviours.

▶ **Modelling:** This relies on learning through observation and imitation and can be used within mentoring or buddying schemes for children or with people with learning difficulties.

Cognitive behaviour therapy (CBT)

CBT builds on behaviour therapy by adding in a cognitive component. It works to change maladaptive thinking in order to change feelings and behaviour. CBT, developed from the work of Albert Ellis in the mid-1950s and Aaron Beck a decade later, is a way of talking about:

▶ how a person thinks about themselves, the world and other people

▶ how what they do affects their thoughts and feelings.

CBT can thus help to change how people think ('cognitive') and what they do ('behaviour)'. Like behaviour therapy and unlike some of the other 'talking treatments', it focuses on the 'here and now' rather than on possible causes of the problem. CBT has been shown to be effective for a wide range of problems, especially anxiety, depression, panic attacks, phobias, stress and OCD. It can also help with anger and self-esteem issues and even pain management.

CBT works by breaking seemingly overwhelming problems down into smaller parts. This makes it easier to see how they are connected and how they affect the person. These parts might include an event or a situation that led to maladaptive:

- thoughts
- emotions
- physical feelings
- actions.

The underlying assumptions of CBT are that emotions and behaviour are determined by thinking processes. Problems arise from maladaptive thinking which is negative, unrealistic and unhelpful. By altering these ways of thinking, the emotional problems can be alleviated.

CBT uses various means to challenge maladaptive thinking. Techniques include:

- questioning
- giving information
- analogies
- humour
- role reversal
- self-instructional training.

Spotlight: Computerized CBT

Computerized cognitive behavioural therapy (CCBT) has been described by NICE (the National Institute of Clinical Excellence) in the UK as a 'generic term for delivering CBT via an interactive computer interface delivered by a personal computer, Internet, or interactive voice response system', instead of face to face with a human therapist. It has proven effectiveness and in 2006 NICE recommended that CCBT be made available for use within the NHS across England and Wales for patients presenting with mild to moderate depression, rather than immediately giving them antidepressant medication.

One of the most distinctive features of maladaptive thinking is that thoughts are often very negative. People can get stuck in a cycle of thinking negatively and these thoughts often have specific qualities:

▶ They appear automatically.

▶ They are often distorted, so don't fit the facts or match reality.

▶ They tend to be unhelpful because they make the patient feel bad or depressed.

▶ The thoughts are plausible so it doesn't occur to the patient to question them.

▶ They are involuntary, which means that they are very hard to control.

The negative thoughts often reflect negative opinions of oneself, self-criticism and self-blame, a negative interpretation of events and negative expectations of the future. Part of CBT, then, is challenging these thoughts; the patient is often asked to keep thought diaries in which they record their thoughts in relation to certain events and then they bring those diaries to the sessions where the therapist will challenge them (eventually the client will learn to challenge their thoughts themselves) by asking:

▶ What is the evidence for your views?

▶ What alternative views could there be?

▶ What is the effect of thinking the way you do?

▶ What thinking errors are you making?

Thinking errors refer to the erroneous ways of thinking about oneself, the world and the future (such as all-or-nothing thinking, self-blame, double standard, etc.); some of these were outlined in Chapter 14 in the section on depression.

Case study: Beth

Beth suffered from depression and lack of self-esteem. She was convinced that no one liked her and that she had nothing interesting to say or to contribute to a conversation. She felt that she had no friends and that she was 'useless'. CBT was used to help her challenge her cognitive distortions. For example, she was asked to carry out 'experiments' to test out her claims that no one 'liked' her to see whether they were based in reality. She was asked why she thought no one liked her and she said that no one spoke to her, smiled at her or asked her to join them for coffee and so on.

So, she was asked to test this out by smiling and saying hello to someone to test out her conviction that no one 'liked' her. She found that people did respond and say hello back. This then allowed the therapist to challenge her assumptions that no one liked her and look for other explanations for people not smiling/talking to her – Beth realized that it could be that other people were shy, preoccupied or, perhaps, when she didn't smile and avoided eye contact, they were put off from approaching her.

A further 'experiment' was encouraged in which Beth was to ask friends to meet for coffee. She predicted that they would make excuses but in fact they didn't. This allowed her to challenge some of her cognitive distortions (such as mindreading, all-or-nothing thinking). She started to realize that her thoughts were distorted and holding her back, which was the first step in lifting her from her low self-esteem and depression.

Psychodynamic therapies

The roots of psychodynamic therapy lie in Freud's psychoanalysis approach (see Chapter 9), but the work of Carl Jung, Alfred Adler, Otto Rank and Melanie Klein have also influenced the methodology. The aim of psychodynamic therapy is to bring the unconscious mind into awareness. The goals are to increase self-awareness and understanding of how the past can affect the present. Psychodynamic therapy helps people to unravel and understand hidden, subconscious and deep-rooted feelings, which it is felt is required if the problems they cause are to be fully resolved. Psychodynamic therapists believe that our unconscious mind suppresses painful feelings and memories, using defences such as denial and projections (see Chapter 9). Although these defences protect in the short term, in the longer term they are often harmful and prevent us from dealing with difficult situations and resolving them.

The basic assumptions underlying the psychodynamic approach are that:

- ▶ most of our behaviour has its root in the unconscious
- ▶ *psychic determinism*, which means that all behaviour has a cause/reason
- ▶ different parts of the unconscious mind (e.g. the id, ego and superego) are in constant struggle with one another
- ▶ our behaviour and feelings as adults (including psychological problems) are caused by our childhood experiences
- ▶ we develop defences in order to avoid the unpleasant consequences of conflict.

Techniques used in psychoanalytic therapy include **free association,** which is where the client talks freely to the therapist – saying the first things that come to mind without any attempt to censor ideas and thoughts. This is thought to allow true feelings to emerge and thus uncover defences. Sometimes the therapist will read words out (e.g. mother, father) and the patient has to say the first things that spring to mind. For this technique to work, the patient has to feel confident that the therapist is not going to judge them for what they say.

> 'The importance of free association is that the patients spoke for themselves, rather than repeating the ideas of the analyst; they worked through their own material, rather than parroting another's suggestions.'
> Pamela Thurschwell, *Sigmund Freud*, 2nd edition (London: Routledge, 2009), p. 24

Freud called free association 'this fundamental technical rule of analysis... We instruct the patient to put himself into a state of quiet, unreflecting self-observation, and to report to us whatever internal observations he is able to make' – taking care not to 'exclude any of them, whether on the ground that it is too disagreeable or too indiscreet to say, or that it is too unimportant or irrelevant, or that it is nonsensical and need not be said.'

S. Freud, *Introductory Lectures on Psycho-Analysis*, Penguin Freud Library vol. 1, new edn (Harmondsworth: Penguin, 1991), p. 328

The use of free association was intended to help discover notions that a patient had developed, initially, at an unconscious level, including:

▶ **transference:** unwittingly transferring feelings about one person and applying them to another person

▶ **projection:** projecting internal feelings or motives by ascribing them to other things or people

▶ **resistance:** holding a mental block against remembering or accepting some events or ideas.

Spotlight: Freudian slips

Freudian slips are typically errors of speech that are interpreted as occurring through the interference of unconscious thoughts. Thus, these slips are thought to be more revealing of the speaker's true feelings. They are named after Sigmund Freud, who, in his 1901 book *The Psychopathology of Everyday Life* described and analysed a large number of seemingly trivial, bizarre or nonsensical errors and slips. However, he never coined the term 'Freudian slips' and it is not known who did. Examples of such gaffes include thanking a host for their 'hostility' (rather than 'hospitality') or asking for 'bed and butter' (rather than 'bread and butter').

President George W. Bush made a now-famous gaffe in 1988 that would have given a psychoanalyst a lot to work with: 'For seven-and-a-half years, I've worked alongside President Reagan. We've had triumphs. Made some mistakes. We've had some sex ...

uh ... setbacks.' Did this reflect a desire to have sex with President Reagan? Not necessarily; a skilled psychoanalyst working with the President (Bush) might well uncover that he connects ideas like triumphs or mistakes with sex, rather than with President Reagan (though such an observation might still be rather insightful).

Here are some other famous Freudian slips:

Gordon Brown, former Prime Minister of the UK, may have secretly considered himself to be a superhero when he told MPs that 'we not only saved the world' before quickly correcting himself, saying 'er, saved the banks...'

Manchester City boss Manuel Pellegrini's assertion in 2014 that 'To manage a big team like Manchester United and to have pressure in all the competitions is very good' may have reflected a hidden desire to manage the competition.

UK Prime Minister David Cameron gave his opponents real ammunition for attack when he claimed in 2012 that 'We are raising more money for the rich.'

'Almost invariably I discover a disturbing influence from something outside of the intended speech. The disturbing element is a single unconscious thought, which comes to light through the special blunder.'

S. Freud on slips of the tongue in
The Psychopathology of Everyday Life (1904)

Humanistic therapies

Humanistic therapies, originating with the American psychologist Carl Rogers (1902–87), focus on holistic approaches to human development and on the role of self-development, growth and free will. They aim to help individuals recognize their strengths, creativity and choices with a focus on **self-actualization** (reaching one's potential). This drive to self-fulfilment is what motivates much of our behaviour. Humanistic approaches tend to focus on the 'here and now' – looking at where the patient is now rather than how they got there or what the future might hold. There are various schools of humanistic therapy, including:

GESTALT THERAPY

Gestalt therapy, developed by Fritz Perls (1893–1970), Laura Perls (1905–90) and Paul Goodman (1911–72) in the 1940s and 1950s, focuses on the whole of an individual's experience, including their thoughts, feelings and actions. In gestalt therapy, self-awareness is key to personal growth and developing one's full potential. Problems can occur when this self-awareness becomes blocked by negative thought patterns and behaviour that can leave people feeling troubled and unhappy.

Gestalt therapy focuses on the skills and techniques that a person needs to develop in order to be more aware of their feelings. According to the gestalt approach, it is much more important to understand what individuals are feeling in the 'here and now' than to spend a lot of time worrying about why they are feeling the way they do, as other therapies do (e.g. psychodynamic approaches).

The goal, then, of gestalt therapy is to develop self-awareness – of feelings, thoughts, ideas and beliefs. This can be achieved with a range of techniques:

▶ **Role-play:** the therapist might play the role of spouse or parent and ask the client to interact within those roles. Sometimes, the client might take on the role of the other person so that they can experience different feelings and emotions that can aid their own self-awareness.

▶ **The 'empty chair' technique:** here, the client sits opposite an empty chair and imagines that it is occupied by someone significant (e.g. their parent, spouse or even themselves). They then interact with this imaginary person – asking questions and talking to them. They then switch chairs so that they are now sitting in the empty chair and the roles are reversed as the interaction continues. The aim is to help the client become aware of suppressed feelings that might be fuelling conflicts or distress.

HUMAN GIVENS THERAPY

All humans have a common set of innate physical and emotional needs coupled with appropriate physical and emotional resources (see the table below). We deploy our 'given' resources in order to meet our 'given' needs in the environment in the course of our daily lives. When our innate needs are met we will be satisfied and content but when they are not met (especially our emotional needs) we get distressed or depressed. The human givens approach believes that we will be happier if we are more aware of and more sensitive to our innate needs and resources.

Needs	Resources
Security	Memory
Autonomy and control	Rapport
Status.	Imagination
Privacy	Instincts and emotions
Attention	A rational mind
Connection to the wider community	A metaphorical mind
Intimacy	An observing self
Competence and achievement	A dreaming brain
Meaning and purpose	

A human givens therapist then uses techniques such as deep relaxation, visualization, guided imagery and use of metaphors to help their client to identify their unmet emotional needs and then to find ways to meet these needs using their own resources.

PERSON-CENTRED THERAPY (ALSO KNOWN AS 'CLIENT-CENTRED' COUNSELLING)

Person-centred therapy is a humanistic approach developed by Carl Rogers during the 1940s and 1950s that views the therapist and client as equal partners in trying to solve a problem, rather than as an expert treating a patient. The client takes responsibility for changing their life rather than the therapist.

Client-centred therapy (sometimes referred to as **Rogerian therapy**) operates according to three basic principles:

▶ The therapist is congruent with the client, which means that they act in a genuine and authentic way (rather than offering the more blank façade of the psychodynamic therapist).

▶ The therapist provides the client with unconditional positive regard; the therapist should care and have deep concern for the client and must show acceptance and non-judgemental attitudes.

▶ The therapist shows empathetic understanding to the client.

It is important to note that Rogers was deliberate in his use of the term 'client' rather than 'patient' as he felt that this implied a more equal relationship than that of the 'sick' patient being cured by the all-knowing doctor. While psychodynamic therapy focuses on trying to interpret the unconscious issues that would appear to have caused the problems, the person-centred approach is far less directive; the therapist does not direct the client, judge them or offer solutions to problems. Rather, the therapist tries to help the client come to their own conclusions.

When people embark on client-centred therapy, they are said to be in a state of **incongruence**, meaning there is a difference between how they see themselves and the reality. A key aim of client-centred therapy is that the client gains 'congruence' – that is, an accurate view of themselves and good self-awareness. The therapist aims to help the client reach congruence so that there is a better match between their self-concept and reality. The therapist achieves this by helping the client identify their own mismatch rather than by directing it themselves. In this way, there are some similarities between person-centred approaches and CBT (although CBT is more directive than CCT).

SOLUTION-FOCUSED BRIEF THERAPY (SFBT)
Also known as solution-focused therapy or brief therapy, this approach focuses on solution-building rather than problem-solving like most other approaches. Other therapists can spend a great deal of time thinking, talking and analysing problems, while the problems simply continue. The aim with SFBT is to stop analysing the problems and work on developing solutions instead, using the client's strengths and skills. Typically, this therapy involves only three to five sessions, which is far less than most other therapies. During sessions the therapist asks questions that encourage the client to find their own solutions to problems. Types of questions used include:

▶ **The miracle question:** this is where the client is asked to imagine a miracle occurring at night while they are asleep that solves the current problem; the client is asked to think about how they will know that the problem is solved when they wake up in the morning – what will be different? What would you notice? This helps the client see a clear picture of how a future without the problem might look – and it is this vision that drives the client forward. This paves the way for a solution in small, practical steps.

▶ **Exception questions:** problems do not always remain with the same intensity all the time for everyone – sometimes we feel better or have brief periods of respite. Often, those better times are caused by us mobilizing our own coping resources. Exception questions, such as 'Tell me about a time when you felt happy', allow people to identify these times and to think about what resources they used to help. By exploring how these exceptions to the current difficult times happened, and highlighting the strengths and resources they used to move into an 'exception period', a therapist can help the client to find their own solution.

ECT (Electro-convulsive therapy)

Although this therapy is little used today, it is worth a mention here as it was once used quite commonly for severe depression and other mental health illnesses. Nowadays, more effective treatments have been developed, and between 1985 and 2002 its use in England, for example, more than halved.

The treatment developed in the 1930s when doctors noticed that some people with depression or schizophrenia, who also had epilepsy, seemed to feel better after having a fit. Based on this idea, ECT operates by passing an electrical current through the brain to produce an epileptic fit. ECT might be offered today if medications for treating severe depression have not helped or if the patient cannot tolerate the side effects. ECT is not, however, without risk of side effects, which is why it is now rarely used.

Eye movement desensitization and reprocessing (EMDR)

EMDR is increasingly being proved an effective treatment for a range of conditions – primarily PTSD (post-traumatic stress disorder) but also phobias and other anxiety conditions.

Developed by the American clinical psychologist Francine Shapiro in the 1980s, it uses a natural function of the body, rapid eye movement (REM – see Chapter 18), as its basis.

EMDR requires clients to firstly focus on the main aspects of the traumatic event that is causing the problem – the visual image that usually pertains to the most disturbing part of the trauma and the negative thoughts that relate to the trauma.

The client then tracks the therapist's finger across their visual field in rapid abrupt eye movements (the eye movements can also be created using a 'light bar', in which you follow a light that moves back and forth across a metal bar). During this procedure, a decrease in the emotional impact of the traumatic memory usually occurs. It is thought that the alternating left–right stimulation of the brain by the eye movements made during EMDR activates the frozen or blocked information-processing system. There is some evidence that the eye movements during EMDR perform a similar function to those that occur during REM sleep (when we dream), which we already know to have a vital information-processing function. When trauma is extreme, this process breaks down and REM sleep doesn't bring the usual relief from distress. EMDR is thought to be like an advanced stage of the REM processing. Using eye movement, the brain processes troubling images and feelings, so that resolution of the issue can be achieved.

Mindfulness therapy

Mindfulness therapy is a rather new approach that helps clients pay attention to the present moment without judgement, using techniques such as meditation, breathing and yoga. Mindfulness training can help individuals become more aware of thoughts, feelings and their body so that these are no longer overwhelming.

Mindfulness-based stress reduction (MBSR) is a mindfulness-based cognitive therapy programme developed by Jon Kabat-Zinn at the University of Massachusetts Medical Center, which uses a combination of mindfulness meditation, body awareness and yoga to help people become more mindful. **Mindfulness-based cognitive therapy** (MBCT) is a psychological therapy designed to help prevent a relapse of depression, and uses traditional cognitive behavioural therapy (CBT) methods combined with mindfulness and mindfulness meditation.

A particular type of mindfulness is **acceptance and commitment therapy** (ACT), which is based on the two key ideas of accepting what is out of your personal control and committing to make changes to improve. The focus is on creating a rich and meaningful life without actually trying to reduce symptoms – recognizing that sometimes those symptoms need to be accepted in order to enhance one's existence.

Medication

There are different medications to treat a range of other mental health conditions and psychiatrists or general practitioners usually prescribe them, rather than psychologists. Often psychological therapies will be carried out in conjunction with drug interventions.

Dig deeper

Website of the Human Givens Institute:
http://www.hgi.org.uk/archive/human-givens.htm#.VXimC0_BwXA

Be mindful:
http://bemindful.co.uk/

Institute for Solution-Focused Therapy:
http://www.solutionfocused.net/

Fact-check

1 Which of the following is *not* a form of behaviour therapy?
   a Token economy
   b Modelling
   c Thought-stopping
   d Systematic desensitization

2 CBT works by breaking seemingly overwhelming problems down into smaller parts. Which of the following is *not* one of these parts?
   a Thoughts
   b Feelings
   c Actions
   d Self-esteem

3 Which of the following is a CBT technique?
   a Token economy
   b Questioning
   c Thought-stopping
   d Aversion therapy

4 Maladaptive or distorted thoughts that CBT tries to change are:
   a Unhelpful
   b Summoned up consciously by the patient
   c Implausible
   d Within the patient's control

5 Which of the following is a thinking error?
   a Realizing that things can change
   b Recognizing the positives
   c Being kind to oneself
   d Mindreading

6 The basic assumptions underlying the psychodynamic approach are:
  a None of our behaviour has its root in the unconscious
  b Different parts of the unconscious mind (e.g. the id, ego and superego) work in harmony with one another
  c We develop defences in order to avoid the unpleasant consequences of conflict
  d Our behaviour and feelings as adults (including psychological problems) are completely independent of our childhood experiences

7 Which of the following is *not* a humanistic therapy?
  a Human givens
  b Person-centred
  c Gestalt
  d Mindfulness

8 Which of the following is a need in human givens approaches?
  a Intimacy
  b Memory
  c Imagination
  d Emotions

9 Which of the following statements about therapies is true?
  a Solution-focused brief therapy analyses a client's childhood experiences
  b ECT is a preferred treatment for depression
  c CBT and mindfulness are often used in conjunction with each other
  d Mindfulness involves providing solutions to problems

10 Which of the following statements about medication therapies is true?
  a Psychologists tend to be against the use of prescribed medication to treat psychological problems
  b Psychological therapies are often used alongside medication
  c Medications are good because they have no side effects
  d Psychologists often prescribe medications

17

The brain and nervous system

The brain and nervous system are the hardware that are responsible for every single human function. It is thus useful to have some understanding of how these systems are structured and how they operate. This chapter will thus outline the most important parts of the brain to be aware of as well as the structure of nerves and neurotransmitters. A brief exploration into the endocrine system is also useful to understand some of the ways that the brain exerts its effects on the body.

The brain and the nervous system make up the body's 'command centre' and are responsible for its every function (see the diagram below). These are made up of two main systems: the central nervous system (CNS) and the peripheral nervous system (PNS). The CNS contains the brain and the spinal cord while the PNS contains the nerves, which leave the brain and the spinal cord and travel to different areas of the body. The PNS also sends information (via sensory nerves) gathered by the body's sensory receptors to the CNS as quickly as possible. Once the CNS has interpreted this information, the PNS will relay the specific orders back out to the body (via motor nerves).

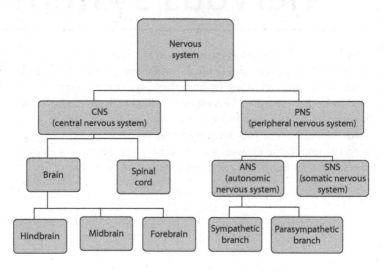

Diagrammatic representation of the nervous system

The central nervous system

The central nervous system (CNS) is so named because it gathers and integrates information it receives from all parts of the body and sends this information to the PNS. The brain processes and interprets sensory information sent from the spinal cord. The brain consists of three main components: the forebrain, the midbrain and the hindbrain (see the diagram below).

The **forebrain** is responsible for a range of functions including receiving and processing sensory information, thinking, language and motor function. The forebrain contains structures such as the thalamus (a relay station for all sensory stimuli), hypothalamus (which controls the body's internal environment, eating, drinking, sexual behaviour and emotional arousal), amygdala and hippocampus (together these structures make up the limbic system that is often referred to as the 'emotional brain') and it also contains the largest part of the brain, the cerebrum or cerebral hemispheres.

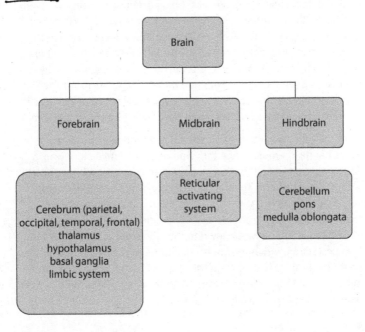

Diagrammatic representation of the brain

The **cerebrum** or **cortex** is the largest part of the human brain, associated with higher brain function such as thought and action. The cerebral cortex is divided into four sections, called lobes, and is highly wrinkled to make the brain more efficient, because it can increase the surface area of the brain and the number of neurons.

Case study: Hippocampus and memory

Henry Molaison, known as 'HM', was 27 years old in 1953 and had suffered from severe epileptic seizures for many years. In an attempt to cure his epilepsy, a Hartford neurosurgeon, William Beecher Scoville, removed the hippocampus that lay within each temporal lobe. The operation was successful in that it significantly reduced Henry's seizures, but it left him with severe memory loss. He was unable to remember new words, songs or faces after his surgery; he would forget who he was talking to as soon as he moved away; he didn't know how old he was or if his parents were alive or dead; and he could not remember any events that had occurred, such as parties. He could learn at a subconscious level (his working memory and procedural memory were intact) and he learned to use a walking frame, but had no conscious memories of having used the frame, even though he retained the ability. As an experimental subject, HM was ideal, because he never grew bored of the repetitive memory tasks he was set because they always seemed new to him.

Unitl then it had not been known that the hippocampus was essential for memory. Once this was realized, HM's story was widely publicized so that this operation to remove both hippocampi would never be done again. HM has been mentioned in almost 12,000 journal articles, making him the most studied case in medical or psychological history. Henry died in 2008, at the age of 82. Until then, he was known to the world only as 'HM' for his own protection, but on his death his name was revealed. After his death his brain was dissected into slices and digitized as a three-dimensional brain map that could be searched by zooming in from the whole brain to individual neurons.

Lobe of the cerebrum	Function
Frontal lobe containing the motor cortex	Reasoning, planning, parts of speech, movement, emotions and problem solving
Parietal lobe containing the somatosensory cortex	Movement, orientation, recognition, perception
Occipital lobe containing the visual cortex	Visual processing
Temporal lobe containing the auditory cortex	Auditory processing, memory and speech

> 'The brain is a monstrous, beautiful mess. Its billions of nerve cells – called neurons – lie in a tangled web that displays cognitive powers far exceeding any of the silicon machines we have built to mimic it.'
>
> W. F. Allman, *Apprentices of Wonder: Inside the Neural Network Revolution*
> (New York: Bantam, 1989)

The cerebrum is divided into two halves, known as the **left** and **right hemispheres**. Each of these has a slightly different function; the **corpus callosum** connects the two.

The **midbrain** and the **hindbrain** together make up the brainstem. The midbrain is the portion of the brainstem that connects the hindbrain and the forebrain. The midbrain is the smallest region of the brain and it acts as a sort of relay station for auditory and visual information. The midbrain contains the reticular activating system, which is the portal through which nearly all information enters the brain.

Spotlight: Parkinson's disease

Parkinson's disease is one of the most common disorders of the midbrain. This progressive illness develops when dopamine-producing nerve cells in this area die off in large numbers. The midbrain may also be involved in some forms of mental illness; the **dopamine hypothesis of psychosis** is so called because dopamine production is often abnormally high in people with certain mental illnesses, including schizophrenia.

The hindbrain extends from the spinal cord and contains structures such as the pons and cerebellum. The **cerebellum**, which is associated with movement, posture and balance, is similar to the cerebrum in that it has two hemispheres and a highly folded surface or cortex. The **pons** is partly made up of tracts connecting the spinal cord with higher brain levels. The hindbrain also contains the **medulla oblongata**, which transmits signals between the spinal cord and the higher parts of the brain and is responsible for controlling such autonomic functions as respiration, heart rate and digestion. Damage to this area would thus be catastrophic.

Case study: Phineas Gage

Phineas P. Gage (1823–60) was an American railroad construction foreman remembered for his survival of a horrific accident in 1848 in which a large iron rod was driven completely through his head, destroying much of his brain's left frontal lobe. Phineas Gage influenced nineteenth-century discussions about the mind and brain, and was perhaps the first case to suggest that damage to specific parts of the brain might induce specific personality changes.

Gage's initial survival would have ensured him fame enough, but what really turned him into a celebrity were the observations made by John Martyn Harlow, the doctor who treated him for a few months afterward. 'Here is business enough for you,' a still-conscious Gage told the first doctor to treat him after his accident, in what is probably the greatest understatement in medical history.

Cage became the most famous patient in the annals of neuroscience, because his case was the first to propose a link between brain trauma and personality change. Gage certainly displayed some kind of change in behaviour after his injury although the exact nature, extent and duration of this change have been difficult to establish. Harlow described the pre-accident Gage as hardworking, responsible and 'a great favorite' with the men in his charge, his employers having regarded him as 'the most efficient and capable foreman in their employ'. But these same employers, after Gage's accident, 'considered the change in his mind so marked that they could not give him his place again' since he was reportedly unreliable, partial to swearing and often making inappropriate remarks – a description that would later be termed 'disinhibited', a classic term for what can occur after damage to the frontal lobes.

Gage survived for 12 years following the accident but became ill with epilepsy (a condition now thought to be related to his injury). When he died, Phineas was buried with the tamping iron that, once removed from his head, had accompanied him wherever he went. Seven years later, he was exhumed at Dr Harlow's request – and now both his skull and the tamping iron are on display at the Harvard Medical School.

The other part of the CNS is the spinal cord. This is a cylindrical bundle of nerves that runs down the middle of the protective bony spinal column from the medulla oblongata in the brainstem to the PNS. The spinal column is made up of bones called vertebrae and although the spinal column is fairly flexible, some of the vertebrae in the lower parts of the spinal column become fused. The spinal cord is surrounded by a clear fluid called cerebral spinal fluid (CSF), that acts as a cushion to protect the delicate nerves.

Spinal cord nerves relay information via millions of nerve fibres from inside and outside the body to the brain and back again; the nerves connecting the spinal cord to the rest of the body are referred to as the peripheral nervous system (PNS).

Spotlight: The spinal cord

The spinal cord is about 45 cm (18 inches) long in men and around 43 cm (17 inches) long in women. It is about the diameter of a human finger.

The peripheral nervous system

The peripheral nervous system (PNS) refers to all the neurons of the body outside the brain and spinal cord (the central nervous system). It is the brain that makes the decisions about how to respond to the information that it receives via the PNS – and the brain uses the PNS to send out responses for action to muscles, glands and so on.

All cells of the nervous system are comprised of neurons (or nerve cells), which are the basic units of the nervous system. The nervous system contains around 10–12 billion neurons and around 80 per cent of them are found in the brain. Neurons contain **nerve processes,** which extend from the nerve cell body outwards. The nerve processes consist of **axons** and **dendrites,** which are able to conduct and transmit signals; axons transmit signals away from the cell body while dendrites, which are shorter than axons, carry signals towards the cell body. There are three kinds of neuron:

- **Motor** (or **efferent**) neurons transmit signals from the CNS to organs, glands and muscles.

- **Sensory** (or **afferent**) neurons send information to the CNS from internal organs or from external stimuli.

- **Interneurons** (relay) transmit information between motor and sensory neurons.

> 'In proportion to our body mass, our brain is three times as large as that of our nearest relatives. This huge organ is dangerous and painful to give birth to, expensive to build and, in a resting human, uses about 20 per cent of the body's energy even though it is just 2 per cent of the body's weight. There must be some reason for all this evolutionary expense.'
>
> S. Blakemore, 'Meme, myself, I', *New Scientist*, 13 March 1999

The other kind of cell within the NS other than neurons are **glial cells,** which provide structural support to the neurons, insulate them, nourish them and remove waste products.

All neurons share the same structure, described in the table below.

Neuron component	Function
Cell body or soma	Contains the nucleus
Dendrites	Branch out from the cell body allowing connection with other neurons
Axon	Transports signals received. Nerves are bundles of axons coming from many neurons.
Myelin sheath	Insulates the axon and speeds up rate of conduction of signals down the axon. The myelin is produced by the glial cells (see earlier).
Node of Ranvier	These are the gaps formed between myelin sheath cells along the axons. Since fat serves as a good insulator, the myelin sheaths speed the rate of transmission of an electrical impulse along the axon. The electrical impulse jumps from one node to the next and thus speeds the rate of transmission.
Terminal buttons	At the end of each axon, they release neurotransmitters (see below). The junction between an axon of one neuron and the cell body or dendrite of a neighbouring neuron is called a synapse.

The somatic and autonomic nervous systems

The PNS consists of two systems: the somatic and the autonomic nervous systems. The somatic nervous system (SNS) transmits sensory information as well as that needed for voluntary movement via the sensory and motor neurons referred to earlier.

The autonomic nervous system (ANS) regulates the internal body functions that are not under voluntary control, such as blood flow, heartbeat, digestion and breathing, and is further subdivided into the sympathetic and parasympathetic nervous systems. The sympathetic nervous system controls activities that prepare the body for action, such as increasing the heart rate and increasing the release of sugar from the liver into the blood – activities generally considered to be part of the fight-or-flight reaction (used to cope with emergency situations – see Chapter 14). The parasympathetic nervous system activates less active functions needed when the body is at rest, such as the production of saliva and digestive enzymes. The ANS produces its effects in two ways: either by direct stimulation of body organs or by stimulating the release of hormones from the endocrine glands (see below).

Neurotransmitters

Nerve cells or neurons communicate and send messages by transmitting nerve impulses. It was once believed that neurons communicated with one another by sending electrical impulses across the gaps (the synapses) between them. However, it is now known that, while the electric impulses travel down the nerves, they do not jump across the gaps between the nerves; instead, neurons mostly communicate across synapses via electrochemical means by releasing chemicals called neurotransmitters. They are produced by glands such as the pituitary and the adrenal glands.

The synapse has three parts to it:

▶ the presynaptic membrane of the neuron sending the message

▶ the postsynaptic membrane of the receiving neuron

▶ the synaptic cleft.

When a nerve signal reaches the presynaptic membrane of the presynaptic neuron, neurotransmitter molecules are released into the synaptic cleft. The neurotransmitter molecules then diffuse and float across the synaptic cleft, so that they can bind to the receptors in the postsynaptic membrane. These receptors are shaped to receive only one type of neurotransmitter, which fits it like a key in a lock. This then sends the signal across to the new neuron.

If not enough neurotransmitters are produced for some reason (e.g. stress, drugs or poor nutrition might affect neurotransmitter production), or if they are blocked from reaching their proper receptors, this can result in certain difficulties and conditions for the individual.

Spotlight: Acetylcholine

The first neurotransmitter was discovered in 1921 by the German pharmacologist Otto Loewi (1873–1961) and was named acetylcholine. It is responsible for stimulating muscle activity (among other functions). Loewi won the Nobel Prize in Physiology or Medicine in 1936 for his work on neurotransmitters (shared with another scientist, Sir Henry Dale).

There are three types of neurotransmitter:

▶ amino acids

▶ peptides

▶ monoamines.

Within each category are different neurotransmitters that are each responsible for specific functions. Neurotransmitters can also be classified as excitatory or inhibitory. **Excitatory neurotransmitters** (e.g. epinephrine and norepinephrine) are those that excite the neurons and stimulate the brain, while inhibitory neurotransmitters (such as GABA and serotonin) have a calming effect on the brain. Inhibitory neurotransmitters help control the spread of excitation through the nervous system.

There are four main criteria for identifying chemicals as neurotransmitters:

1 The chemical must be synthesized in the neuron or otherwise be present in it.

2 When the neuron is active, the chemical must be released and produce a response in some target.

3 The same response must be obtained when the chemical is experimentally placed on the target.

4 A mechanism must exist for removing the chemical from its site of activation after its work is done.

Spotlight: Epilepsy

Epilepsy is a disorder of the central nervous system characterized by recurrent seizures. Excitation and inhibition of electrical activity in the brain are normally carefully balanced. Neurons will usually fire singly or in small groups in order to achieve a desired aim and then stop firing. In epilepsy, a seizure happens if too many neurons fire at once so that neuron excitation and inhibition become unbalanced; either there is too much excitation, or too little inhibition. This causes a wave of abnormal activity between neurons or groups of neurons and can lead to other neurons nearby or throughout the brain also firing. If the electrical activity is confined to one part of the brain, this results in a partial seizure. If it spreads through the entire brain, this results in a generalized seizure.

Many of the drugs that treat epilepsy act by either increasing activity in the inhibitory systems or decreasing activity in the excitatory systems. The drugs may affect the neurotransmitters responsible for sending messages, or attach themselves to the surface of neurons and alter the activity of the cell by changing how ions flow into and out of the neurons.

The endocrine system

The endocrine system is made up of glands that produce and secrete hormones – chemical messengers that regulate the activity of cells or organs. The endocrine system is the collection of glands that produce hormones that regulate, among other things, metabolism, growth and development, tissue function, sexual function, reproduction, sleep and mood. The endocrine and nervous systems are intimately linked; the endocrine glands are controlled directly by stimulation from the nervous system. By regulating the functions of organs in the body, these glands help to maintain the body's homeostasis. The nervous system provides a very fast system to activate specific glands and muscles throughout the body. The endocrine system, however, is much slower-acting, but has very widespread, long-lasting effects. Hormones are distributed by glands through the bloodstream to the entire body, affecting any cell with a receptor for a particular hormone.

The main glands that make up the endocrine system are outlined below:

▶ **Hypothalamus:** this is located in the forebrain (see above) and is responsible for the direct control of the endocrine system through the pituitary gland (see below) by secreting important hormones.

▶ **Pituitary gland:** this is a small area connected to the hypothalamus of the brain. The pituitary gland is actually made of two completely separate structures: the posterior and anterior pituitary glands.

▶ **Pineal gland:** The pineal gland is found just posterior to the thalamus of the brain and produces the hormone melatonin that helps to regulate the human sleep–wake cycle known as the circadian rhythm (for more on the sleep–wake cycle, see Chapter 18).

▶ **Thyroid gland:** this is located at the base of the neck and produces three major hormones.

- **Adrenal glands:** the two adrenal glands are located just above the kidneys and are each made of two distinct layers, each with their own functions: the outer adrenal cortex and the inner adrenal medulla.

- **Pancreas:** this is a large gland that produces the hormones glucagon and insulin, which are responsible for maintaining blood glucose levels. When the pancreas fails to produce insulin, diabetes results.

- **Gonads:** the gonads – ovaries in females and testes in males – produce the sex hormones of the body, testosterone in males and oestrogen in females.

Dig deeper

Epilepsy and medications:
http://www.epilepsy.com/learn/treating-seizures-and-epilepsy/seizure-and-epilepsy-medicines

Henry Molaison – the amnesiac we'll never forget:
http://www.theguardian.com/science/2013/may/05/henry-molaison-amnesiac-corkin-book-feature

Mo Costandi, 'Phineas Gage and the Effect of an Iron Bar through the Head on Personality', *The Guardian*, 8 November 2010:
http://www.theguardian.com/science/blog/2010/nov/05/phineas-gage-head-personality

Fact-check

1 Which of the following is *not* part of the CNS?
   a The hindbrain
   b The spinal cord
   (c) The sympathetic nervous system
   d The forebrain

2 Which of the following is *not* part of the forebrain?
   a The medulla oblongata
   b The thalamus
   (c) The hypothalamus
   d The limbic system

3 Which of the following descriptions of the cerebrum is correct?
   a The parietal lobe contains the visual cortex
   b The occipital lobe contains the auditory cortex
   c The temporal lobe contains the somatosensory cortex
   (d) The frontal lobe contains the motor cortex

4 Which of the following statements about the spinal cord is correct?
   a The spinal cord connects the midbrain to the hindbrain
   b The spinal cord connects the medulla oblongata in the brainstem to the PNS
   (c) The spinal cord is part of the sympathetic nervous system
   d The spinal cord contains the visual cortex

5 Which of the following is *not* a kind of neuron?
   a Dopamine
   b Motor
   c Sensory
   d Inter

6 Which of the following is *not* a component of a neuron?
   (a) Pons
   b Dendrite
   c Terminal button
   d Axon

7 The purpose of the nodes of Ranvier are to:
  a Slow impulses down
  b Speed impulses up
  c Provide insulation
  d Release neurotransmitters

8 Which of the following statements about the PNS is correct?
  a The sympathetic NS is part of the somatic NS
  b The somatic NS controls involuntary processes
  c The parasympathetic NS controls voluntary movements
  d The sympathetic nervous system controls activities that prepare the body for action

9 Which of the following is part of a synapse?
  a The post-synaptic membrane
  b The neurotransmitter
  c The axon
  d The electric impulse

10 Which of the following is *not* a part of the endocrine system?
  a The hypothalamus
  b The thyroid gland
  c The pancreas
  d The kidney

18

Sleep

Sleep, essential for health and functioning, is a naturally recurring state in which we experience skeletal muscle relaxation and an altered state of consciousness. During sleep we are less reactive, experience altered hormone production and are unable to use our voluntary muscles or interact with the environment. Three additional criteria – reversibility (i.e. sleep is not permanent), recurrence (it occurs regularly) and spontaneity (it is not always intended) – distinguish sleep from that of other dormant states such as hibernation or coma. Human sleep occurs as repeating periods, in which the body alternates between two distinct modes known as non-REM (rapid eye movement) and REM sleep.

Why we sleep

Scientists do not know exactly why we sleep but there are three key theories:

▶ **The Repair and Restoration Theory of Sleep:** according to this theory, sleep allows our physiological and psychological functioning to be maintained – for example, it is known that during sleep the body increases its rate of cell division and protein synthesis. This could explain why newborns sleep so much – an average of about 16 hours in each 24-hour period; the first few months of a baby's life are marked by rapid growth so this suggests that sleep allows these functions to occur.

▶ **The Evolutionary Theory of Sleep:** also known as the Adaptive Theory of Sleep, this approach suggests that periods of activity and inactivity evolved as a means of conserving energy and that we sleep at a time when being active would be most dangerous for us (if we cannot see predators as easily, or if it is colder so we would use up more resources if we were active). Support for this theory comes from the fact that animals with few natural predators, such as bears and lions, sleep for much longer periods (between 12 and 15 hours each day) than those with many natural predators (four or five hours each day). On the other hand, if sleep protects us from predators (by keeping us curled up and out of harm's way), you might expect those lower in the food chain to sleep more, so this theory is conflicting.

'If sleep does not serve an absolutely vital function, then it is the biggest mistake the evolutionary process has ever made.'
A. Rechtschaffen, quoted by E. Mignot in 'Why We Sleep: The Temporal Organization of Recovery', *PLOS Biology* 6/4 (April 2008): 106

▶ **The Information Consolidation Theory of Sleep:** this theory suggests that sleep allows us learn and to process information from the day and to prepare for the day to come. Long-term memories are thought to be laid down at night and, indeed, studies of sleep deprivation suggest that a lack of sleep can have a detrimental effect on memory.

Spotlight: Different animals need different amounts of sleep

Adults typically sleep between six and nine hours per night, while bats sleep more than any other animal – a massive 20 hours per day. This could be due to the fact that their food source is only available for a short period of time (at dusk), so they are awake long enough to feed – then sleep to conserve energy. This supports the evolutionary theory that sleep allows us to conserve energy when food is scarce.

We may not know exactly why we sleep but we do have a good idea of _how_ we sleep. The **ventrolateral preoptic nucleus** (VLPO or VLPN) in the hypothalamus is one area of the brain that is important in the sleep response. Neurons here induce sleep by inhibiting activity in areas of the brainstem that maintain wakefulness. Various neurotransmitters are also involved in the sleep–wake response, including histamine, dopamine, norepinephrine, serotonin, glutamate and acetylcholine. Histamine is sometimes thought to play a particularly vital role as it shows high activity during wakefulness, decreasing activity during non-REM sleep, and its lowest levels during REM sleep (which is why histamine-blocking antihistamine medications cause drowsiness and increase non-REM sleep). Another neurotransmitter, serotonin, is also released in the brain throughout the day; serotonin is used to produce melatonin, sometimes called the 'sleep hormone'. Melatonin production is inhibited by light (and therefore stimulated by lack of light, or darkness) and jetlagged travellers who have difficulty sleeping may take melatonin to help adjust their sleep cycles to their new location.

Spotlight: Sleeping like a baby

While newborn babies can sleep for up to 17 hours each day (though, sadly for their parents, often in short bursts of a couple of hours at a time), their sleep cycles (see next section) are far shorter than those of adults. Babies also spend more time than adults in rapid eye movement (REM) sleep (which means they dream a lot more than adults). Because this is a lighter state of sleep, newborns are much more likely to wake up in response to noises, changes in temperature and movement. When they are dreaming, newborns can make quite a few little noises and their eyes, facial muscles, arms and legs will move a lot – this can even wake them up, which is why swaddling is thought to help babies sleep. Dreaming allows vital brain development to continue even when the baby is asleep.

Newborns also do not seem to develop effective circadian rhythms until they are around six weeks old, or later (which is why they make no distinction between day and night).

Towards the end of the night, the body starts to secrete cortisol in preparation for the anticipated stress of the day, in what is known as the cortisol awakening response.

Stages of sleep

Adult humans sleep in periods of approximately 90 minutes in four to five cycles per night of REM and non-REM (NREM). During the NREM stage, body temperature, heart rate, breathing rate and energy use all decrease, while brain waves get slower and bigger. The American Academy of Sleep Medicine (AASM) divides NREM into three stages: N1, N2, and N3, the last of which is also called delta sleep or slow-wave sleep. The whole cycle normally proceeds in the order: N1 → N2 → N3 → N2 → REM. Each stage may have a distinct physiological function. There is a greater amount of deep sleep (stage N3) earlier in the night, while the proportion of REM sleep increases in the two cycles just before natural awakening.

▶ **NREM (N1):** this is the stage of sleep that usually occurs between sleep and wakefulness. Sudden twitches and jerks may be associated with the onset of sleep during N1. During non-REM1, the organism loses some muscle tone and most conscious awareness of the external environment. This stage typically lasts only around five to ten minutes and a person awakened from this stage might feel that they have not actually been asleep.

- **NREM (N2):** in this stage, sleepers become gradually harder to awaken. During this stage, muscular activity as measured by EMG decreases, and conscious awareness of the external environment disappears. This stages lasts about 20 minutes.

- **NREM (N3):** this stage is called slow-wave sleep (SWS) or deep sleep. The sleeper is less responsive to the environment; many environmental stimuli no longer produce any reactions. Slow-wave sleep is thought to be the most restful form of sleep, the phase which most relieves subjective feelings of sleepiness and restores the body. Bed-wetting and sleepwalking are most likely to occur at the end of this stage of sleep.

- **REM:** Entering rapid eye movement (REM) sleep, where most muscles are paralysed and heart rate, breathing and body temperature become unregulated, the sleeper may experience vivid dreams. REM sleep is activated by acetylcholine secretion and is inhibited by serotonin-secreting neurons. An adult reaches REM approximately every 90 minutes, and remains in REM sleep for longer during the latter half of sleep.

Dreams

Dreams are successions of images, pictures, scenes, ideas, feelings, motions and sensations that occur usually involuntarily in the mind during certain stages of sleep (mainly during REM sleep when brain activity is high). The length of a dream can vary; it may last for a few seconds or up to 20–30 minutes. Most dreams are instantly forgotten, although we are more likely to remember the dream if we wake during the REM phase.

There are various theories that attempt to account for why we have dreams:

- **The Psychoanalytic Theory of Dreams:** according to Freud, in his well-known 1900 book *The Interpretation of Dreams*, our dreams represent the unconscious desires, wishes and thoughts that we normally suppress. They are thus an outlet for our real feelings.

▶ **The Nudity Activation-Synthesis Model:** this theory, proposed by J. Allan Hobson and Robert McClarley in 1977, suggests that areas in the limbic system of the brain that are involved in emotions and memories (such as the amygdala and hippocampus) are activated during REM sleep. The brain attempts to find meaning in these signals, which results in dreaming.

▶ **Information-processing theories:** some theorists believe that dreaming facilitates the information-processing that is thought to be a function of sleep. Some dream experts suggest that dreaming is simply a by-product or even an active part of this information-processing. This is why we often solve problems during our sleep – our minds are freed from the logical constraints of wakeful thoughts. Some believe that dreams allow us to mentally prepare for change or rehearse for new events that might happen in our lives. This is why we often dream about events that are going to happen to us in the future.

Sleep disorders

Sleep is such a vital part of our life that, when things go wrong in that department, it can cause a lot of stress. Most people at some point in their lives will have some difficulties with sleep, the most common of which are to do with problems getting or staying asleep; according to the NHS, a third of people in the UK will experience this. Insomnia can be short term (up to three weeks) or long term (above three to four weeks) and can lead to memory problems, depression, irritability and an increased risk of heart disease and driving-related accidents.

Spotlight: The effects of sleep deprivation

In rats, total sleep deprivation is lethal after two to three weeks; they lose weight despite increasing food intake, and progressively fail to regulate their body temperature. They also develop infections, suggesting an impairment of the immune system. In humans, lack of sleep leads to impaired memory and reduced cognitive abilities, mood swings and even hallucinations. The longest documented period of voluntary sleeplessness is 264 hours (approximately 11 days).

The *DSM-5* criteria for insomnia include the following:

▶ Difficulty getting to sleep

▶ Difficulty staying sleep, characterized by frequent awakenings or problems returning to sleep after awakenings

▶ Early-morning awakening with inability to return to sleep.

In addition, to be classed as insomnia, the sleep disturbance should also cause clinically significant distress or impairment in social, occupational, educational, academic, behavioural or other important areas of functioning; it should occur at least three nights per week; it should persist for at least three months, and it precludes those times when there is not the opportunity to sleep (e.g. with a newborn baby in the house) or when drugs or medication are involved.

Causes of insomnia are varied but the most common reasons for people seeking psychological help are often centred around anxiety. Sleep is a deep state of relaxation, so it is difficult to fall asleep if you are not relaxed. Individuals may experience anxiety-provoking events that stop them relaxing, but often anxiety about not sleeping contributes to the condition, too. The other important condition for sleep is that the individual must be tired! This might sound odd, but people with sleep difficulties often doze during the day and may thus not be tired enough at night. Dozing during the day can affect circadian rhythms (see below), which can make it harder to fall asleep at night.

Treatment for insomnia can be pharmaceutical, with benzodiazepines such as temazepam and diazepam (best only for the short term as the benefits wear off as tolerance builds up) or by using psychological techniques such as relaxation therapy, sleep hygiene methods (e.g. ensuring that a bedroom is quiet and dark, that no caffeine is consumed during the evening, that there is no daytime dozing, etc.) and **paradoxical intention**. Paradoxical intention is a cognitive reframing technique where the insomniac, instead of attempting to fall asleep at night, makes every effort to stay awake (i.e. essentially stops trying to fall asleep). This can be effective because it relieves the 'performance anxiety' that arises from the perceived need or requirement to fall asleep.

Spotlight: Alcohol and sleep

Alcohol is often used as a form of self-treatment of insomnia to induce sleep. However, using alcohol in the long term to induce sleep can actually be a cause of insomnia as it is associated with a decrease in NREM stage 3 and 4 sleep as well as the suppression of REM sleep.

Hypnosis

Hypnosis, while appearing to hold quite magical powers, is merely a state of deep relaxation. It involves an altered state of consciousness during which the client is focusing their attention totally on the therapist and is thus receptive to receiving suggestions and instructions from them. During a hypnotic state, the person is so relaxed that their subconscious processes can be accessed. Hypnosis is normally preceded by a 'hypnotic induction' technique, traditionally viewed as a means of putting the subject into a 'hypnotic trance'.

The origins of hypnosis go back many millennia; indeed, many ancient cultures and civilizations knew of hypnosis and used it as a therapeutic device. Although there was some documented use of hypnosis by the druids in ancient Britain and Gaul, the development and introduction of hypnosis to the modern world is attributable to Islamic scientists of the Middle Ages.

From the fifteenth and sixteenth centuries onwards physicians from many nations further developed and refined the concept of hypnosis and its uses. Even though this knowledge spread throughout the European continent and to the British Isles, it remained mostly confined to a small group (scientists, physicians and universities) and never quite reached the attention of the masses. However, in the eighteenth century the Austrian physician Frantz Anton Mesmer (1734–1815) used magnets and metal frames to perform 'passes' over the patient to remove 'blockages' (i.e. the causes of diseases) and to induce a trance-like state.

'The real origin and essence of the hypnotic condition, is the induction of a habit of abstraction or mental concentration, in which, as in reverie or spontaneous abstraction, the powers of the mind are so much engrossed with a single idea or train of thought, as, for the nonce, to render the individual unconscious of, or indifferently conscious to, all other ideas, impressions, or trains of thought.'

J. Braid, *Hypnotic Therapeutics: Illustrated by Cases: with an Appendix on Table-moving and Spirit-rapping* (Edinburgh: Murray & Gibb, 1843)

It is from this that the verb 'mesmerize', which means to hold someone's attention to the exclusion of anything else so as to create a trance state, originates. After Mesmer's death in 1815 one of his disciples, Amand-Marie-Jacques de Chastenet, Marquis de Puységur (1751–1825), carried on his work and took it one step further. He discovered that the spoken word and direct commands induced trance easily and noticeably faster than 'mesmeric passes' and that a person could be operated upon without pain and anaesthesia when in a trance. This technique was used for many following decades by surgeons in France; Dr Récamier performed the first recorded operation without anaesthesia in 1821.

Soon after, chloroform was discovered and mesmerism dropped out of favour as an anaesthetic; it was much faster to inject a patient than induce a state of trance!

In 1841 the Scottish optometrist James Braid (1795–1860) discovered by accident that a person fixating an object could easily reach a trance state without the help of the mesmeric passes advocated by Dr Mesmer. He named his discovery 'hypnotism' based on the Greek word *hypnos*, which means 'sleep'; it was a total misnomer as hypnosis is not sleep; yet the name remained and mesmerism became hypnotism.

Hypnosis was officially approved as a tool in medicine by the British Medical Association in 1955 and three years later the American Medical Association recognized the therapeutic use of hypnosis.

Case study: Joe Thompson

A 12-year-old schoolboy from Weston-super-Mare, in Somerset, Joe Thompson, was so afraid of flying that he was stranded in the United Arab Emirates for 18 months. He was only able to return home thanks to hypnotherapy.

Joe had travelled to Abu Dhabi with his family in 2009 after his father began work as a manager at a private hospital. In 2012 the family planned to return home, but Joe developed such a fear of flying that their plans were scuppered. Not only did he develop this debilitating fear of flying but he was also afraid of any form of long-haul transport, which meant he was trapped in the UAE. After four separate attempts were made to get Joe to board a plane, the rest of his family returned to Somerset, leaving Joe with his father abroad. His parents spent about £40,000 trying to cure Joe's fear and on cancelled air fares and accommodation in the UAE, but his distress was so severe that he was simply unable to board the planes; he was so terrified as he approached the departure gate he would slump to the floor sobbing with stomach cramps.

Joe was finally able to return to the UK after undergoing three months of hypnosis therapy (in combination with CBT – see Chapter 16) from the therapist Russell Hemmings.

Circadian desynchronization and shift work

As we become an increasingly 24/7 society, more and more of us work some kind of shift pattern. It is thought that 4 million people in the UK – 17 per cent of employees – work shifts. What used to be the domain of medical personnel has now become endemic to many other professions such as retail workers, care workers and even call-centre employees. Yet rotating shifts are known to cause mental and physical health problems stemming mainly from working in opposition to the body's normal circadian rhythms, especially the sleep–wake cycle. Documented problems of shift work include the following:

- ▶ Incidence of peptic ulcer disease in shift workers eight times higher than that of the rest of the population

- ▶ Increased risk of obesity

- ▶ Increased risk of cardiovascular mortality

- ▶ Other physical problems including chronic fatigue, excessive sleepiness and difficulty sleeping

- ▶ Increased divorce rate

- ▶ Higher rates of substance abuse and depression.

There are other phenomena associated with shift work:

▶ Shift workers are much more likely to view their jobs as extremely stressful.

▶ Accidents are known to increase as a result of working shifts. Many major disasters attributed to human error (the *Exxon Valdez* oil spill, Three Mile Island, the Bhopal chemical plant explosion, Chernobyl) occurred on the night shift.

▶ Shift workers are more likely than non-shift workers to have a life-limiting longstanding illness; they are also more likely to have more than one longstanding illness.

▶ Men and women doing shift work are more likely than non-shift workers to have diabetes (possibly due to the disruption in insulin production).

▶ Cigarette smoking prevalence is higher among shift workers than non-shift workers.

▶ Fruit and vegetable consumption is lower among shift workers than non-shift workers.

'The main physiological consequence of such shift schedules is disruption of circadian rhythm which can have a deleterious effect on performance, sleep patterns, accident rates, mental health, and cardiovascular mortality.'

J. M. Harrington, 'Health Effects of Shift Work and Extended Hours of Work', *Occupational and Environmental Medicine* 58 (2001): 68–72

Much of these effects are thought to be due to the disruption in circadian rhythms that happens when we don't get chance to sleep at regular times. The term 'circadian' originates from the Latin words *circa* (about) and *dia* (day) and refers to the physical, mental and behavioural changes that follow a roughly 24-hour cycle. Sometimes these are referred to as our 'biological clocks' and they regulate sleep–wake cycles, hormone release, body temperature, heart rate, digestion and other important bodily functions. Circadian rhythms are vital to the sleep–wake cycle.

The key area of the brain that controls the sleep–wake cycle is the **suprachiasmatic nucleus** (SCN) in the hypothalamus, which contains thousands of nerve cells. This region controls the production of melatonin, the hormone that makes us sleepy. When there is less light, the SCN tells the brain to make more melatonin. Overnight, melatonin levels remain high. They drop at daybreak and remain low during the day. During the day, other chemicals (neurotransmitters) – such as noradrenaline and acetylcholine – increase in the body and keep us alert. Thus, shift workers will find it hard not to feel sleepy and less alert at night. However, the SCN is also influenced by other factors – such as our place in the circadian cycle. This explains why jetlag occurs; even if it is dark, if our internal body clock says it is daytime, it is hard to sleep.

Night-time shift workers are expected to be alert when their brain is secreting melatonin and yet to sleep during the day when it is not. People rarely sleep during the day for the same amount of time as they would at night; daytime sleep is typically one-and-a-half to two hours shorter than a nocturnal sleep period and it is REM that is the casualty. In addition, society is built around the expectation that we sleep at night; there are thus noises and activity during the day that make sleep for the shift worker difficult. This compounds their difficulties. The night worker must contend not only with the dip in energy levels and alertness that are the result of circadian rhythms but also with sleep deprivation from poor-quality daytime sleep.

Many attempts are made to reduce the impact of shift work by moderating shift patterns in terms of how many nights in a row an individual is expected to work. Long patterns (e.g. four to six weeks) would seem to be the best in terms of circadian desynchronization; these allow circadian rhythms to be adjusted and time to get used to the new pattern before readjusting again. It takes about ten days for the body to adjust to night-shift work. The optimum pattern would be to always work nights, of course, since then there is no readjustment needed (but the social and emotional effects are likely to be too detrimental for most people).

Alternatively, it might be best to just do the occasional night shift so that the body never has to actually adjust. Working four to seven night shifts in a row is generally thought to be the worse possible shift pattern, resulting in someone who is permanently 'desynchronized' – never really adjusting to either night or day wakefulness.

Dig deeper

National Sleep Foundation (United States):
http://sleepfoundation.org/sleep-disorders-problems

Journalistic article: 'Why shift work is linked to so many health problems such as cancer and diabetes: Study finds it damages 1,500 genes':
 http://www.dailymail.co.uk/health/article-2542780/Working-shifts-damage-1-500-genes-New-finding-explain-shift-work-associated-health-problems.html

British Society of Clinical and Academic Hypnosis:
http://www.bscah.com

Fact-check

1 During sleep we:
- **a** Are always paralysed
- **b** Snore
- **c** Are relaxed
- **d** Always dream

2 Which of the followings statements about sleep is correct?
- **a** We experience non-REM sleep once during the night
- **b** Once we are in deep REM sleep we stay in it until we wake
- **c** We sleep in cycles each lasting three hours
- **d** We sleep in cycles of around 90 minutes in four to five cycles per night of REM and non-REM (NREM).

3 Which of the following statements about dreams is correct?
- **a** Dreams are voluntary
- **b** Each dream can last up to 30 minutes
- **c** We are more likely to recall a dream if we are woken up during non-REM sleep
- **d** If we don't recall a dream it is because we are subconsciously suppressing it

4 Which of the following is not a theory of dreams?
- **a** Psychoanalytic Theory of Dreams
- **b** Activation-Synthesis Model
- **c** Rehearsal Theory
- **d** Evolutionary Theory of Dreams

5 Insomnia can involve:
- **a** Difficulty getting to sleep
- **b** Difficulty staying a sleep, characterized by frequent awakenings or problems returning to sleep after awakenings
- **c** Early-morning awakening with inability to return to sleep
- **d** All of the above

6 Which of the following is a name associated with hypnosis?
- **a** Franz Mesmer
- **b** James Braid
- **c** Carl Jung
- **d** Dr Récamier

7 What is hypnosis?
- **a** A miracle cure for many problems
- **b** A deep state of relaxation
- **c** A deep sleep
- **d** Dangerous

8 Which of the following statements about shift work is correct?
- **a** Fewer and fewer people are doing shift work these days
- **b** Shift work causes circadian rhythms to get out of sync
- **c** Shift workers sleep the same amount as non-shift workers but at different times
- **d** It is rare to get ill from shift work

9 Shift workers are more likely than non-shift workers to:
- **a** Smoke
- **b** Be slim
- **c** Eat fruit and vegetables
- **d** Have stable relationships

10 The best shift-work pattern to have is:
- **a** Two nights a week
- **b** Three nights a week
- **c** One week of nights followed by one week of days
- **d** Four weeks of nights followed by four weeks of days

References

Allport, G. (1954). *The Nature of Prejudice* (Reading, MA: Addison-Wesley)

Argyle, M. 1988. *Bodily Communication*, 2nd edn (London: Methuen & Co.)

Atkinson, R. C. and Shiffrin, R. M. (1968). 'Human memory: a proposed system and its control processes', in K. W. Spence and L. T. Spence, *The Psychology of Learning and Motivation*, vol. 2 (New York: Academic Press), pp. 89–195

Baddeley, A. D. and Hitch, G. (1974). 'Working memory', in G. H. Bower (ed.), *The Psychology of Learning and Motivation: Advances in Research and Theory*, vol. 8 (New York: Academic Press), pp. 47–89

Bandura, A. (1977). *Social Learning Theory* (Englewood Cliffs, NJ: Prentice Hall)

Bandura, A., Ross, D. and Ross, S. A. (1961). 'Transmission of aggression through the imitation of aggressive models', *Journal of Abnormal and Social Psychology* 63(3): 575–82

Beck, H. P., Levinson, S. and Irons, G. (2009). 'Finding Little Albert', *American Psychologist* 64: 605–14

Bern, D. J. (1996). 'Exotic becomes erotic: a developmental theory of sexual orientation', *Psychological Review* 103: 320–35

Bouchard, T. J., Lykken, D. T., McGue, M., Segal N. L. and Tellegen, A. (1990). 'Sources of human psychological differences: the Minnesota Study of Twins Reared Apart', *Science* 250(4978): 223–8

Bowlby, J. (1999) [1969]. *Attachment,* vol. 1 of *Attachment and Loss*, 2nd edn (New York: Basic Books)

Broadbent, D. (1958). *Perception and Communication* (London: Pergamon Press)

Burnstein, E. and Vinokur, A. (1977). 'Persuasive argumentation and social comparison as determinants of attitude polarization', *Journal of Experimental Social Psychology* 13: 315–32

Campbell, D. T. and Stanley, J. C. (1966). *Experimental and Quasi-experimental Designs for Research* (Chicago: Rand McNally)

Cannon, W. B. (1927). 'The James–Lange theory of emotion: a critical examination and an alternative theory', *American Journal of Psychology* 39: 10–124

Cattell, R. B. (1971). *Abilities: Their Structure, Growth, and Action* (New York: Houghton Mifflin)

Chomsky, N. (1965). *Aspects of the Theory of Syntax* (Cambridge, MA: The MIT Press)

——— (1968). *Language and Mind* (New York: Harcourt Brace Jovanovich)

Cialdini, R. (1984). *Influence: The Psychology of Persuasion* (New York: Harper Business)

Condry, J. and Condry, S. (1976). 'Sex differences: a study of the eye of the beholder', *Child Development* 7: 812–19

Craik, F. I. M. and Lockhart, R. S. (1972). 'Levels of processing: a framework for memory research', *Journal of Verbal Learning and Verbal Behavior* 11(6): 671–84

Duckitt, J. (1992). *The Social Psychology of Prejudice* (Westport, CT: Praeger)

Duncker, K. (1945). *On Problem Solving*, Psychological Monographs 58 (Washington, DC: American Psychological Association)

Dutton, D. G. and Aaron, A. P. (1974). 'Some evidence for heightened sexual attraction under conditions of high anxiety', *Journal of Personality and Social Psychology* 30: 510–17

Ekman, P. (1972). 'Universals and cultural differences in facial expressions of emotions', in J. Cole (ed.), *Nebraska Symposium on Motivation* (Lincoln, NB: University of Nebraska Press), pp. 207–82

Festinger, L. (1954). 'A theory of social comparison processes', *Human Relations* 7(2): 117–40

French, J. R. P. (1953). 'Experiments in field settings', in L. Festinger and D. Katz, *Research Methods in the Behavioral Sciences* (New York: Holt, Rinehart & Winston), pp. 98–135

Gibson, J. J. (1966). *The Senses Considered as Perceptual Systems* (Boston: Houghton Mifflin)

Gibson, J. J. (1972). 'A theory of direct visual perception', in J. Royce and W. Rozenboom (eds), *The Psychology of Knowing* (New York: Gordon & Breach)

Gregory, R. (1970). *The Intelligent Eye* (London: Weidenfeld & Nicolson)

Guilford, J. P. (1950). 'Creativity', *American Psychologist* 5(9): 444–54

Guilford, J. P., Christensen, P. R., Merrifield, P. R. and Wilson, R. C. (1978). *Alternate Uses: Manual of instructions and interpretations* (Orange, CA: Sheridan Psychological Services)

Herzberg, F., Mausner, B. and Snyderman, B. B. (1959). *The Motivation to Work*, 2nd edn (New York: John Wiley)

Hobson, J. A. and McCarley, R. W. (1977). 'The brain as a dream state generator: an activation-synthesis hypothesis of the dream process', *American Journal of Psychiatry* 134(12): 1335–48

Janis, I. L. (1972). *Victims of Groupthink* (New York: Houghton Mifflin)

Jack, R. E., Garrod, O. G. B., Hui Yu, Caldara, R. and Schyns, P. G. (2012), 'Facial expressions of emotion are not culturally universal', *Proceedings of the National Academy of Sciences of the United States of America* 109(19): 7241–4

James, W. (1884). 'What is an emotion?' *Mind* 9, 188–205.

—— (1890), *The Principles of Psychology*, vol. 2 (New York: H. Holt and Company), pp. 449–50

Jiangang Liua, Jun Lib, Lu Fengc, Ling Lia and Jie Tianb (2014) 'Seeing Jesus in toast: neural and behavioral correlates of face pareidolia', *Cortex* 53 (April): 60–77

Katz, D. (1960). 'The functional approach to the study of attitudes', *Public Opinion Quarterly* 24: 163–204

Kraft, T. L. and Pressman, S. D. (2012). 'Grin and bear it: the influence of manipulated facial expression on the stress response', *Psychological Science* 23(11): 1372–8

Latané, B. and Darley, J. M. (1968). 'Group inhibition of bystander intervention in emergencies', *Journal of Personality and Social Psychology* 10(3): 215–21

Latiné, B. and Rodin, J. (1960). 'Lady in distress: inhibiting effects of friends and strangers on bystander intervention', *Journal of Experimental Psychology* 5: 189–202

Locke, E. A. (2005). 'Why emotional intelligence is an invalid concept', *Journal of Organizational Behavior* 26(4): 425–31

Loftus, E. (1974). 'Reconstruction of automobile destruction: example of interaction between language and memory', *Journal of Verbal Learning and Verbal Behavior* 13(5): 585–9

Maslow, A. H. (1943). 'A theory of human motivation', *Psychological Review* 50(4): 370–96

Miller, G. A. (1956). 'The magical number seven, plus or minus two: some limits on our capacity for processing information', *Psychological Review* 63(2): 81–97

Money, J. and Ehrhardt, A. A. (1972). *Man and Woman, Boy and Girl: Differentiation and Dimorphism of Gender Identity from Conception to Maturity* (Baltimore, MD: Johns Hopkins University Press)

Moscovici, S. and Zavalloni, M. (1969). 'The group as a polarizer of attitudes', *Journal of Personality and Social Psychology* 12: 125–35

Orne M. (1962). 'On the social psychology of the psychological experiment: with particular reference to demand characteristics and their implications', *American Psychologist* 17: 776–83

Orne, M. T., and Whitehouse, W. G. (2000). 'Demand characteristics', in A. E. Kazdin (ed.), *Encyclopedia of Psychology* (Washington, DC: American Psychological Association and Oxford University Press, 2000), pp. 469–70

Plutchnik, R. (2002). 'Nature of emotions', *American Scientist* 89: 349

Premack, D. (1959). 'Toward empirical behavior laws: I. Positive reinforcement', *Psychological Review* 66: 219–33

Quadagno, D. M., Briscoe, R. and Quadagno, J. S. (1977). 'Effect of perinatal gonadal hormones on selected nonsexual behavior patterns: a critical assessment of the nonhuman and human literature', *Psychological Bulletin* 84(1): 62

Rhodes, M (1961). 'An analysis of creativity', *Phi Delta Kappan* 42(7): 307–9

Rundus, D. and Atkinson, R. C. (1970). 'Rehearsal process in free recall: a procedure for direct observation', *Journal of Verbal learning and Verbal Behavior* 9: 99–105

Russell, J. A. (1994). 'Is there universal recognition of emotion from facial expression? A review of the cross-cultural studies', *Psychological Bulletin* 115(1): 102–41

Schachter, S. and Singer, J. (1962). 'Cognitive, social, and physiological determinants of emotional state', *Psychological Review* 69: 379–9

Schwabe, L. and Wolf, O. T. (2009). 'The context counts: congruent learning and testing environments prevent memory retrieval impairment following stress', *Affective and Behavioral Neuroscience* 9(3): 229–36

Skinner, B. F. (1938). *The Behavior of Organisms: An Experimental Analysis* (New York: Appleton-Century).

——— (1953). *Science and Human Behavior* (New York: Simon & Schuster)

——— (1957). *Verbal Behavior* (Acton, MA: Copley Publishing Group)

Sternberg, R. J. (1999), 'The theory of successful intelligence', *Review of General Psychology* 3: 292–316.

Stoner, J. A. F. (1968). 'Risky and cautious shifts in group decisions: the influence of widely held values', *Journal of Experimental Social Psychology* 4: 442–59

Treisman, A. (1964). 'Monitoring and storage of irrelevant messages in selective attention', *Journal of Verbal Learning and Verbal Behavior* 3(6): 449–201

Tuckman, B. (1965). 'Developmental sequence in small groups', *Psychological Bulletin* 63(6): 384–99

Wetherell, M. (1987). 'Social identity and group polarization', in J. C. Turner (ed.), *Rediscovering the Social Group* (New York: Basil Blackwell), 142–70

Young, P. T. (1966). 'Distilled water and tap water as factors in taste preference of the rat', *Psychological Reports* 18, 159–62

Zajonc, R. B. (1965). 'Social facilitation', *Science* (American Association for the Advancement of Science) 149(3681): 269–74

Index

Answers to fact-checks

CHAPTER 1

1 d	6 a
2 c	7 d
3 c	8 d
4 a	9 a
5 d	10 d

CHAPTER 2

1 b	6 a
2 a	7 d
3 c	8 d
4 d	9 a
5 c	10 d

CHAPTER 3

1 c	6 c
2 d	7 d
3 b	8 d
4 a	9 c
5 d	10 c

CHAPTER 4

1 a	6 d
2 b	7 d
3 b	8 a
4 a	9 c
5 c	10 d

CHAPTER 5

1 d	6 a
2 b	7 c
3 c	8 d
4 a	9 b
5 b	10 d

CHAPTER 6

1 a	6 b
2 d	7 d
3 c	8 d
4 c	9 b
5 d	10 a

CHAPTER 7

1 c	6 d
2 d	7 b
3 c	8 c
4 a	9 d
5 d	10 a

CHAPTER 8

1 d	6 b
2 c	7 d
3 a	8 b
4 d	9 a
5 d	10 d

CHAPTER 9

1 a	6 d
2 d	7 a
3 b	8 a
4 a	9 d
5 b	10 d

CHAPTER 10

1 b	6 a
2 d	7 a
3 c	8 d
4 a	9 b
5 c	10 d

CHAPTER 11

1 c	6 a
2 c	7 a
3 d	8 b
4 c	9 c
5 c	10 a

CHAPTER 12

1 a	6 a
2 b	7 c
3 a	8 c
4 d	9 b
5 a	10 d

CHAPTER 13		**CHAPTER 15**		**CHAPTER 17**	
1 a	6 b	1 c	6 c	1 c	6 a
2 d	7 d	2 d	7 d	2 a	7 b
3 a	8 a	3 b	8 b	3 d	8 d
4 b	9 d	4 d	9 d	4 b	9 a
5 a	10 d	5 a	10 d	5 a	10 d
CHAPTER 14		**CHAPTER 16**		**CHAPTER 18**	
1 d	6 c	1 c	6 c	1 c	6 c
2 b	7 c	2 d	7 d	2 d	7 b
3 a	8 d	3 c	8 a	3 b	8 b
4 c	9 c	4 a	9 c	4 d	9 a
5 d	10 a	5 d	10 b	5 d	10 d